PRAISE FOR

Butterflies Over Africa

"*Butterflies Over Africa* is a vivid memoir, a deep meditation, and a stirring manifesto for Integral leadership in Africa. Yene Assegid is a stirring storyteller, whose poignant memories and vignettes introduce us to a series of amazing characters. In her eyes, the "poor and disenfranchised" of Africa emerge as three-dimensional human beings, and the reader can't help but begin to share her passionate love for Africa, as she unfolds the evolution of her life mission to create an Integral education for the next generation of African leaders."

—Terry Patten
Co-developer & co-author, with Ken Wilber, of *Integral Life Practice*
www.integralheart.com

"I have had the privilege on many occasions of being mesmerized by the stories that illustrate the remarkable life of Yene Assegid. Reading *Butterflies Over Africa* touched my heart and brought forth tears of joy, compassion and laughter. As you immerse yourself in this colorful tale of Yene's life, you will begin to see the world and the continent of Africa through the eyes and heart of this emerging African leader and global citizen. Her stories are both deeply personal and universal, told in the same voice and style as if you were sitting across the table from this beautiful and courageous woman. Yene's vision for the future of Africa and the world is both inspired and pragmatic. May this vision inspire you to action and may it be realized

in her lifetime!"
—Dana Carman, Principal, Pacific Integral, www.pacificintegral.com

"*Butterflies Over Africa* represents an innovation in writing on development, weaving personal experience with theoretical frameworks and practical thoughts and guidance on new ways to approach human development and understand leadership in African contexts. It tells a story that many Africans working in international development have often not told, about some of the oversights and negative practice in the aid industry. It also proposes a genuinely holistic way of reconceiving development, as a process of transforming lives and not simply a game of chasing 'outputs.'"
—Jessica Horn, women's rights consultant and philanthropic advisor

"I've now finished your amazing book, and am so deeply grateful you've shared it with me. My spirit soared and marveled at your courage, creativity, and nobility. I treasured the spellbinding stories of the countless ways you've persisted in your quest to help Africa include and transcend its history and cultural values. They are a powerful human thread woven through the solid theoretical underpinnings of your work. Integral Africa will indeed be supported and clarified by this important articulation of your personal history, your mission, your passion, and the human face of the continent you know as home. Though I am not part of your blood family, the warmth and generosity of your words have captured my heart, and spontaneously included me in your lineage. It's a very powerful feeling that gives me a profound sense of home and hearth."
—Deborah Boyar, Ph.D
Somatic Educator & Senior Teacher, Walking Down in Mutuality
www.deborahboyar.com

"An important and extremely informed new voice for troubled times. Assegid sows stories and with them, nurtures original ideas and philosophies, and does so with enormous passion and disarming honesty."
—Joan Baxter, author of *Dust in Our Eyes: an unblinkered look at Africa*

"Ms. Yene Assegid has a gift of amiably articulating the truth from the heart so evident in *Butterflies Over Africa*. The book reveals truths she has learned and experienced in Africa, scrutinized with eyes like an eagle, a heart of empathy, and the intelligence of a visionary. The result: inspiring hopes and dreams for change and transformation in Africa.

She proposes the key for its transformation in a new style of African leadership; leadership rooted in indigenous African culture and traditions and infused with modern thinking and technology. Otherwise, Africa will wallow in the shallow waters of poverty and mediocrity and never reach the deep waters of prosperity and growth.

Ms. Assegid urges African's to rise to their full potential by rediscovering their self-identity and stop being victims to traumatic periods of their history. Africans must not live in the past always blaming others for their mess. The truth is only Africans can develop their continent and they must seize the initiative to create change instead of waiting on others to do so.

This masterpiece of a book *Butterflies Over Africa* wisely articulates the way forward. It opens a door of hope, of nurturing our imaginations to create a continent where good governance, justice, prosperity and well-being will be a reality for all Africans."

—The Rt. Rev Dr. Trevor Mwamba
Bishop of Botswana
Author, *Dancing Sermons*

"*Butterflies Over Africa* releases a multi-perspectival view of Africa that unfolds like the life-cycle of the butterfly. In an entertaining and developmental way Assegid reveals her deep kinship with a continent which was her birthplace but is also her heart. Assegid's observations and reflections come to life through the personal stories she tells, the advice she receives from her grandmother, and the leaderful insights she shares from her integral studies. *Butterflies Over Africa* offers profoundly new options for transforming a continent that are culturally sensitive, organizationally strategic and globally complex. We would do well to support this leader of leaders."

—Marilyn Hamilton PhD CGA
Author, *Integral City: Evolutionary Intelligences for the Human Hive*
Founder & President : Integral City Meshworks Inc.

"J'ai trouve ce livre particulièrement intéressant et stimulant. Il est à la fois un condensé de "vie" et une analyse de "pratiques de développement".

[I found this book particularly interesting and stimulating... It is at the same time an intense summary of a life and a practical analysis of development.]
—Ibrahim Mayaki, PhD, CEO NEPAD

"In *Butterflies over Africa* I saw and relived much of what I had talked about with Yene one evening long ago about making the difference at the point of "contacta" - making the difference with the person here with you at this time, building the connections over space and over time. To build connections, we have to recognize where we are starting from, who we are, where we stand and what we should keep from our heritage and what should be discarded in order to advance to the next level of consciousness. There is no movement/advancement without loss. A swimmer who does not push air out of his lungs pretty soon cannot swim."

"We all have two time frames—our lifetime and eternity.
We have a life time to plant the seed that will grow in eternity.
What is your timeframe?

What is the real time frame of the Integrated Africa? I think we have only just started."
—Rita Mazzocchi, PhD
Human Rights Lawyer

BUTTERFLIES OVER *Africa*

PERSPECTIVES ON CHANGING AND TRANSFORMING THE CONTINENT

YENE ASSEGID

Integral Publishers

Published by Integral Publishers
http://www.integralleadershipreview.com
http://www.integralpublishers.com
733 Mermaid Avenue
Pacific Grove, California, USA 93950
831 333-9200

Cover design and text layout by Terry Ann Hayes
Cover photograph by Matthias Reusing, 2009
View from Imet Gogo (3,926 meters), Simien Mountains, Ethiopia

For more information about Integral Publishers:
russ@integralleadershipreview.com

ISBN: 978-0-578-03993-0

To Almazesha

"I would like to leave behind me the conviction that, if we maintain a certain amount of caution and organization we deserve victory [....]
You cannot carry out fundamental change without a certain amount of madness.
In this case, it comes from nonconformity, the courage to turn your back on the old formulas, the courage to invent the future.
It took the mad men of yesterday for us to be able to act with extreme clarity today.
I want to be one of those mad men. [...]
We must dare to invent the future..."
(Thomas Sankara, August 21, 1983)

Contents

TEXTE ORIGINAL

Preface

Un continent dont la moitie de la population a moins de vingt ans doit inventer des modes de gouvernance originaux et adaptes, adaptes a ses défis démographiques et de développement.

Ces modes de gouvernance ne pourront se construire sans un leadership conscient de notre réalité afin de favoriser des situations de sécurité et de progrès. La question qui doit être posée, pour l'Afrique, est de savoir si nous disposons aujourd'hui de cette capacité de leadership et sinon, comment peut-elle être créée ?

Le livre de Yene Assegid pose cette question essentielle et y apporte des réponses avec raison et passion. Sa vie, comme acteur de base du développement, lui a fait voir et analyser les écueils des politiques et des stratégies destinées à créer du progrès et à transformer des sociétés.

Elle a côtoyé le meilleur et le pire des contextes, elle a analyse des théories et vécu des pratiques.

Face à un pessimisme ambiant et généralisé, elle offre des pistes neuves qui tranchent avec les théories des « professionnels du développement » en remettant les femmes et les hommes au cœur du « débat » sur leur devenir.

Je considère ce livre comme un instrument essentiel de progrès car il permet de se poser des questions de fond sur nos approches de développement et de comprendre les vrais obstacles à l'appropriation.

Cette réappropriation du politique par les populations africaines est une condition sine qua non pour relever les défis du siècle à venir ou alors notre marginalisation risque de s'accentuer.

Mon propre vécu me fait ressentir intuitivement que sa quête est non seulement salutaire mais aussi féconde de créations stratégiques et institutionnelles correspondant a ce que nous sommes et non pas conduites par des systèmes qui pensent pour nous.

Bien entendu, il ne s'agit pas de réfléchir en termes de «fabrication de miracles » mais de construire intelligemment un leadership responsable, démocratique et ouvert à l'écoute. Parler de techniques dans ce domaine est certes provocateur mais en même temps innovateur : notre jeunesse doit être formée à assumer ce leadership dont nous avons tant besoin et les programmes décrits dans ce livre doivent constituer une inspiration a ce projet

Rappelons –nous que l'invention du « développement » au sortir de la seconde guerre mondiale a trace les voies dans lesquelles se sont engouffrées les stratégies de nos pays : stratégies mimétiques pour l'essentiel qui ont asséché nos imaginations et donne un rôle secondaire a nos populations.

Une des causes majeures de la faible qualité de nos indicateurs socio-économiques tient à cette propension que nous avons eue de « regarder vers l'extérieur « sans vraiment « réfléchir a partir de l'intérieur ».

En remettant en cause les approche habituelles par lesquelles nous avons jusqu'à présent pense nos stratégies et mis en œuvre nos pratiques, nous faisons preuve non seulement de résistance a l'échec mais en même temps libérons notre sens de l'innovation.

Quand Yene Assedig aborde ces questions, elle le fait avec la passion d'une Africaine convaincue que l'investissement dans les personnes est la clé de notre « présence au monde ».

Nous ne pouvons pas dire que nos élites ont véritablement permis aux peuples auxquels elles appartiennent d'être des acteurs de leur progrès au XX eme siècle : construisons le XXI eme siècle en ayant a l'esprit qu'une autre gouvernance est possible.

—Ibrahim Assane Mayaki,
CEO, Nepad
Ancien Premier Ministre du Niger

ENGLISH TRANSLATION

Preface

A continent with half of its population under the age of twenty owes it to itself to invent a new way of governance, adapted and contextualized to the challenges imposed by its demography as well as its development.

This way of governance would only be able to emerge with a leadership that is conscious of our reality, in order to create an enabling environment for security and progress. The question that we would ask for Africa, is whether or not we have such leadership capacity and if not, how we could possibly create it?

Yene Assegid's book asks this key question and brings us a range of answers that come both with reason and passion. Her life as a development practitioner at the grassroots level has given her a particular vantage point allowing her to see and analyze the policy and development strategies aiming to bring progress and transformation within the African societies and communities.

She has seen the best and the worst of situations in the given context, she analyses theories and experienced the practice.

Despite the common and generalized pessimism, she offers new approaches that cut away from the mainstream theories of "development professionals"; that rather reinstate women and men in the heart of the debate about their own future.

I consider this book to be an essential instrument for progress because it probes us to ask ourselves deeper questions about our approach to development and to reflect on the true core issues, causes and obstacles obstructing our way forward.

This need to innovate development policies by African peoples for African peoples, is a precondition for us to face up to the challenges of the coming century, without which our marginalization only risks further accentuation.

My own personal experience makes me feel intuitively that her quest is not only worthy of consideration but also ripe with necessary institutional strategies corresponding to whom we are as a people as opposed to strategies and systems that think of and on behalf of us.

It goes without saying that it is not only about thinking in terms of "fabrication of miracles" but rather of intelligently building a leadership that is responsible, democratic and open to dialogue. To speak of technical tools and methods in this field of leadership might of course be a bit of a provocation but we must also appreciate the innovation that it brings. Our youth must be groomed to assume this leadership that we so dearly need and the programs described in this book must constitute an inspiration to our leaders.

Let us remember that the invention of "development" at the end of the Second World War lined the way in which our respective national strategies were entrenched: essentially desktop strategies that have dried out our imagination and creativity and given only backstage roles to our populations.

One of the major causes of the weak quality of our socioeconomic indicators is very much related to our propensity to look for solutions "outside first" without really "reflecting and thinking from within first."

By putting our usual approaches, the usual ways of formulating our strategies and implementing our practice, back on the table for reflection and evaluation, we not only say "No" to failure, but at the same time, we give way to our sense and capacity to innovate.

When Yene Assegid embarks on such questions, she does it with the passion of an African with the conviction that the key to our "emergence and presence in the world" is in our commitment to invest in our people.

We cannot fully say that in the twentieth century, our leaders have let their peoples become actors of progress; now for the twenty first century, let us move forward with the spirit and belief that another kind of governance is possible.

—Ibrahim Assane Mayaki,
CEO, Nepad,
Former Prime Minister of Niger

Prelude

This book is about hopes and dreams for change and transformation in Africa. It is about exploring what else is possible on this wonderful continent. It is a reflection on what I have learned and experienced in Africa. It is one voice amongst the millions of voices. I wrote this book to present a case arguing that unless we find a way to change and transform African leadership, it is unlikely that the African continent will reach its potential to flourish.

I grew up as a child with stories. I grew up very close to my family and grandparents, and stories were the main mode of discourse; hence, this book is filled with stories, which I hold inseparable from the theory and the praxis I discuss. Here in the Preface, I offer the story of my own beginning, my awakening.

In October 2008, my parents put our Brussels apartment, Avenue Brugman, up for sale. My parents and sisters, my family and I had been in that apartment for so long that it had a name—it is the first place we landed when we uprooted ourselves from Ethiopia in the mid-seventies after the Communists overthrew Emperor Haile-Selassie. This apartment, our first home outside of Ethiopia, would be leaving our family after all these years—the news made me think of the time my family first came to Brussels, some thirty plus years earlier, and the events leading up to our emigration.

I was eight years old when my family emigrated to Belgium, and that was when my awareness about Africa emerged. I was old enough to know, to remember, to sense fear around me. At the same time, I was young enough not to really know how to process this fear. I felt the air squeezed out of me as we left our home country to go and settle in Europe, like someone ripping me off my roots and putting me in a vase with some water when I really belonged planted in the earth. We were transplanted to another world with one single aircraft flight. At the time, I didn't appreciate the world I was leaving because it was the only thing I had ever known; over time, my roots have refused to relocate themselves, remaining deep in African soil and keeping my life focused on the continent where my life took shape.

LOVE, LAUGHTER, AND LIFE: THE ROOTS OF CHILDHOOD IN COMMUNITY

I was born in Addis Ababa[1] *the capital and largest city in Ethiopia. It sits on a plateau with the Entoto mountain range on the north, and the Blue Nile and Awash River basins on the south. Addis Ababa means "new flower" which describes it perfectly: a fragrant delight, which held all of the beauty in the world to me.*

I spent most of my early life in my grandmother's house, a large compound with an entire life of its own. She was a sage figure for the community and the surrounding areas as well, part of an ancient family that is well known and lovingly respected. She is most famous for her generosity and immense wisdom and passion for justice and humanity. Family, friends, and even outsiders go to her to help resolve their issues, then and now.

At that time, my grandmother owned a number of houses, some of which were on the same block, and my family lived in one. We referred to her house as "Lie–Bet," which literally means "upper house." Her home was the larger upper part in relation to the part of the compound that housed the larger kitchen, stables, and the warehouses for grain.

---

[1] Addis Ababa is the capital of Ethiopia and its largest city. It is currently the official diplomatic capital for Africa with more than ninety embassies and consular representatives. In 1963 it became the headquarters of the Organization of African Unity (OAU). And in 1988 Addis Ababa became the headquarters for the UN Economic Commission for Africa (UNECA). Also the African Union (AU), founded in 2002, is based in the Ethiopian capital.

Most houses in Ethiopia and other African nations are in compounds, meaning walled and gated properties. Homes are walled for security and privacy reasons. I suppose that initially these gates also ensured security against wild animals such as hyenas and leopards. Today there are not that many wild animals in urban areas. One might be able to see hyenas late at night, but leopards are never seen in town; even during night safaris, one must be lucky to see a leopard.

The gate of my grandmother's home was a quiet presence at the bottom of the street. It stood tall, emoting strength and security. There were gatemen whose job it was to stay at the gate at all times, and to open the gate for family, friends, and guests and then to immediately close the gate behind them. A car would honk its horn as it approached the gate—some of the drivers would frantically honk their horn just to tease the gatemen. The opening and closing of the gate was a stately ritual, and there was always excitement when a car came into the compound, the anticipation of families and friends coming to visit.

Once through the gate, on the left was the main house with a beautiful garden. Near the gate on the right was another, smaller garden. From the upper level of our home, we could look down into the courtyard and enjoy the rainbow of colors from the flowers that adorned our veranda. Driving down the steep road you could see my grandmother's home and my godmother's home as well. Lie-bet was not so huge, but the compound had many little stations or micro-neighborhoods. There were smaller homes for the cooks and the other help, and also a barn/stable structure and a storage house for the grain.

In the tradition of the African community, Lie-bet was filled with children, relatives, neighbors' children, and the children of the men and women who were working in my grandmother's home who had become family. It was a micro-system. There were rules and regulations and you just knew them by default from living there or being there. Respect was a factor of age: you went up the ladder of commanding respect from those who were younger, and there was no bypassing this rule. Arrogance, showing off, or being rude was the utmost crime; should you be found displaying any of those behaviors, the penalty could be anywhere from being verbally corrected all the way to the stick. It all depended on how badly you behaved, whom you behaved that way toward, and also the state of the compound (meaning whether all was peaceful or whether there was some crisis at hand).

Almazesha (Almaz Haile-Mariam), my maternal grandmother, is a unique and exceptional woman. She is a woman of substance—the pure essence of strength and character who has always followed her heart. She has been and is a role model for many. Almazesha comes from a family of intellectuals and warriors: a family where principles and the code of conduct apply to all, regardless of age. Her strong will and courage come through in all aspects of her life. She comes from a very old lineage of women. She is the first-born daughter and oldest child of Berhane ("my light"). Berhane was also the first born daughter of Gessessech Hagos, who herself was the oldest daughter and traced her line back to Emperor Yohanes IV, who was the last Emperor in the world to die in battle while defending his country from invaders. My mother is the first-born child and oldest daughter, and I too, am the oldest daughter in this line.

Somehow, this line might have contributed to my friendship and attachment with Almazehsa beyond that of the usual grandmother–grandchild relationship. At Lie-Bet, my grandmother kept a beautiful rose garden—she loves roses and prunes her plants herself. Each time she went in the garden, I followed, and this was my time alone with her. She told me stories. She told me what was going on. She asked me questions, and even though I was a child she gave me the same attention as if I were an adult. She always says that it is important to recognize that children are full souls in a little body and that speaking with them should not be in baby language, as this will inhibit their evolution and maintain them in a state of intellectually and emotionally stunted growth. What I loved most was how she treated me as a sovereign person, an adult, not a child. She paid attention to what I had to say and was respectful and supportive. She understood and even enjoyed the mischief we did as children. In my relationship with her there is an expectation of living up to all the women who came before and passing on that same wisdom to all who will come in future.

After the Communist revolution, when the new authorities put a ban on the ceremonies for mourning the dead, Almazesha was among the few who cried and mourned overtly, despite the fact that violating the ban could pos-

sibly cost her her life. She mourned because she refused to break the tradition of her ancestors and the culture of her country. She cried because she had to express her grief and loss, even if expressing it meant that she might be the victim of a spare bullet.

Almazesha's bravery and courage led her to play a key role in the establishment of one of the few independent parties for our current Ethiopian government. She worked to build a nation and defended the existence of diverse communities. Her empathy for others, her good heart, and her innate wisdom passed on from a line of ancestors who fought in wars, have made her my shining star and the main person who has shaped my soul.

My grandfather, Ababi (Ato Makonnen Yetemegnu) was a grand beautiful man; tall, with beautiful olive skin, demure in his ways and very reserved. He was the complete opposite of my grandmother who is a woman of energy and constant excitement. Together they set the tone in our family and instilled the value of education. Ababi spent close to 75% of his modest salary on the education of his eight children, my mother and her brothers and sisters. He used to tell me how he had a motorbike with a seat attached next to it, like those the Germans used in World War I and II. Every morning he would take the first three daughters to school and every afternoon he would bring them back. I am not sure what he used to take the others to school when their time came around.

What I know in my heart is that the wealth I inherit from my family is in the education I was given. All of our resources were always put into education. We could ask for as many books as we wanted, and even any special program—if it had to do with our education there was never an issue. Short of that, there was not much. We did not have many toys, expensive clothes, or treats, but we did have a love of learning and a wonderful, sharing family.

Every afternoon during the workweek, we children would wait by the gate for Ababi to come home from work. We would all pile into his Volkswagen bug and drive to Enrico's, a famous pastry and sweet shop and restaurant. (It is still there!) Enrico's always had Italian gelati (ice cream). I would usually choose strawberry; my sisters and cousins would have their own favorites. On the way home, we would lick our cones, all messy and sticky, and smiling happily. These were wonderful times.

My father, Assegid Tessema, has the same attitude toward education. He shares with my sisters and me his story of how he went from growing up in a rural area all the way to becoming an international businessman. He continues to tell us how it all got started with the scholarships he received to go from primary school to his post-graduate degree in Geneva. He had to run away from home to be able to go to primary school on the scholarship he received from the Emperor Haile Selassie. He tells us about the Jesuits who kept the school and all the care they gave to their students. These scholarships were the Emperor's way of creating intellectuals and spreading education through the nation. As long as the student was able to study and willing to continue, the Emperor maintained the scholarship, and that is how my father was educated from primary school in Harar all the way to doing his post-graduate work in Geneva. My father always ends the story of his early life with his insistence that education was the key to being self-sufficient and creating choices and possibilities in life. Together with my mother, Selamawite Makonnen, they gave my sisters and I the best anyone could ever wish for, albeit not always in comfortable circumstances.

I remember sitting on the veranda of my grandparents' house in Lie-Bet around mid-morning, while looking out at the mountain ranges beyond our family compound and seeing the smaller hills and valleys nearby. It made me feel peaceful, serene and secure. The air felt dry and clean, and I could smell the fragrant flowers from the courtyard below. These moments held some of my favorite memories with my grandparents.

When I would sit with my grandfather, Ababi, we would hold hands and he would invite me to drink a café-au-lait with him. Sometimes I would even have a doughnut! He would tell me about his cows, the ones he had before they built this upper house. He said the cows would all stop whatever they were doing to greet him when he came back from work. He loved his cows and he is sure they loved him back. He swears they knew him well and that they would communicate with him. The story would always end with "well, and one day I came home and they were no longer there, Almaz [my grandmother] had sold them." By the end of the story his voice would have a sadness and resignation that goes with the loss of a wonderful life gone by, as he stared out into the mountains that filled the horizon. Then he would pick up my hand and holding it say, "Your hands are warm, Mamishet." He was the only one who called me Mamishet or Mamay, his pet name for me. I would tell him his hands were warm, too. And we would sit a while longer in contented silence. This was our ritual, and it never changed throughout my life. It was the same ritual until the end.

When I sat with Almazesha, it was totally different. She would laugh a lot and found humor in all things in life. Each time someone passed in front of the veranda, they would greet her warmly. The greetings were in Amharic (the official language of Ethiopia) and Afan Oromo (the second language in Ethiopia, mostly spoken amongst farmers). She speaks both languages fluently. She knew the name and life story of every person who greeted her. The people of Lie-Bet were special to her and she was special to them. She is caring and filled with love and humor.

These were the first years of my life. Lie-Bet was the center of my universe—I would go back to my parents' home just to sleep. On some weekends I would stay over at my grandmother's with my sister, Fofi. My other sisters Noel and Lily were not born yet. We would sleep right in the middle between our grandparents.

LOSS OF INNOCENCE: CHANGE, CONFLICT, AND EMIGRATION

Before the revolution, I never thought about safety. Rule of law, safety, code of conduct and the like—I took all that for granted until I experienced what it is to live in the absence of security, law, or a humane code of conduct. The only things that might have worried me before the revolution were stray dogs or the hyenas we heard in the night.

After the revolution, things were very different. Even at that young age, I became fearful of people in uniform. I became uncomfortable when people gathered around the entrance of a home or gathered in the streets—I always felt things would take a turn for the worst.

After the revolution, things changed at school and at home. There was a different texture to life. Everything was quiet, hushed. The father of one boy at school was a colonel in the new government—if you did not do as Johannes said, he would threaten to get your parents shot. I thought I was cursed be-

cause Johannes was in my class. I was scared that if I ever upset him, he might get my mother or father killed, or both! Looking back now, maybe some of the stories in school were fabricated, but at the time it felt and sounded so real and added to the stress of my young life.

We felt the stress at home, too—the children of Lie-Bet met in secret councils to make our plans for the best way to avoid the bullets we felt would certainly come. Our "plans" were ill-informed and we felt our impotence, but we had to do something to react to the tension. We wanted to feel safe.

It was in this atmosphere that my parents made plans to leave Ethiopia. I heard my parents whispering one evening when we were at my grandmother's house. Most of my aunts and uncles were there and, as usual, I was the last child to go to bed. I would always lie on the sofa on my grandmother's lap and she would lightly scratch my scalp and run her fingers through my hair. This would make me feel so happy and safe that I would soon fall asleep. My eyes were shut when I heard my parents speaking in English. My aunts and uncles asked each other whether I was truly asleep. "She must be asleep because her eyes are closed." Still speaking in English, in hushed tones, they all agreed they did not want me to hear what they had to discuss. They did not want me to hear because they feared that children would be used against their own parents as informers. It was true, I was going to the French school, but I knew what they were saying. I understood them. I chose to pretend to be sleeping because I was hurt that my parents did not trust me anymore. This is what the government had done—it brought enough paranoia and fear that children, parents, brothers, and sisters no longer trusted each other.

My family discussed the departure of my father who was going to leave for Europe. I heard the word "Europe," but had no concept of it. I thought they might have meant Nairobi because I had heard of Nairobi, but I did not know where it was either. In Amharic we often refer to someone traveling as going "out" or "towards out," which to me meant out of our community and into foreign lands. I assumed that we were leaving for either Europe or Nairobi; regardless of which place, the fact was that we were going "towards out." I never talked about it.

One morning, very early, my father came to my room to kiss me goodbye. He thought I was asleep, and gave me a kiss on my forehead. The plan was for him to leave ahead of us to prepare for our arrival. He was expecting us to leave within thirty days and had managed to get a visa to go to Belgium. I felt such a deep sadness seeing him go. It was the kind of sadness that chokes at your throat, hits hard in your stomach, and makes your body feel like one hollow space.

As most daughters, I love my father very much, so much that my throat gets tight just thinking about him and his goodness. My father is a modest, humble man and to me, he is the greatest of all. That morning, when he was leaving, it was easier for me to pretend to be asleep so I would not be wimpy and cry; but at the last moment I needed to say something to him, anything to feel one last connection. So, I opened one eye and asked him for a quarter so I could buy a crochet needle, to crochet a decoration for my room. I know it makes no sense, yet it was my way of having one more moment with my father. I had to have a reason to talk so my tears would not come out first. He did not give me a quarter, but instead, he gave me an Ethiopian Birr. It was a lot of money then, I could not believe it!

As I looked down at the dollar my father gave me, nothing seemed the same. He was gone. I was sad and empty when my father left, but those feelings were soon pushed aside as the next few weeks were filled with activity. My mother started selling all of the furniture and household appliances. People were constantly coming to buy, and some things my mother gave away, and soon the house was empty. Our voices resonated as echoes throughout the hollow home.

One night our guard, Hussein, banged on my bedroom window. He was banging so hard he startled me and my sister, Fofi. I opened the window slightly to hear him better—he was ordering us to open the main door. He was screaming, "Open the main door! Open the main door!" He was panic-stricken. Fofi and I went out to the living room together to open the main door.

I remember we were wearing our pajamas: little white nightgowns with a big doll on them and writing that said, "Hello Sweetie." Off we went to the living room together, because we always followed each other.

Looking through the glass door, I knew that more than one person was standing outside, but I could not see who they were. From the shadows, I thought I could see that it was my Aunt Koky being dropped off by her husband Yigezu. He was a pilot and he often used to drop her off early in the morning when he had to fly out. Since we thought it was Aunt Koky, my sister and I confidently opened the door.

We were wrong.

There stood many soldiers in their fatigues. A shotgun was pointed straight at us. All I saw was a barrel. It was the barrel of a rifle, eye level to my face. I do not know if I was in shock, but I do not remember being very afraid. I did not know if he would really shoot me. I just remember wondering, why do they have their rifles pointed at my face? Even then, I made sure my younger sister Fofi was behind me. I tried to protect her.

The men seemed tall and their military fatigues looked new. Perhaps they were not that tall, but being seven years old at the time, they just seemed huge to me.

It was so cold outside that the air felt very fresh, almost wet.

House searching had become a common practice. Soldiers would search homes randomly or because someone had reported the family to the kebeles, or community authorities. The search process could be just a search, but it could also end with arrest and sometimes even executions of men and women found to be against the revolution.

There were six or seven of the soldiers, and they pushed me over as they opened the door to our living room. They stated flatly: "We have come to search the house." They nodded to each other and went in various directions. Some stood guard while others searched, and there was one who gave orders to the others. They were looking for weapons or any incriminating imperialist material. These infractions were punishable by immediate execution on the spot or, at the very least, imprisonment. It depended on the whim of the lead soldier.

The soldiers headed straight for my mother's room where she was sleeping. My parents' room was not so big, but it seemed huge to me back then. I remember it had wall-to-wall red carpet. My mother woke quickly and came out in her nightgown, a beautiful gown with a matching robe. When the soldiers saw her and the red carpet, they bad mouthed her and mumbled: "Look at this Imperialist with the red carpet." By this time, I was so frightened that

I thought they would start shooting right away. Thank God, my mother was very calm. It is funny now that I think about it. She just looked at them and said: "Yes, eh, how can I help you?" How can anybody say that at four o'clock in the morning when soldiers have just barged into your room? It was her calm and staid manner that saved our lives.

The soldiers restated their purpose of looking for weapons and Imperialist material. They encouraged my mother to surrender any weapons before the search began because if we said that we did not have weapons and the soldiers found them, the penalty would be costly, even death.

My mother said, "We don't have any weapons because our one and only protector is God himself, not man-made rifles." The soldiers stopped her in the middle of her declaration and began shaking their heads, stating that they did not want to hear this religious rubbish. Religion was discouraged because it did not support the efforts of the revolution. They gave her a warning look that said: if we find anything, you will be in serious trouble.

They looked, searched, and made the path of a desert windstorm as they turned over furniture, threw clothes from the closets, emptied drawers, and pulled pictures from the wall.

I followed them and watched.

Then, they went into my room, the room where I played. In that room, up in the closet, there were two suitcases where we kept Christmas decorations. All of our suitcases were the same: a greenish color, all leather with nice buckles. I guess if I had them now, they would be considered beautiful antiques. Back then, they were just suitcases. Pointing at the suitcases, the soldiers said: "What's up there? What's up there?" My mother said: "Christmas decorations." I am not sure if the soldiers understood or could not relate to the Christmas experience complete with Santa and the tree—they did not seem to know what Christmas decorations were and they really did not care to know. All they wanted to know was whether there were Imperialist products from the bourgeois in our suitcases. At this point, they ordered our compound guard, Hussein, to climb up and get the suitcases. Hussein's knees were shaking so badly that he could hardly stand. I do not know what they had done to him, if anything. Perhaps it was just the fear of what they could do. They motioned again for him to climb up and pull down the suitcases. Hussein was so scared that he pulled down the wrong suitcase. The entire suitcase came down on him, spilling its contents of Christmas decorations onto his head, leaving him looking like a Christmas tree! How funny and sad it all was. I know the soldiers wanted to laugh, but they did not. Hussein certainly did not want to laugh. He almost had a heart attack. He thought he was going to be shot on the spot. However, he was not, and the soldiers left my room and continued their search.

They went through the service rooms where the cook and the housecleaner were sleeping. Then the soldiers noticed a door leading to an underground room. It was where we kept the supply of grain. They ordered us to open the door, but unfortunately, we could not find the key. Maybe it was panic or the stress of the moment, but that key was nowhere to be found.

All of the adults, who had been following the soldiers, had told them repeatedly that it was the supply room; however, they needed to see it for themselves. They insisted again that we open the door, but the harder we looked, the more insistent the key was on staying lost! So there we were, standing on the stairs looking into the backyard. I remember my mother looked over to one of the soldiers and said: "Would you care for some cognac?" He looked at her, puzzled. I was puzzled too! She continued: "Well, you know, it is cold outside. It will help you with the weather. Even the Russians drink." I guess she meant vodka, because the Russians were not known for drinking cognac. The soldier looked at her and said he did not drink when he was on duty. He was starting to warm up to us but he was still very strict and severe-looking. Watching the two of them and feeling the mood of the night, I was not sure if this was all real or some sort of macabre game.

I had built a little path to go through the shrubs to my grandmother's house. I asked the soldiers if they wanted to go visit my grandmother's house. I do not know what compelled me to ask them. By nature I was very shy, so speaking up to adults, let alone soldiers, was not within my usual behavior. I may have been trying to distract them from the missing key to the supply grain room. In any case, taking them to my grandmother's home was irresponsible.

In a matter of minutes we were on our way to Lie-Bet. I was leading the soldiers through the little passageway through the plants that I had built big enough for my little cousins and me. The soldiers had to bend down and crawl painfully as they followed me through the passageway. When we arrived at the gate (where I usually called out for the other children to open the little passage that locks on the side of my grandmother's house), I called out for Almenesh. She was part of our band, my circle of friends and cousins. She lived there, but did not respond. Then, suddenly someone else opened the door and there I was, walking into my grandmother's compound with the soldiers following close behind! I assume now the delay was due to my mother calling my grandmother to warn her of the search. My grandmother ordered her staff to remove any weapons, as most people did have weapons at home, small revolvers and rifles.

The soldiers were elated. They thought they were going to get an easy catch or an easy victim. My grandmother's compound was very big and it would take them three hours to search. This was something I will never forgive myself for because it could have ended very badly.

The soldiers went straight for the main house in Lie-Bet. They headed to my grandparents bedroom. My grandmother had let go of all of the weapons, except for a small bird rifle, a BB gun that my Uncle Essayas would use to hunt birds. When we walked into my grandmother's bedroom, my Auntie Koky was also sleeping there. She had recently had a baby, Timmy, who was sleeping in his crib in my grandmother's room. My grandfather, Ababi, was also there. The BB gun was there, too. My grandmother knew if they found the BB gun that anything could happen, especially since the soldiers' operation was to rid the nation of imperialists and landlords. They set about completing their mission with a vengeance, with my grandparents being an ideal situation to set an "example."

My grandmother opened the door of her room, let the soldiers in, and waited for them to continue searching. I was walking around with the soldiers and I remember my Auntie Koky almost fainted when they left.

Now many years later I found out the rest of the story.

As it turned out, Almazesha still had the BB gun when the soldiers were searching the room. She had put it under the baby. My grandmother is a brave woman and this bold act saved her family.

About a week or so after that horrible night, it was time to leave. The night before we left, everyone came to say good-bye. Some people were teas-

ing us, saying that there was no Ethiopian food where we were going and that we would be stuck with fries and pasta! "Eat all you can now," they said, "because you won't get this kind of food ever again. All you will eat is hamburgers." Belgium, however, was not the land of hamburgers that they thought it was.

Some of our friends were crying so hard that I thought someone had died or was about to die. The amount of crying was comparable to that of a funeral. True, in some ways this was like a funeral. We might not ever come back, or have anyone to come back to. The future looked dark and unpredictable. I really did not understand the intensity of the sadness, but I did have such heaviness in my heart that it hurt when I took a deep breath, and I choked.

My sister, Fofi, and I decided to cry along with everyone else because we were the only ones not crying. People cried all night long. They fell asleep crying and woke up crying. There had been days that our family and relatives cried about our departure. On this particular morning, the crying was even more acute. In fact, I think the crying might not have been exclusively for us, but for the situation in general. People might have been crying for their eminently unpredictable destinies, for the country, for the irreversible change that was taking place.

We said goodbye systematically. We moved from one Aunt to the next, from one Uncle or Cousin, kissing and briefly hugging. Some were faking a smile or even cracking jokes to lighten up the mood. No sooner did we kiss and hug to say our goodbyes, then a series of grunts, coughs, or deep sighs mixed with illegitimate tears[2] flowed out, warping and distorting any semblance of last minute conversations. Often the last words that came out, straining to make it through vocal cords coiled up in tight throats, were: "May God guard you" or "May He guide you." Then a heavy sigh followed, as if from relief of having been able to blurt out the last blessings.

Now the time to say goodbye had truly come. In order to avoid the big crowd of family and friends at the front door, I jumped out the bathroom

[2] We were all supposed to be very brave and not cry. It was implicitly understood. As much as for funerals, we in Ethiopia even have an entire crying ceremony—but this time, crying was not really welcomed. We had to be brave, despite the wrenching feelings of separation. So, we all pretended to be brave. When some tears erupted, we accused the dust and the wind, or shrugged it off like it didn't happen.

window and went through to my grandmother's house because I knew that the cars taking us to the airport would leave from Lie-Bet. I soon realized that I had not escaped anything because everyone—my mother, uncles, cousins, and friends—were all there at Lie-Bet, crying. I was trying to hold it in and be strong, but when I turned and saw my mother and grandmother hugging and crying, I cried, too.

That was the moment, the realization—the one where my world that had "wholeness" like a complete egg in the safety of its shell, was gone. My heart and emotions were cracked open and raw.

It was not goodbye. It was Farewell and May God Be With You.

Before long, we were all in the Fiat that my Grandmother had bought for my Uncle Essayas. He is my youngest uncle and was my best childhood friend in so many ways. Only eight years older than I am, he was my big brother who grew up with Fofi and me. He seemed so "old" to us then, when in reality he was only in his late teens.

On the day that we actually left the country, the ride to the airport was a slow and unforgettable ride. Before the revolution, I only knew rides to the airport as a time to either pick someone up or as a family outing to go get pastries or ice cream and watch the planes land and take off. It was always a very special treat when my aunts or uncles or parents took us to the airport. I suppose for me it compared to a child, nowadays, going to Cape Canaveral to see the rockets and the space shuttles.

The morning we left Ethiopia, going to the airport was no longer an outing; it was rather a painful memory of being ripped out of that which gave us a sense of belonging, a sense of community and security. It was an unforgettable and traumatic experience. It was still dark when we woke up, and by the time we were ready to go to the cars and say goodbye, the morning mist had still not lifted. For me, it was only the second time in my life to be up so early. (The first time was when my sister and I had been flower girls for our Aunt Koky's wedding, just about a year earlier than this time.)

We drove out of my grandparents' home. I remember that as the engines started and cars started moving, my heart was just ripped out of my rib cage. I felt hollow, empty, floating, dizzy, afraid and also brave, and even more so, very sad. These were the moments that would remain with me for ages, the minutes that I drove out from Lie-Bet. It was like being thrown out of a nest without being fully formed.

There were a number of cars that followed us to the Bole Airport; some were needed to carry the suitcases, others cars were just full of family members wanting to be with us until the last minute. The cars followed each other up the hill to the main street and down on the large and deserted road leading to the airport. We had driven the same route so many times for so many routine things of life. Now, the images on the street looked like shots from a silent movie with no actors in it, just images containing a million stories and even more questions.

I had not been to the airport since the revolution had started. The drive to the airport now was frightening and strange. Everyone in the car was eerily quiet as was the road and the usually bustling landscape.

There was a checkpoint on the road to the airport. When we got close to it, there was a belt of nails lying in the middle of the street to force the cars to stop, as if the soldiers with their rifles were not intimidating enough to make you stop. This meant that should you dare to continue without stopping your tires would pop, and you would probably be shot as well.

This was the first roadblock I had ever seen. It was more than a road-block; it was a block to our human rights and humanity. The soldiers on duty opened the car to look in the trunk, the glove compartment, under the seats. They looked everywhere. I do not know for what or why. It was just another example of the paranoia from the revolution. Photos, cassettes, and books were not allowed out of the country without a specially obtained license—this was one of the ways that the government managed to keep much of the cruelty that took place in the country, hidden from the rest of the world.

The feeling of insecurity was intense. To this day, I tense up each time I see a roadblock or a detour. We had to go through each one and feel our hearts beat in the tips of our fingers as the checks were conducted by well armed soldiers. I was not sure exactly what they were looking for, and I was not sure if we had reason to worry or not make it past the checks.

The same engine sound that had ripped my heart from my rib cage when we departed Lie-Bet anointed my heart with oil each time we made it through one roadblock after the other. There was no guarantee that we would make it through the roadblocks, and the worst part was not knowing exactly what the soldiers were looking for.

Finally, we arrived at the terminal. This time it was not pleasant to be at the airport. It was a place of anguish and painful separations overseen by an airport staff and guards whose dark, piercing eyes that only added to the feelings of fear and dread.

Once at the airport, my sisters and I just followed my mother. We did not ask questions. We just had to move along through the process of checking in and boarding a plane that would fly us to another life. I remember boarding the plane with so much curiosity. But it was not really seen as polite or good manners for children to engage in adults' conversation, except when adults invited them to speak or take part. So, I just followed instructions and kept everything else inside my heart. It was not that my parents or elders were strict; it was just the way it was. Children listen, learn, and follow; grown-ups speak, teach, and lead the way.

Koky's husband, Uncle Yigezu, came all the way into the airplane. I remember that so clearly. He always had a spring in his step and a smile. Uncle Yigezu made sure that we were well-seated and comfortable. He gave us a sporty wave (Air Force style) that made me happy, and I smiled my brightest.

This was the last time that I would ever see my Uncle Yigezu. He came all the way into the plane because he was a pilot and had special permission. He gave my mother a big hug and waved to us—his last wave. He passed away a few years later.

When the plane took off Fofi and I were still crying. We had been on a plane only once before to go to Harar, to visit my paternal grandmother's house, and this plane was bigger than that one. It lasted what seemed an eternity, but the flight to Europe did not take more than 7-8 hours.

I boarded as a child, and disembarked as a pseudo-adult under siege in a particular circumstance, a person yanked into the hierarchical operational ranks of the household. As the oldest child, I automatically assumed my role to help out with my younger sisters and any other household things I could help with. I had grown up on the spot. My departure from Ethiopia also marked the first time that I was left face-to-face with my parents. I say this because before leaving Ethiopia, I spent my days either in school during weekdays or mostly at Lie-Bet. I only came home to sleep—all the rest of the time I was at Lie-Bet with all the other children.

THE COUNTRY OF THE FOREIGNERS: ARRIVAL AS AN EMIGREE

We were supposed to land in Brussels; however, I learned years later that we landed in Amsterdam because the weather was so severe. There the seven of us were: my mother, my Uncle Essayas, Abaye (my adopted oldest sister), my sisters Fofi, Noela, and Lily; and me. There were four children under eight years of age, two teenagers, and my mother who was in her late twenties at the time.

We were all in a state of shock and uncertainty as we sojourned into the unknown. My mother was the only one who knew anything about the Western world, having gone to school in the United States—for the rest of us, it was a series of "firsts."

When we arrived in Amsterdam, we had to go down escalators. We had never seen escalators before, not even on TV. Abaye, my older sister, was carrying Lily, our youngest sister who could barely walk. As Abaye stepped on the down escalator, she lost her balance and almost fell along with Lily, but Essayas quickly snatched Baby Lily from her hands, which allowed Abaye to regain her balance. The three of us, Fofi, Noela, and I just watched, stunned by what took place. I guess we sort of froze and did not know how to manage the escalators. We could not move, because the near fall of Abaye scared us all. Essayas, very caring and thoughtful as usual, went up and down the escalator to help us go down one at a time. This was our first encounter with the Western world.

What struck me the most about this airport and this new country where we landed were the smells and scents. It was different than what I knew in Ethiopia. It looked different, smelled different, and felt different altogether. The light was very different as well—bright lights, but all in neon. The airport looked desolate and abandoned because it was so late.

We boarded a bus in Amsterdam and headed to Zaventem (Brussels Airport). The trip was so long that it did not seem to have an end, continuing seemingly forever. In another first, we saw snow, and what I remember most was the cold. It was the unforgiving kind of cold that starts with your fingers and toes and seems to go right through to your very soul, rattling every bone.

By the time we arrived at Zaventem, we were all drained, but none of us admitted to being tired. We had to keep on going and we kept on going. Then I finally saw my father's silhouette—he was wearing a raincoat like Colombo's, the popular television detective. I remember I was holding my little sister, Lily, who had just turned one that day. It was her birthday, December 28th.

I was so happy to see him! Seeing my father meant, in my young heart, that everything would be okay. I felt secure. I thought he could do all things and that if he was around, then all would be well. I wanted to run to him and hug and kiss him, but I was too shy, so I waited for him to walk over to me. My emotions, my heart, were all twisted in my throat making me feel like I could not breathe. Then I started to cry: desert tears, the kind of tears that brim the eye and never go any further, like the desert rain in a distance—you feel the wind, see the torrent, but it never comes any closer.

My strongest memory of that first night is the smells. I smelled the cold, the snow, the air, the car—even the people smelled different. There was not a cat or soul to be seen. It was late in the night, but still, I was stunned by how quiet the whole place was. We drove through streets and boulevards, each with their own set of smells.

In the car, I kept on thinking, "now we are in the country of the foreigners." I did not yet understand that now I was the foreigner. Back home, white people were called "ferenge." I don't know where this word comes from, but maybe it comes from people trying to either say "foreigner" or "Français." In my mind, it was only logical that upon seeing so many white non-Ethiopians in our travels that day, I assumed we were in their country.

Finally, the car was parked and we were at our new home. We went on a small elevator to the third floor. There were only two apartments on our floor, ours and one other family.

When we walked into the apartment, I remember seeing apples on the top of the refrigerator—red, beautiful apples! Apples were just not a common fruit in Ethiopia; they were a luxury, a special treat that really made me aware of the ones sitting on top of the fridge. I could not believe it, eight apples sitting right there!

We all had a light meal and a little conversation, and then it was time to go to sleep. It was snowing. It seemed as if we were suspended in mid-air on the third floor. There was no compound to protect us. There was no sun. It was cold. It was dark. Quiet. I suddenly felt trapped in this new place with the smells that were so different from my home, my Africa.

In my young mind, I was not aware of the distance we had traveled. I fantasized that all of my friends would come driving down the street and I would wave to them from the window and go running down the stairs to welcome them.

What I did not understand, at that time, was that my mother and father had left Ethiopia for good, or let's say, indefinitely. Many years later, they told us that they had left with all their savings, amounting to not more than 10,000 USD with four children under 10 and two adolescents in their care. There is a proverb in Ethiopia that says that "smoke will always find an outlet." It means that if you try, you always will find a way to survive and come out of your circumstances.

The apartment had four bedrooms, a living room, a dining room, and two bathrooms—it was large, but we were a large group. That Avenue Brugman apartment became our home, and stayed in our family for thirty years; the sale truly marked the closing of a cycle.

Leaving one's country by force and for survival requires one to hold a particular, complex set of feelings. The ability to leave the country is not always granted for all, so when we get the chance to leave a situation of conflict where our lives are at stake, we feel grateful. At the same time, we are aware that we cannot all leave—an entire community cannot leave—so there is a sense of rupture, a sense of being ripped apart from the collective of those we love the most and from the environment that we have always known. There is often no looking back. You pack, you go; sometimes you don't even pack, you just go. We are never sure of seeing our loved ones again or finding anyone again, should we return home one day. So, we leave it all to God, to Jesus, to Allah, to the One who is all capable and omnipotent.

For me, leaving always had a taste and a particular physical state. There is a bitter taste that emanates from the back of the tonsils, something that pulls on my gut, and always a sense of tingling in the body with a heart rate racing in silence. Leaving brands images and emotions that one can never really get rid of, these deeply rooted images and emotions affect us the rest of our lives. And forever thereafter, each time I leave from a place that I had made into a home, I know to take a deep breath and negotiate with my emotions, as you would negotiate the gear box of a stick shift driving up a hill, to avoid clashing gears or reaching dramatic states of sadness. I focus on knowing that nothing is permanent—all things will pass and I too will pass one day.

This time of emigration and re-settlement marked a great shift in my life. After leaving Ethiopia, life would never be the same again. I would never really be in a place that I belonged to. I would always be a visitor, a guest, maybe at best a long-time guest. And if I ever returned to my country, I would be the "returnee"—another sort of guest. Such is the basis of my life and the lives of hundreds of other families that have had to leave their countries looking for peace, safety, and opportunities elsewhere. As an eternal global nomad, I would have to learn to make the best of the situation, especially in deepening my understanding of the circumstances that led my own family and so many other families to be displaced, to emigrate, to be uprooted from their homes.

Looking back on my life's journey, I realize that I did not have any awareness of my ethnicity until I left Africa. Until I moved to Europe, I was just "I"—not from here or there, "I" just "was." It had never occurred to me that there were different kinds of people, differentiated by origin or ethnicity. Once I was in Europe, the recurrent question of "where are you from?" made me more aware and more conscious of the differences among people based on their national origin or ethnicity. Later on, I came to learn that these differences, which start with a very seemingly innocent question, create much of the conflicts and hardships in the world.

This background filters through my life each day and affects how I try to understand what the core issues of economic and human development might be: beyond the numbers and the statics; beyond the policies and the programs; beyond the words, the conferences and the politics, at the end of the day I often wonder, "what is it all about?" What will it take not to have displacement, migration, and mass movement anymore from Africa? And when will we Africans make the choices to leave our countries, based on the kind of work we aspire and the education we hope to pursue, rather than for the sake of survival?

DEFINING AFRICA: DIFFERENCES IN PERCEPTION

As a child growing up in Europe in the seventies, I was proud of the Africa I knew, regardless of the perception of others. I was just so proud for some reason. Then in time I learned that in fact that my perception was based on the truth I knew. In a very short time I also learned that people like me in Belgium and many people around the world had a different perception of the continent. Often people considered Africa poor, miserable, and a place where life was below the basic standards of living in other parts of the world — but that is not my Africa, the one I know and love. And when I say that it is not my Africa, I am not referring to material wealth and comfort, but to what I know is so harmonious on the continent. I am referring to the stories, the conversations, the traditions, the laughter, and also the tears that bond families and communities together.

Africa is vast and, actually, as it has been said many times before, there is no such thing as Africa. It may be *"Les Afriques,"* as it is said in French—a collection of peoples, traditions, histories, and communities. All these nations share a common ground together, a history of migration and movement, a story of tragic wars and epic legends, a story of a village and a hospitable home.

My perspective about South Africa has changed dramatically over time, and it is those changes that have informed my understanding of what it is to be African. There was a time when I could not relate to the country. I remember that as an Ethiopian, our passports stated, "Valid for all countries, except South Africa," and this has not changed since the end of Apartheid. I never thought I would go to South Africa, because it was a country where blacks/Africans are unwanted, and I found it revolting that black Africans could be segregated on their own land. In the mid-1990s, however, I did go to South Africa, to Durban to attend a conference, and there I felt strange, conscious for the first time of the color of my skin, which had never really been an issue in my life before. In Belgium foreigners, *"les étrangers"*, were seen as a mass grouping of all non-Belgians, and thus details of appearance were not significant—I was just a foreigner like all the other foreigners. But in South Africa, I was suddenly seen as black, in a country that had once segregated blacks/Africans from the rest of their society. It felt weird to me to be in a place where, because of my skin color, I would have not been able to fully be free to go where I pleased to be. This was very different from the racism that I had seen in Belgium; in Belgium I did not see it so overtly. In the years following, I continued to wonder how people of Asian and European descent all called themselves "South African" or "African" instead of using what I then considered their "true ethnic identity."

I was blessed to have the chance to travel to South Africa many more times, and little by little, I understood that the country gradually evolved and that it was not about the skin color anymore. It was rather the culture and quality of leadership in the country that aimed to bring together all peoples that make up the country. I also learned in time that the struggles for liberation were not exclusively fought by black South Africans, but that they included many whites and Indians as well. So, when in South Africa they speak about a Rainbow Nation, it shows us the heart they act from. It does not mean that the country is free of its own share of challenges, but it means that the leadership in the country, together with its people, has built a new nation.

The idea of "Africa" seems intangible, because other than the common denominator of skin color, for sub-Saharan Africa it seems there is very little else in common. And today we can't even bring skin color as a common denominator—Africans, as the rest of the world, are made up of beautiful people of all colors, creeds, and ethnicities.

So, what is Africa? To me, it is made up of the people who stand for the improvement, the development and welfare of the continent and its people, to join the rest of the world in making this planet a better place to live for the next generations. That is Africa to me. It is not about what color you are. It is not about whether your parents are black or not, or what ethnic group you belong to, but rather how deeply you carry the concerns of the issues facing the people of this continent.

South Africa calls itself the Rainbow Nation, and although we look at South Africa in awe for its progress and its capacity to integrate all people of all colors and creed, Africa has in the meantime become the Rainbow Continent. For that matter, the world has become a Rainbow World. The times of being able to look at someone and state his or her ethnicity are over; many people look one way, and yet they could pass for so many different nationalities. It gets even more complex when we take into consideration the mixed marriages and the children of dual or multiple heritages. In my own life and within my own family, fully African, there are so many members of my family that represent the entire array of ethnic diversity. My own daughters have come to this world very fair and blond—does this make them less or more African? My nephews look entirely South-East Asian; some fully African friends of mine can pass for Scandinavians, but they count themselves as part of Africa.

It is not about color anymore—Africa is about where our heart lies and what we are willing to do to support her progress toward development. Being African should therefore no longer be limited to an ethnic heritage, but rather evolve to a political and social identity. It is how we feel and what we stand for that makes us Africans or not. Being African is really about doing what one can to contribute to bettering the situation on the continent. It is about caring for the people. It is about putting forth our efforts despite the odds to make things happen that matter and change lives.

LOOKING FORWARD: EXPANDING INTO A NEW PARADIGM

My leaving Africa was and always will be a defining moment in my life. It was a major turning point that has shaped and defined the person I am today. This book is about the experiences acquired through my journey in this life as an uprooted child who left "Shola sefer"[3] not really knowing where my family was headed. It is the story of discovering the concept of Africa as a result of being a foreigner in a land where Africans were not al-

[3] *Sefer* in Amharic means "neighborhood," and the neighborhood where I grew up was called Shola. Within Shola Sefer, where everyone knew each other, the home of my grandparents was the center of our community.

ways accepted; it is the story of my dreams, albeit at times naïve, of the day that African nations will enjoy and offer the same quality of peace, health, and life opportunities for their people as do most modern states.

It seems that today, many years after that life-changing morning when we arrived in Brussels after an exhausting journey, we are still going on, still ticking—none of us is admitting that we are tired. We just keep on going. No one is admitting that it is time to go home, that it is time to right the wrongs and adjust the clock. However, inside my heart for all these years, I have been wondering, "why, Why, WHY do some of us have to leave our houses and families and settle in a land that might or might not welcome us? Why do we have to find opportunities elsewhere and why are we unable to create those same opportunities at home? How long do I have to answer to people asking me where I am from? What will it take to allow people not to be forced to emigrate, but allow them to make a life right where they are?"

Of course, all of these questions are mainly pointing to us, the people of the Global South—the so-labeled Third World countries or developing countries. Often times we are the people who must find a new home somewhere else, because our governments and systems fail to offer us security and basic opportunities. We leave, because we feel we can have a better life abroad. We seek new homes, because it is not possible to have peace or sustained peace in our own countries. So we go. We go looking for life somewhere else. This is normal. It is human.

But what if we stop one moment and just reflect on what is possible at our own personal level? Yes, it is clear that we might not change the world overnight. We cannot stop conflict, single-handedly take our communities out of poverty, or create new opportunities in our Third World nations. But one thing we can do is to share ideas and possibly reflect on how we can co-create the future that we hope to have in 20, 50, or 100 years from now. What seed can we plant today to avail another, better reality for our children and their grandchildren? If we collectively put our minds to this task, what would then be the outcome? What is stopping us from envisioning this future? What is in the way of our planting seeds of change? What will it take to gather the collective responsibility and transform it to a joint effort towards development?

When growing up, my grandmother Almazesha would always talk with me of the future and our responsibilities today in order to create the reality of tomorrow. When she spoke of the future, it was like speaking of a horizon — tomorrow could literally be the day after today or it could be many years later. She spoke to me about our Fathers (Abatochachen) and our Mothers (Enatochachen), her way of referring to our ancestors and forefathers, reminiscing of the work they had done and implying that it falls on us to now continue the journey and the work of our forefathers. This is her way of looking at the world we live in from the moment in which we are born. Her philosophy is cognizant of the greater scope of time and its eternity. She used to tell me that the future happens a moment at a time. That is why each moment is precious, and that is why we have to be conscious about everything we do or say—because it is what we do with our moments that define the colors of our tomorrows.

Almazesha instilled in me the knowledge that in this eternity of time, it is a humbling experience to know that whatever we do in our life, as long as we do it in deference to knowing how insignificant or impermanent we are, then the quality of our contribution might emerge truly in line with the needs and opportunities on the ground. Because of her teaching, I had the audacity to put this book together, despite my awareness of the modest impact my own experience might contribute to African development. Yet, I took the plunge to share what I have seen that works and what I have experienced that does not work, in order to find innovative solutions and approaches to improve the situation. All visions are enacted this way, with each of us doing our small part, one contribution building on the other.

However, one thing is certain to me: we Africans cannot leave the development of our countries to others. It is we Africans who have to invest in our lands in order to build a foundation for future generations. The late President of Tanzania, Julius Nyerere used to say, *"My generation fought and won political independence, but unless our generation fights and wins economic independence, our nations will continue in bondage."* It is economic independence that will earn us our freedom; that is what we must strive for at all levels.

So, when speaking of co-creating the future and working "today" on the kind of future we want to see in 20, 50, or 100 years, I say that in recognition that our work should be a continuation of the efforts of our ancestors. We co-create, hoping and intending to bring in the next generations to follow on the bit of work that we do, and their children to follow up from there. The stories in this book focus mostly on the opportunities for change and transformation that are at the doorsteps of African nations across the continent, albeit with apparent challenges that can jeopardize the overall success.

It is with immense recognition of all the souls who have borne the pain of war and internal conflict, in recognition of all the mothers' tears for their sons and daughters' shed blood, in recognition of the millions of orphans of AIDS, of war, of genocide, in recognition of the soldiers, the activists, and the workers who have lost their lives for the cause of change towards better living conditions — that I write each line in this book. At the same time, as I write the stories, I do so as my call to the heavens to allow the power of forgiveness to emerge in our communities and our peoples, to ease the pain of loss and trauma of all sorts and open the path for a new life. We owe it to them—all of those who have fought and paid with their lives for making human life better in Africa, whether in politics or in development work, whether in fighting conflict or working towards peace — to do the best we can to change things for this continent. We owe it to ourselves and certainly to future generations. It is about taking a step at a time, a day at a time, but persistently moving towards that horizon that holds a better future we all wish for.

This book is also a call to you, the reader, to contribute in whatever capacity to a better future in Africa and other developing countries throughout the world. Excellence in our work can only come when our contributions are based on the essence and truth of our commitment. It is when we are balanced and grounded that our hearts can open up and lead our minds to holistic and bold and innovative solutions. Through our stories, our minds and our determination, with our truth, whether with love or with fear or anger; to see our truth from a position of surrender; to see our truth from a standpoint of possibilities and abundance instead of scarcity and limitation—we can make the ground ready to host the process of change so it can enter into our communities across the continent.

It is about time that we dare to ask for a new quality of leadership to uplift the lives of so many men and women and children who today live much below any acceptable level of living standards. It is about time that we Africans, individually and collectively, coordinate our efforts and pull our wisdom and knowledge together for the sake of our common future. It is about time that we mobilize ourselves to take on our responsibilities as Africans.

Introduction

It was only after leaving my country and living as an immigrant in Belgium that I became conscious of the situation in Africa. My own experience with displacement—with uprooting to settle somewhere else, with finally realizing that I may never find a place that I call home—led me on a journey seeking insights and understanding about my own life, my community, and the continent of Africa in general.

When I first emigrated from Ethiopia, I did not realize that the tables had turned and I had become "the foreigner," the unusual person of a different color. It was in school in Brussels that I realized my African-ness.

We were admitted into a very small school in Uccle, called "Ecole Primaire du Doyenée" on Rue du Doyenée. Very few of the students knew of a country called Ethiopia and close to none knew Addis Ababa. People identified with me as an African. "Tu viens d'Afrique," they use to say to me. The next question would be, "Zairoise, Métisse?"[4] *All the students knew was Zaire (Congo). And if someone was not fully dark skinned, then, that person was suppose to be a Métisse. "Tu es Métisse?" was the usual question. Or, they would ask if both my parents were truly black. I stopped replying to such questions mainly because I did not understand what they meant.*

Some would call me and my sisters "les nouvelles" (the new students). It was annoying—but I understood that we had now entered a new space and

[4] Métisse refers to someone of multiple heritage, most commonly applied to those with both African and European heritage.

that it was up to us to set the boundaries of the relationship with the school and the students. Amongst all the noise, the movements and the chaos that follows a family move, I found my peace in stepping fully into my origins and in establishing it with anyone that crossed my path. I was proud to be an African. The teachers would sometimes ask me to tell the class about where I came from and I would just be so proud to tell them, "We, in Africa, have everything. We have animals of all sorts, we have fruits and vegetables all over the place and most of all we have sun!"

One day in class a boy made a presentation about racism. I was the only black student in the class. Actually, in the entire school the only Africans were my sisters and I. I had no clue what he was talking about. I had never heard of racism before. At the end of the presentation, the teacher asked me to share my experience with racism. I thought that it might be a political ideology like communism, socialism, imperialism, etc. I had been well-trained in Ethiopia not to talk about politics — you end up either locked up, tortured, or killed. So, I told the teacher I would rather abstain from commenting. They thought that I said that because I was so affected by racism and took my silence as a deep, profound, and thought-provoking moment. I was just rather relieved that they stopped their questioning. For a moment, I had wondered if this country of foreigners had also experienced a coup and a change of government, like my own country—although I had not yet seen armed soldiers or heard machine gun fire around town.

In the years that came I learned very quickly about racism. I learned very quickly about what it meant to emigrate and how once in another person's country we often lose our right to demand equal treatment. It is like being a guest in someone's house and demanding to be treated equally as the children of the master of the house. It is not possible to make such demand; it is up to the host to realize the needs and initiate the integration.

Racism took on a whole new meaning for me at that time. I cannot say that I experienced it directly, but I did see a lot of it. Part of subtle racism is when we are treated just as numbers, just as random individuals without a story, without roots or a place of belonging. There is a way that people look at you and you realize that to them you mean nothing more than a figure, a label, another item, nothing more. You have no story, neither soul nor spirit. There is not that warmth or even just recognition that others get. Such moments of subtle racism gave me a hollow feeling inside my gut. I felt like a ghost, present but invisible, not counted.

Often, I would think to myself that even though our neighbors, schoolmates, and teachers did not know where we really came from, did not know our history and our stories, there was a place somewhere in the world where people knew me, my story and family history. And until I got back there, I would have to work hard and be the best I could be, so that I could find my way home one day. This constant quest for home haunted me much of my life, and still does at times.

In more recent years, in 2006 in Freetown, Sierra Leone, someone asked me why I felt so attached to this continent. I did not quite understand the question, because I did not know what else could be more important for an African other than to see that Africa progresses, that living conditions became adequate for all, that we have educational opportunities and health care. I really did not understand what this friend was trying to get at. I was offended by the question, because the person asking—although of African descent—did not associate with this continent at all. I was further upset at myself for being so sensitive about just one question.

Until my friend asked his question, I had never realized that I was always bringing up the issue of the greater context of Africa. I found ways to relate all things to the greater unfolding of the continent and continuously brought up the issue of African reality, African economy, its resources and potential, and so on. It really bothered me that the question irritated me, and I wanted to understand why such a question would even bother me. I had to find for myself the reasons why the question hit a sore spot and why, after all, this continent is so important to me.

Africa is important to me because this is where I belong. This is my home. This is where my spirit is at rest. It is through knowing this continent and allowing it to live within me that I experience my full-blown self in both my greatness and my misery. Africa is my identity, and I talk about it because in it I find a place for myself and I can reclaim energy that was snatched away years ago. This is the continent where I can go anywhere without fearing anything. It is important to me, because this is where I am from. I feel that while I was born in Ethiopia (and I take that as a neighborhood address), I consider myself even more as an African. I don't see the borders between countries. And in the greater scale of the world, I realize that I only see people. Rarely have I seen someone and associated them with their ethnicity or their communities. I see the world in neighborhoods or areas without borders per se. In my personal case, I find my community in Africa—not to exclude the rest of the world—but this is where I feel at home.

However, families such as mine will continue to leave Africa in search of a better life elsewhere in the world as long as the overall situation on the continent remains unchanged.[5] So many people have and will continue to live without quite fitting in, either in their adopted country or in their country of origin. Since my own emigration, I have felt a need to make sense of the current reality, but more so to find the means to bring change. How do we bring change in such a complex reality? I refuse to stop entertaining the idea of possible change and transformation just because the complexity of our reality is so intricate and the odds of success are seemingly so low. By change, I am talking about change in the overall paradigm in African countries—a change in the mindset of the people—that might bring a transformation of the African reality. Such a transformation would open the path for economic and human development and create true opportunities to improve living conditions for African men and women. We would have the option of staying in our home countries as opposed to feeling obliged to leave and find our livelihood somewhere else in the Western nations.

This book is about my journey in understanding African development. It is a personal perspective based on my life and experience. The process of writing this book allowed a deeper reflection and hence an opportunity to deepen my own understanding; in addition, in sharing my journey I hope that many others within and outside Africa can find the time to reflect

[5] Once we leave home for another place, we lose our home on two counts: we can never really fit in to the new place because we are always branded as "other," and even if we choose to come back home, we don't really have the option to return and fit in as we used to before we left, because we have changed and the reality at home has also changed.

on their own experiences. It is my vision that this book will reach change agents across the world so that we can create a platform of collaboration and harmonization, to coordinate development effort in a natural and integrated organic way.

When our social systems are not strong enough to provide social safety for the population, and children end up on the street fending for themselves, then there is a problem. When we have development workers who cannot quite understand what poverty looks and feel like, but who are responsible for designing programs for the poor (without really understanding the core issues), then there is a problem. When highly paid consultants write about poverty in air-conditioned offices without ever leaving their desks or even knowing what the poor woman looks like, then there is a problem. Often our knowledge of poverty is limited to statistics and figures. But is this enough of a basis to formulate policies, design programs, and call ourselves development practitioners? Is this enough to allow us to forego opportunities for deep self-inquiry and reflection about what else might be needed within our policies and programs to truly address the situation on the ground?

Most of my professional life is related to work in Africa, at times working with humanitarian organizations, at times doing consulting work for the public sector, and at times working with multi-lateral organizations. In all these years I found myself being part of multiple worlds, worlds of wealth and plenty, alongside worlds of sheer poverty. The greatest gap in living conditions I witnessed during my work with Médecins Sans Frontières (MSF) was in the project for women surviving from prostitution in Addis Ababa, the capital of Ethiopia.

Once, in the late nineties, I was invited to a very exclusive reception in Addis Ababa filled with big names from Ethiopian society and the international community. The reception took place at the Hilton Hotel. Highly groomed waiters and waitresses waltzed around the cocktail hall with drinks and finger foods, serving all the delegates and guests. Conversations flowed. Most conversations seemed to be just polite chit chat, but if one was perceptive enough, one was able to see which conversation was just casual courtesy and which conversation would actually turn into some action. Some guests were just trying to pick up someone to warm their bed for the night or the weekend. This I found completely shocking. I had come to the reception thinking that it was a place to exchange words and ideas about work, that it was a place to network where I could find mutual support. But I was wrong.

I remember that I arrived at the reception after a long day of work. At that time, I was in charge of one of the largest projects in Ethiopia, aiming to empower destitute women who were surviving from prostitution in Addis Ababa. I could not relate very well to the crowd that I found at the reception. An official from one of the donor agencies started up a conversation with me, and before I knew it, he proceeded to say that in Ethiopia he could sleep with any woman he picked up at a bar. I was stunned. For a moment I just stood there with anger and revolt at the situation. I had no idea what to say to him that would make me feel avenged. I told him that the country's economic situation may have sadly forced many women to resort to men to make ends meet, but that it is not something for him to boast about. I added that as far as he is concerned, he should know that the women certainly would not go with him for his looks! All I could think of was the ladies in the red light district that I worked with. They would have to endure such men and sometimes even worse men, just to feed their families. In a nutshell, it was all about money and what money can buy.

When I considered that it is such type of men who would sit in their offices to decide how to bring aid to the country or speak about our national policies, it left me so broken. I could not breathe properly, I was so revolted. I had expected a minimum ethical and moral standard among aid agencies in terms of the kind of individuals they send out as so-called experts. But as my mother would say, it's their money…so they can do as they please.

I was happy to leave the reception when it was time to go. I felt empty and drained. I felt disillusioned. Most of the people gathered were working on one aspect of development or another, but at this reception and at most receptions in general, it seems that the issue of development is often left on the side bench for many practitioners. Maybe my disillusionment was reflecting a shadow of righteousness on my part or a lack of understanding of how things are really done, or maybe I was just still in a stage of consciousness where I believed that hard work and good intentions were the only ingredients nec-

essary for successful accomplishments. I felt guilty about the plenty that I saw around me, almost thinking that if we worked on development then we should not indulge in the comforts of modern society. I was not sure. I might not have been ready to look at the truth of my own mindset.

On my way back home that night, I was stopped by some of the street children I knew from night outings for our project. It was cold, so I told them to jump in the car for a few minutes until we finished talking. They ranged in age from about 10 to almost 17 or 18. The back seat of my car was built with benches along the sides, so one by one close to twelve or thirteen kids and teenagers squeezed into the car, and we talked and talked...and talked. Coincidentally, the entire conversation was about their perspective of what it would take to eradicate poverty, not only in Ethiopia but across the continent. They all had a lot to say about it. There were great debates and arguments, there were such ideas and thought coming forth, I was just amazed to listen to all of these kids we call Street Children. I remember looking up at one point and seeing some joggers, and only then did I realize that I had spent the entire night out talking to these girls. They were equally surprised and ended the conversation abruptly. One of them grabbed his Gaby (warm traditional shawl) and said, "Well, I better get back to work." I was surprised to know that he had a job. He then clarified and said, his job for now is begging, and he better get to the early cars because they tend to give more money than the rest. On my side, I had to rush home, take a shower, change clothes, and drive straight to work.

In this one day, I had seen and been with the entire spectrum of social strata and development issues were the common anchor of the conversations I was part of. It is somewhat strange to be in an environment of plenty one minute and be in the midst of utter poverty in the next moment. To see and witness the world from all sides is an experience that is hard to deal with, because it forces us to stretch our boundaries in order to make sense of this reality. It is frustrating to see all the perspectives until we learn how to ride the wave of perspective in a way that benefits the whole. The children in my car all have a name, a story, and dreams that they hope to attain. Their world also has its own power dynamics and rules. It has its own regulations, and for them it makes sense. From their point of view, they see the outside as "the rich people," "the police," "the foreigners," and so on, not knowing that all those they refer to as such also have their own names, their own stories, and their own challenges to deal with. And the same goes for the development workers who talk about "the street children", putting them in the same bag. But that is what we do as humans, we tend to put people in categories, we sort them and arrange them on a nice virtual shelf in our minds—stick them in a box, so the complexity is easier to manage.

Until we can put ourselves in the shoes of the other, it is not possible to fully appreciate the life of that person. A lot in development work depends on our ability as practitioners to put on the other's shoes and see the world from their perspective, and then establish programs that are in harmony with what we have witnessed, felt, and intuitively known is the right thing to do.

Many seasoned development practitioners are very astute about what is needed on the ground and how to attain it. Many are open to the subtle ways of knowing, and use such means to enrich the programs they design—but they are not as many in numbers as they should be. Instead, there are a large number of development practitioners who just focus on their own individual career path, forgetting that working in development is almost like working in medicine, in that you take an oath to serve and do your best to service the communities. It should not be about a career path or finding some work for a couple of years just to add to your CV. It is not about being a technocrat who produces masses of papers that will hardly be read but will rather collect dust on the shelf. It is about service, and service to the communities. It is about using the knowledge and skills we have to better another life.

There is a need to raise the awareness of policy-makers and development practitioners to the reality of what non-development means in real human life, and not just in virtual statistics. Only when we find out what the texture of poverty actually is, when we experience the taste of hunger or the stench of blood in war zones or the scent of a fired bullet, only then we know. Then we can write, we can work, and we can make things happen. Short of that, it's like teaching swimming without having ever been in the water ourselves.

Many management or personal development seminars and programs call us to try and think "outside the box" in order to create innovative and creative products, programs, and so on. However, it might be more productive finding means to think and operate not only outside the box, but also to think consciously of the box we are personally in—conscious of the societal box in which we operate and conscious of the space outside that box. Such an approach would allow us, as development practitioners, to deepen our understanding of the dynamics at play beyond the statistics, numbers, figures, and projections. Such a level of understanding would by default put us in a place where the policies and programs we create come not from our intellect only, but also come from our whole being. It is when our entire being is engaged that we can effectively respond to the reality at hand in a holistic, comprehensive, and innovative way.

When managing MSF's HIV/AIDS communication program for the women surviving from prostitution, we came up with a different, unconventional approach. The program was based on the perspective and understanding that most of the women are working in the red light district because of financial and social stress; and that often it is their sheer inability to provide for their families that takes them to the street, looking for other means of survival such as selling sex for money or for a roof over their head. In essence, our mandate was to create Information, Communication and Education (ICE) programs to increase the knowledge of these women about HIV/AIDS and to encourage them in leading healthier lives. As a comprehensive approach to the issue, we decided to build a component into the program where the women could have a chance to stop and reflect on their own lives.

Each woman had to make a decision about whether she wanted to continue working in the red light district or whether she wanted to try another way of earning her living. Once they made their decision, then the training to support them in their chosen line of work would start. The process of reflection took about 10 days of workshops with a consultant we brought in from Germany. The consultant knew the subject well as she, personally, had worked for years in the red light district but had managed to transform her life and escape the red light district, becoming an activist for women's rights.

In short, the workshop allowed the women to reflect on and to decide whether they wanted to continue as sex workers or whether they wanted to try to get out of this business. And, whatever choice they made, we helped them to see how they could sustain a healthy life, how they could manage their income, and how they should think of their enterprise (regardless of the product sold). Needless to say, I faced problems, from some team members and from some officials of the regional government bodies, because this program was too far out of the box and way beyond conventional thinking in Ethiopia during this time. But in the end, because the program was successful and served the women, we were able to go forward. Many chose to have a different lifestyle, but those who chose to remain in the red light district also left the workshop knowing how to protect themselves and still run their work as a strictly business.

This example illustrates a concrete case of success. And this is what can happen when programs are designed with a full understanding of the situation, an understanding beyond numbers and inclusive of the human factors behind the figures. Such a comprehensive response to any development issue might face criticism or even resistance from many, but in fact if we are able to sustain our stand, then we would inevitably be in a position to witness the transformation that happens when we work from both within and beyond our box of existence, when we can define reality by what we know but also acknowledge the existence of the space we do not know. Not only should we be aware of the things we know we don't know, we should also be aware of the things we don't know we don't know.

Unfortunately, many who live at the bottom of the social pyramid think that the responsibility to improve their living conditions rests solely with the government and international organizations they can name or whose logo they recognize. This belief is equally part of the challenge. How do we pass on a message that it is not only the role and responsibility of the governments and international organizations, including the NGO community, but also the responsibility of people at all levels to work towards improving living conditions and creating opportunities within their communities and countries? It is also equally necessary to raise the awareness of the greater populations that it is not only up to the governmental bodies or the international organizations to bring change to the ground. —It is rather up to each one of us, each individual, to contribute our share within our capacities so that the collective can raise the living conditions. Such change might not happen overnight, but if we each take responsibility and if action is taken, then change is bound to happen. With the right policies and intentions in place, we may be able to witness change, maybe even within a decade or so.

This is a book about perspectives on what it might take to bring about change and transformation to Africa, with all its diversity of nations and peoples. This book represents the voice of one African among millions, and it includes my reflections from many years of working, living, and traveling in various parts of the continent and beyond. I have tried to mesh together my experiences, the lessons I have learned, the mistakes I have made, and the successes and the failures along the way, to bring forth stories and insights for African development progress.

Most of my career was centered on working on HIV/AIDS programs at all levels, starting from the grassroots and community level to the policy and national level. The greatest frustration in my work was however not being able to concretely touch and feel the results we all labored to achieve. If we created a great communication program about the use of condoms, well, we could only possibly see the effects of that campaign many months later, if at all. And if we did see tangible results, then that would mean that we had already set up processes to tightly monitor our target areas. I could see the number of the people we were losing to AIDS, but I could not see how many people remained alive living with AIDS or those who managed not to contract HIV as a direct result of our work.

At some point in my work, I started to feel more and more that HIV/AIDS might not be the problem per se, but might be instead a symptom of a dysfunctional system. The fact that the HIV/AIDS epidemic is ravaging so many communities in Africa is a reflection of the flaws of our systems; and who speaks of systems must speak of the structure, the rules and regulations and the nature of the systems. What makes the system work, who is involved in the system, and how does one identify the leverage points within the system? All of these and more questions emerged to me, which I had to answer.

I believe that the weakness in our systems, and this is true for most African nations, is that the entire system is highly linked to the leadership that heads it. It is the top-most influential people within the public sector who hold the key to bringing change and transformation, mainly because they are the ones who dictate what can enter or be built into the system, or who define how one might tweak the system (be it to better serve[6] its members or to better serve those in power—in either case the decisions are taken at the highest levels).

In African societies, which are more based on the collective, the issue of change may often only be approached when the leaders within the community open the way for collective action. My personal experience has taught me that the core issue to bring change in all of the challenges Africa faces is leadership; leadership capacity development, or developing and deepening the capacity of leaders to exercise their role of leading, is the key to most effectively leveraging change. It is through leadership capacity development at all levels that we can create a mindset shift and evolve the dominant paradigm to one that allows harmonious and collaborative work within communities, nations, and ultimately across the continent. The focus must be on developing the "capacities" of the leaders in both their role within the systems as well as in their capacities to design, execute, and follow through with actions to demonstrate and implement their vision for their respective communities. When the leaders — be it at the community or the national level — are open for innovations and different approaches to address the problems at hand, change can take place with ease. On the other hand, if such leaders are not on board with the proposed or needed changes, it often leads to their ostracizing those initiating such change or even to civil unrest, in the worst-case scenario. Starting from the highest respective societal levels allows the change to trickle down to the grassroots level where the benefits of the change (whatever issue may need to be tackled) can manifest effectively.

[6] There can be a sustained debate regarding whether or not our systems, especially the public sector, are designed to serve the community or serve the individuals who hold the key positions, but that is a debate for another book.

In order to further explore the concept of leadership it is important to make a distinction between the terms *leader, leading, and leadership.* A leader can be seen as a role within a system; leading is then the activity of the individual undertaking this role of a "leader." Leadership is thus the whole that integrates the role of the leader, the leading activities of the individual leader, and the context in which the role and activities take place.[7]

So when we speak of the need to have leadership capacity development for change and transformation in Africa, we have to explore the factors that affect the quality and the process of leading. What is the process of leading? What does it entail? What needs to be taken into consideration? It becomes inevitable to mention that the lens or lenses used to explore the concept of leadership are equally very important.

We often talk of leadership, while not really taking the time for introspection about our own definitions of leadership; our understanding is all about the outside, about the role of leading. It might be that the most appropriate quality of leadership will emerge when we collectively take the time to reflect on how we express leadership. It might be necessary to accept each other's worldviews and beings so that we can be open to welcome the various levels of consciousness in the leadership we see around us.

At the same time, what do we mean by "change" and "transformation"? To me, change is the decisions and policies that can be implemented to alter the current reality. For example, change is being able to take the number of children attending schools from 30% to 100%; it is being able to ensure the welfare of women by providing 100% healthcare services and ensuring their human rights 100%. It is being able to have zero tolerance for corruption and have the necessary legislations to make that a reality; it is about modifying what is so today, toward what the reality could be, so that all men, women, and children can have a healthy, safe, and productive life. Transformation, on the other hand, is both the capacity to actually make the decisions to change the reality and also to continuously work toward the manifestation of the change on the ground. Once the change can tangibly be felt on the ground, then transformation has occurred.

---

[7] Volkman, Russ. (2009). Integral Leadership. Publication info?

Development is also a word that may have lost its edge and meaning because it has been used in so many contexts. I refer to development as the meta-processes to implement policies to improve the livelihood of men, women, and children at all levels of the community. Development might be obtaining sources of clean water for people, but it can also be implementing water resource management programs. Development can be making the latest communication and computer technologies available to the populations, as well as programs aiming to provide basic education to all children. Development is about ensuring the economic growth of nations, and also about ensuring human rights, governance, healthcare, peace, sustainable agriculture, and education to places where such elements may not be available. In this book, I refer to development in the greater sense encompassing all the above-mentioned issues.

As far as Africa is concerned, there is great talk about new leadership needed for development; at the same time, little is done to find the wisdom in African leadership itself. Instead, we see the transposition of what Western academics and practitioners have coined as leadership. Our environments here in Africa call for a quality of leadership that is exercised in *being* as oppose to doing—a leadership style that is straight forward and disciplined. One that allows the compassion we know of our elders. Such kind of leadership might look too simple, but it's not. It does not lack complexity, but rather means that in order to truly address the complexities in the environment, we can only provide the needed kind of leadership by flowing with the moment, being more intuitive rather than rational — not thinking, not rationalizing, but flowing and trusting our inner wisdom.

There is a lot that I have inherited from my grandparents and my parents in terms of my understanding of life. My greatest challenge has been to find ways to translate what I have learned so that I could use it objectively in my work throughout the years, and to share this knowledge with my colleagues and superiors. I have found the Integral Theory and the lenses it offers to be one the most effective ways to relate to and define our reality; at least in my experience so far, the Integral theory has been a holistic, comprehensive tool that allows the user to enter a realm of wisdom in a step-by-step way and then apply this wisdom in various aspects of life and work. Emerged in recent times in philosophy, *"[...]the Integral theory itself is a meta-theory [...] in that it is a theory of theories, [...] and as all meta-theories its aim is to provide a wide variety of theories that can be integrated [...] to further our understanding"* (Volkman, 2009, p. 1).

The Integral lens or way of looking at reality is based on the Integral theory, and is the application of the theory as a perspective(s) in practical life. The Integral lens or approach offers a map to attain a comprehensive view of any reality by allowing the user to see the objective and subjective sides of reality and at the same time look into what the territories include in the individual and collective spheres. The Integral approach is, of course, much more complex than this simple definition. This book makes reference to the Integral Theory, lens, and approach throughout the pages, and more specifically in Chapter Four. Change and transformation at all levels, starting from a personal level and ranging to the country and/or regional level, will come as we work toward gaining a quality of leadership that is both transformative and integral, meaning holistic and comprehensive.

I hope this book can allow others who also immigrated under hard conditions to reflect on our lives and their process of making sense. I hope that the stories might inspire all of us to continue our work and maintain our vision for Africa, a vision that we may soon see is substantial for development on the continent. The process of writing brought out something I did not expect — it made it clear to me that beyond our individual actions and projects, there is a need to look at the greater horizon as well as to share thoughts and ideas. We must pave the way for more effective and innovative development schemes, based on a holistic understanding of ourselves and our environment, but for that understanding, we need not turn exclusively to the West. This book offers thoughts and ideas that would allow Integral to further expand its potential for economic and human development and at the same time bring to light the Integral aspect that has always existed in African traditional wisdom and leadership capacities.

The context of the discussion of this book is set in Chapter One where I discuss my personal motivations for choosing HIV/AIDS work, and how the lessons I have learned, along with my life experience, have informed my understanding of the situation in Africa. The question of why Africans emigrate is investigated, with an emphasis on hoping for change.

Chapter Two focuses on the differences in perception that underlie problem situations in Africa. These differences can be on the macro level, such as the gulf between Western and African perspectives on time; they can also be on the micro level, requiring us to examine the shadow side, whether of the individual or of the organization. The concept of perspectives and how it is affecting development work will be discussed in this chapter. I will try to shed light on why there is often discordance in economic and human development policies and programs executed in African communities; and how this discordance might be a direct result of the fact that most of the actors working in the field don't have a wide and integrative perspective as they relate and look at the realities on the ground. The chapter concludes with a consideration of cross-cultural communication difficulties between Africans and Westerners.

Chapter Three concerns the mechanics of change and transformation. I present my own vision of change and transformation for Africa, discuss how to create transformation, and consider the relationship between transformation and time, particularly the concept of emerging transformation, one life at a time.

Integral Theory is the focus of Chapter Four, and a limited set of Integral concepts, theories, and approaches pertinent to the discussion are briefly described. I tell the story of my own experience with Integral in my work and personal life, and examine how we can use the Integral theory and its applications to serve and support African development efforts. I also examine how Integral theory overlaps with African traditional wisdom, and how finding and highlighting this parallel can serve to bring Integral tools to bridge the gap of perspectives among development practitioners.

Chapter Five concerns change within, and faces squarely the difficult topic of coping with complexity, frustration, and pain, with the focus on embracing the shadow side. Through this process, new possibilities for change can be created, more in alignment with African ways of being.

A vision of change for African leadership is the main topic of Chapter Six. I present my own journey in trying to establish Integral Africa,[8] and the subsequent lessons learned through the successes and failures experienced during this journey. I then discuss transformation from the context of the African Wisdom, and speak of the Copper Pot as a metaphor for community efforts. The chapter concludes with a presentation of next steps for me, for you as the reader, and for a vision of change for Africa as a whole.

[8] Integral Africa is a Leadership Capacity Development program I am hoping to launch in service of change and transformation throughout Africa, through a emergent network of African change agents.

CHAPTER ONE

Conditions in Africa

Part of the challenge in development work in Africa is the way we each understand what development is and ought to be. When I say "we," I am referring to development practitioners, each coming from a different cultural and educational background, each with our own particular character and personality. I am talking about the various communities and countries in which work is undertaken—each district, community, and country with its own particularities starting from language and culture to ways of conducting work. And I am also talking about the various institutions and organizations from which we work, each with its' own particular ways of doing things, its own policies and strategic frameworks.

PERSONAL MOTIVATION FOR CHOOSING HIV/AIDS WORK

One of the main reasons why I became involved in the work on HIV/AIDS was when I had my first serology test in 1986. I wanted the test because of a short relationship with a guy in college. I realized later that this guy's favorite sport, at the time, was to score with as many girls as possible and he was very committed in keeping the score high. It would be easier to count the girls that he did not sleep with, rather than find out those whom he had lured into sex. Once I realized that, I thought it would be better to find out what was in store for me than wait to see it emerge slowly, so I decided to go for the test. At that time, testing was not so common. I arranged for the test with my family doctor in Brussels.

It took days to get the results. Each day I would make a new resolution. I started out wanting to commit suicide if the test came out positive. Then I thought of my sisters and my parents and thought it would not be fair to them. So, I thought, if the test is positive, I would just go and live in a monastery somewhere and never come back again.

Finally, I came to the knowing that whether the test was positive or negative was irrelevant, because should I be negative today, tomorrow I could be positive. The whole thing can be different for a number of reasons. Maybe one of my sisters can be positive, or a neighbor or a friend. But the question was about where does one draw the line about whose life we care about? Do I not care anymore if it is not a friend, not a sister or not someone I know? Or does it not matter who ends up infected with the virus, so that we should do all we can to avoid infection for all people? It is in the midst of this reflection that I called my doctor for the results.

"Good morning. I am calling to ask if you have the results?"

"Yes, I have the results. It's affirmative."

My heart stopped.

"It's affirmative that you don't have HIV *in your blood."*

My blood dropped to my feet. I did not know what to believe, whether I was awake or asleep and in some nightmare. The doctor repeated the negative result and I felt a sense of relief, the kind of relief that makes all the colors very bright and all my senses very sharp. I had been close, and got lucky. In this moment it was up to me to choose how to direct my life. Once we are conscious of the preciousness of breath and the gift of waking up in the morning, we discover that it is a state where we cannot just simply live. We are driven to make meaning of our existence and not just live to eat, sleep, and work.

In the time between the doctor saying "it's affirmative" and then saying "you don't have HIV*," I died for a little while. My life ended for a moment. It was like hearing and feeling the door of life slamming, with me out of it. I was still standing there with the slammed door panel a half a centimeter away from my sweaty nose. It's over. Time to go. As I faced my death, I thought about how I did not know it would end this way, losing my chance for life over one or two foolish dates with a foolish man. He was not even worth my time.*

Life took on a whole other meaning. The situation enabled me to make clear and genuine distinctions between mere sex and intimacy, to consciously choose a partner, being aware of each step of the way and re-committing myself to the relationship at each step. My aunt Elene, who literally counts as my second mother and with whom I lived in the United States during my last two years of high school and the first two years of University - used to tell us that if we love someone so much, and that it feels right to express this love other than with words, then it is perfectly fine to have an intimate relationship. Otherwise, she used to say, you can also go to the gym to sweat the hormones out. In a sense, she was telling us that in a moment of love, it is all right to go into intimacy, but for lust, it is better to have awareness of the lust so that we can choose whether we want to have the short gym session with the person, or whether we can just drink a glass of water and let the moment pass. This moment of testing and reflection about life was an invaluable lesson for me both in my work with women surviving from prostitution and also in taking a strong position as to the strategies I would stand by when the great campaign for HIV/AIDS testing started in the early nineties.

A moment later, I came back from the dead. My hair had turned grey in my heart. If souls could be seen, my soul emerged crowned with wrinkles like those of my paternal great-grandmother, from Harar, the one who used to make traps for hyenas.

It is a very strange feeling to get a second chance. All the colors around become brighter. All the words ring louder. All textures become velvet. As I looked around and saw my family, I could only see them with gratefulness for the few more days or years we would spend together.

I had to make sure that my family, too, got a second chance—I had to make sure that everyone gets a second chance. And this is how I got recruited to the work on HIV and AIDS. When I was in college, my HIV-prevention campaigns were just about distributing pamphlets around campus and holding small group meetings to discuss various issues about HIV/AIDS, such as prevention, impact on relationships, trust in relationships, and so on. At MSF, the campaigns were out in the real world—it was not students we talked to anymore, but women surviving from prostitution and the clients who entertained themselves through prostitution. The work took a completely new and complex dimension.

During my MBA studies, I focused on Financial Management/Banking and Investment analysis. This was a double gift: on the one hand, it allowed me to come into the world of public health with a business perspective and a bottom-line approach (profits being health), and on the other hand, it allowed me to come with a beginner's mind and the humility that comes with that. Since I did not know all their jargon, I had to come in with an open mind and learn to draw the solutions that came from my heart's understanding as opposed to my mind's perspectives. It is this "beginner's mind," as they say in Zen, that allowed me to enter a space of creative thinking to bring innovation to the project.

LESSONS FROM THE FRONT LINES OF DEVELOPMENT WORK

When I returned to Ethiopia in the mid-1990s to work on HIV/AIDS, I must admit that my family was slightly disappointed that after all those years of education, after all the money spent on my upbringing, and despite all the opportunities I could have had access to abroad, I chose to return to a future that was completely uncertain. At the time, my parents had a home in Addis Ababa in a well-to-do residential area close to the airport—a big house with all the amenities that come with such a house. The contrast between my home life and my work life was stark. Personally, this was the beginning of my descent into the inner realms to find peace and solace, a time to reckon with shadows, with demons, and with my own constricted view. It took foolishness or audacity, depending on your perspective, to remain in the field of "not knowing."

MSF Belgium hired me to design, implement, and manage a communication strategy for the red light district community (both women and clients). MSF has always been a vibrant organization, full of energy and outspoken souls. My time in MSF would be the coming out or reincarnation into flesh of all that I had been learning in spirit from my surroundings, from my grandparents, friends, sisters, parents, etc. It was through these years in MSF that I could literally soak up that place of immense hope and joy as well as that of surreal sadness and awakening to the texture of suffering. The year when MSF received the Nobel Peace Prize, our project for the

"Women Surviving From Prostitution" was recognized as the best development program of the year. This gave our team as well as the women we worked with, a lot of pride and provided us with even more inspiration and motivation to work harder.

We worked in the office from about 8AM to 6/7PM and we continued working on the streets of Addis between 11PM and about 3 to 4AM. We did our night work at least 3 out of 5 weekday nights. We were plunged into that night time reality. I saw places in Addis that I am sure the Mayor doesn't know about. These were places where things were so bad that the only thing left to do was to draw on humor as a crutch to sustain ourselves and hold back the tears that would emerge often unannounced and unexpectedly. Once I met a young girl about 14–15 years old. She was just so pretty, but only on one side. The other side of her face had been slashed open with a pocketknife by another girl. She laughed and said to me: "the doctor forgot to "sew" me from inside, that is why the scar is so big." She was slashed because she was not willing to accept the offer to be a "virgin for a night," which is when virgins are brought to men who pay up to 1500 ETB (close to 200 USD) as opposed to the usual price of about 30 ETB (4 USD). The money is shared between the girl who brings the virgin and the virgin herself.

This girl did not accept the deal and later had sex with an ordinary street boy for love. Hence, the opportunity cost of this love was about 1500 ETB as per the rules of the street. It cost her personally her face. We sat in the Toyota van, that one that we always see NGOs driving, the one that has the side-facing seats in the back. We sort of laughed along with her about the matter, yet on the inside we wept for her, the situation of so many girls like her and our frustration of not being able to see how we could possibly break this vicious cycle of "a virgin for sale."

In the same vein, when these girls told me about the rapes they experienced, instead of calling it rape they would say that the client used them "for free!" Sometimes they talked of well-to-do men who got together (only among men) to drink and hang out, with the added entertainment of live sex shows (they would bring in the girls to have sex with each other), while the men/guest have their drinks and conversations. All this was happening for a mere 2–5 USD. The men were behaving this way for a number of reasons, ranging from having different sexual outlooks to wanting to avoid possible infection with HIV.

The stark difference of our worlds was hard to bear. I would come with our team of social workers with bags full of condoms and wooden phalluses to demonstrate the use of condoms. For these girls the time they spent with us was more of a momentary break away from giving their lives away. At the same time, our conversation about this sex trade became so ordinary that it was difficult to gauge the severity of human rights violations.

The girls would come and tell us about one, two, or more violent clients, or they would tell us about the rapes that took place. When we spoke of rape, our questions were geared to knowing if she managed to use a condom or not. We had to be deaf and blind to the fact that we were talking to a young woman who constantly lived out moments of rape at the hands of different clients. The laws in the country were not favorable to reporting such incidences. As in many other countries, reporting a case of rape would end up having to re-live the humiliation and pain over again. So, we let it slide and talked about it in a mundane way. I had an agreement with the girls—I asked them not to tell me the names of their clients, their cars, or their license plates. I did not want to know who was involved and wanted to focus on just the women, and not open a Pandora's box in finding out who some of the clients might be.

For the first time ever, I witnessed discrimination in its most brutal forms ranging from hearing from eye witnesses about incidents where whole villages or settlements stoned HIV-positive persons to personally seeing how people with full-blown AIDS were being treated in their everyday lives. Professionally speaking, communication experts who are commissioned to design campaigns on a particular topic may not need to be personally affected by the topic; however, when the campaign is put together by people who actually feel the topic in their gut, then it comes with very effective and real punch lines, with words and formulations that the public will notice.

I took my work on HIV/AIDS as a means to alleviate the pain I felt inside about the entire impact of the epidemic on our lives as a community, whether that community is the immediate family, the village, the nation or the world. It is through my work there that I found peace and could sleep at night. Without my work, I think that the reality and its tragedy would have been just too hard to bear. At times the anger and frustration I felt, because my country did not react to the epidemic as aggressively as it could have (at that time), made me forceful, almost hostile, in my work, at times unsociable and even unpleasant company. I completely forgot that diplomacy works a lot better to get things done. It was too much for me. I could not bear the hypocrisy of going to Church or the Mosque to learn about tolerance and caring for others, and then coming out of worship and forgetting all about tolerance for all and caring for the sick. Instead of seeing the preaching of these religious places as a way to inspire people, what I saw was a double standard of treatment for those who had HIV or those suspected of having HIV. There were few in the communities who did not discriminate against HIV-positive persons. Discrimination was widespread and no one was willing to talk about the fear that we felt in the face of AIDS and how we could deal with this fear. It was fear at its best that fueled discrimination. It was fear that kept the silence among families and the continued denial of the existence of AIDS. To make matters worse, as time went by, I learned how women surviving prostitution were excluded from society, as if they did not exist. I did not know how to deal with the disparities I saw. I struggled to find my peace, and in the process I alienated many in my own community.

There were times when I would go to incredibly large HIV/AIDS conferences, and I felt that we were not working on tackling HIV/AIDS but were rather talking for hours about how we were going to talk about it. At the end of the day, it was only a conference and only those truly affected by HIV, in one way or another, kept the fire burning; often many of the other participants would just flow with the agenda, not necessarily engage with the heart that it would have taken to get things moving and eventually head back home with a new conference bag and some business cards of newly established contacts. Were we working hard enough? I am not sure. In a way, I have to also admit that I was also blind to my own intolerance of those who either had not understood AIDS or those who had chosen to dissassociate from it. I spent so much time in the underground of this big capital called Addis Ababa that when I came up to the surface where normal life took place. I could not bear the stark gap in the living conditions. The worst was that my own life and my own family were living in such comfort, so shielded from the impact HIV infections and AIDS were having on the communities around us. I did not know how to manage the situation and bring my family to see what I saw. So, I withdrew and little by little I closed up. Somewhere along the way I just dissociated myself until my family was willing to recognize the painful realities that existed just around the corner. I wanted people to acknowledge the existence of HIV, the way that it was and is affecting the lives of many, and especially how it was destroying the livelihood of our communities.

One of my cousins visited us from the United States at some point during this time. I had to drop her off somewhere along Bole Road (major road leading to the Airport in Addis). As we sat in my car waiting for the person who was suppose to pick her up, we noticed a couple of girls with short skirts and tight shirts and high heels with fish net stockings. Obviously they were just starting their night shift work. My cousin looked at them, shook her head in dismay and with much disgust told me: "Addis has definitely deteriorated since I left, I can't believe these women on the street." She referred to them with such disgust and such disdain. Never for a moment did she think that maybe these were not women. They were just very young girls. They were possibly out there selling their bodies because they have to feed a family or pay for someone's medical bills or just earn some money to live. What I found most difficult was that society was faster to condemn these young girls trying to survive than it was to question the underlying causes. To what extent would we each go, in a crisis situation, if our children were starving? It is the intolerance that I found so painful. It is the cold hearts that were blind to the suffering on the streets that I found so incredibly frustrating. The fact that these girls were out was just a reflection of the lack of social welfare or employment.

I wanted to hear people to say "yes, we care." But instead, all I often found was either denial or rejection of the reality or harsh intolerance and discrimination. This was in the mid-nineties. Things have changed now, and more work is being done. But I can't help but think about what else might have been possible if our communities and societies truly engaged the challenge of HIV and AIDS with more conviction and commitment way back in the early days of the epidemic. How many lives could have been saved if we reacted earlier and took the right measures in time?

PHYSICIAN, HEAL THYSELF: THE PROBLEM OF BURNOUT AMONG DEVELOPMENT WORKERS

Part of the difficulty in working on development issues in most African nations is the inter-related nature of all the issues to be addressed and the underlying cultural/traditional/societal intricacies that remain either invisible or very subtle to the untrained eye. In addition to these factors, the difficulty of our work is further exacerbated by the lack of resources, lack of education, lack of adequate technology, and lack of adequate communication infrastructure impeding our capacity to network and support each other.

It is crucial to have peer support so that each one of us can find the means to continue working without burning out. Peer support within nations and across borders, within or across the various sectors of work, actually is a way to resource and reenergize ourselves. There are very few places to go to unwind, to resource, reinvigorate, and fill up our soul as energy tanks. By a place to go I am not referring to the usual recreation of bars, nightclubs, or sports facilities—I am referring to a constructive or resourceful platform such as an association or regular forum for discussion and learning.

What I have seen to be common among the lives of my African colleagues/peers is that we end up working until we either burn out or lose efficiency. When I compare this to how most of my European or Western colleagues operate it is very different. They work hard as well; but, contrary to us, they actually take the time to rest and relax. So, they might not burn out as fast because they not only have the support system they need and if they don't have it, they make sure to get it, but most of all they take time out to get the rest they need. There are many professional platforms where one can find peers and get professional support, but often such platforms are only accessible to our Western colleagues, be they professional associations or regularly held industry seminars and gathering. Very simple reasons make such platforms outside the reach of the average African development practitioner: discriminatory contractual arrangements, salaries and the level of daily subsistence allowances, travel facilities, visas or just the time to find out about such platforms. There is also one other thing: what I have seen so far, is that most of the time—and this is not just true for me but many of my peers—when we get time off from work, we often go to attend family matters, visit someone back home, or do something in service of our community. Rarely have I seen my peers just go on vacation to rest in a country or place where they have no other business other than resting.

For me, about a year after we married, my husband Matthias arranged for us to go for holidays with the sole purpose of resting. I agreed to go—but once there, I did not know what to do with myself. I don't know if this is related to where I am from or to being addicted to work or both. I remember we had booked a nice package somewhere in the Canary Islands; we went near the pool of the hotel and sat down on the lounge chairs. After about 10 minutes I looked at Matthias, asking him, "What happens next? How long do you want to sit here?" He said, "Just try to relax for a moment" he said. All I could think of was all the places I could have been in my work or personal matters, and how I could have used the time effectively, instead of just sitting on a lounge chair by a pool and reading a book. Likewise, I couldn't really give into the wonderful trips he organized for visiting historical, cultural other sites of natural beauty, just for sightseeing. I could have instead been with my sister to help her move, or with my parents to help them organize this or that, or I could have been in a short training course on this or that. Having such kind of thoughts in my mind, it was literally close to impossible for me to relax and enjoy our vacation. My mind was restless and racing in all directions. It took me a while to realize that resting your body and your mind is equally important as working.

It is only through resting properly that we can maintain our effectiveness and that we can continue being creative and innovative. Without rest, one can end up having completely stale energy. In addition to resting, the next thing would be to find opportunities to meet and exchange with others working in different part of the continent. It is such exchange that can allow development practitioners to create synergy, to harmonize and maximize efforts. It is also such exchange that can enrich our understanding of each other and thus permit further effectiveness in our work and our capacity to innovate, create and move forward. This is not only for African development workers but it is true for all of us working on the issue of economic and human development. The foundation of the quality of our work starts with our capacity to understand ourselves, understand the other and see clearly the benefits of working together for the sake of the communities we are trying to serve.

ACCESS TO EDUCATIONAL RESOURCES

Part of the challenge that many in Africa face is education; this is true not only for elementary education, but also for higher education and even more so for continuing education. When I talk of education in this context, I am not merely talking of academics. Many times in my career I have witnessed Western consultants visiting Africa for a number of days to assess, support, or design programs. The information these consultants use—most of it, and sometimes all of it—comes from their African counterparts on the ground. Within days, these consultants are able to use their skill as well as the technology they own to transform the data collected into knowledge and useful information. They make their flashy PowerPoint presentations and walk away as the God-sent savior of the day; meanwhile, the African counterparts remain on the ground not even in a position to question how they too could have transformed their raw data into useful processed information. I am talking about skill-building, about the means to come out of our boxes and look at our reality from a different perspective, and then be able to formulate what we see and understand and transmit that knowledge in a coherent and useful way.

In the context of development work, there are "international hires" and "local staff," with "local" often connoting less-educated—and of course, less well paid and having less privileges. As long as the local staff is paid less, their work is not given the same value as that of an expatriate coming to work in Africa (with salary plus all the benefits of house, rent, car, etc.). As long as the local workers do not have access to building their purchasing power, they cannot possibly participate in the global market, be it as consumers or providers of service.

Education affects purchasing power, and purchasing power affects our ability to attain and access the resources needed to work more efficiently and more profitably—this remains true even in the most basic instances of life.

I remember an expatriate woman who lived in Sierra Leone and had come as an accompanying spouse. She offered to take me to town in her car, as I had just arrived. Throughout the ride, she continuously complained about the smell of her driver. "I can't stand this smell," she said to me. "He just smells bad," she continued, over and over. I felt ashamed of her comments. I shrank in my seat listening to her comments and imagining how her driver must have felt. At one point, I spoke up and told her that unlike her, the driver had to wake up, wash up, and iron his clothes very early in the morning so that he could walk or take whatever transportation he could to report to work, and in addition, he did not have access to air conditioning or fancy deodorants. He was doing the best he could to be clean and on time for his work. If he sweats, it is human nature—instead of coming down on the man, maybe she should be giving him a better allowance so he could use better transport and possibly afford to buy a deodorant. That was the end of the relationship with her. She never took me to town again and hardly ever spoke to me again. I didn't care — I was glad I spoke up, and hoped she would not treat her drivers so badly anymore.

In a way, the same dynamics of income disparity apply at the professional level. In most Africans nations, education is not made available to all who are willing to learn, and the main reason is the lack of resources to make such education available. When education is indeed made available, the quality of education is often far below world standards. For example, I have witnessed many instances whereby expatriate professionals complained about African staff's ability to format or design a computer document. Most of these expatriates overlooked the reality that few locally employed staff have access to a computer in their regular lives. Often, they may have taken one or two courses to learn a basic competency, and the rest is left to their capacity to continue learning on the job; whereas, in most Western countries, owning a computer has become a norm of life. Children have computers and learn to work, play, and create with the machine at a very young age, so that the computer becomes second nature to them. When these children then grow up to become professionals, it is obvious that their capacity to use the PC to enhance their work comes naturally. Again, this is about education—access to education and the quality of education/resources available.

The question then becomes, what needs to be done to fill the gap and change the paradigm so that all development practitioners, irrespective of whether they are Westerners or from developing countries, have comparable skill sets. There is certainly a call to bridge the education gap both in quality of education and in access to education. It is true that there are many thousands of highly educated African men and women who graduated from the most prestigious schools around the world. Most of them are recognized leaders in their fields and in very influential position in governments, within international organizations and/or the private sector. But this is not enough. It should be normal to find well qualified men and women throughout all levels and all sectors. It should not be an exception to find such qualified human resource capacity in Africa.

This definite gap in education is often mainly based on the purchasing power of the individuals, which is directly linked to the reality of our economies. It is important to consider this reality, because only in bridging this education gap can we open the way to working more effectively and in a more sustainable fashion.

If we take it a bit further and start exploring opportunities for continued learning through books, software, tools, and so forth, the gap between third world nations and the rest of the world is highlighted further. When I travel in the United States or Europe, I have the chance of accessing a myriad of bookstores, courses, and seminars to further deepen my knowledge in my line of work. Software, resources, and libraries are readily available for all; these resources allow people in the first world to continue to excel. On the African side, these benefits are only available for the privileged few, who have access to the internet; depending on the worldview of each of those few, some share their resources and others keep them to themselves.

At home in Africa, I can visit any online bookseller such as Amazon or Borders to purchase material with my credit card. But despite the fact that I can actually buy the products because I have a credit card at hand, I still face obstacles because I am in Africa and the shipping can be extremely expensive (often more than the value of the product purchased), unreliable and very slow. In addition, it is often a big headache to clear the shipment through the various postal offices, should the products actually make it to the country. It is just not easy for Africans at home to continue learning and continue accessing resources to push our work forward—in a sense, it is difficult for African professionals to remain up-to-date with the latest developments in their fields. So, although we talk of poverty reduction through various programs, it is paramount that we also realize that development efforts need to be coupled with widening the opportunities to learn, to access resources and books or the internet, and to attend gatherings and meetings to continue evolving our minds.

I can tell you of my own struggles to access knowledge: because I choose to focus my work in Africa and at the community level, my income is far less than anyone would believe, despite the fact that I speak five languages, was educated in the best schools in Europe, and hold my share of degrees from very respectable U.S. universities. It is not always easy for me to get books or attend seminars, but I still do it with a lot of effort. But the effort is so huge for me, even with all the privileges I have such as being able to travel when I need to, to have credit cards, to have family and friends abroad, that I can always call on for support — how much harder must it be to access similar learning opportunities for individuals living and working in Africa, without having the network of friends abroad and without the facility of having the foreign currency or necessary credit cards or other payment facilities? How can people in those circumstances continue to learn and update themselves?

What efforts are being made to make books, publications, and seminars available to individuals who can actually take that knowledge to the far corners of the world? How are efforts inclusive of those individuals in places where the Internet might not always work, where the postal system might not always be operational, and where people might not always have a credit card to make online transactions? Even though the responsibility to learn and deepen our understanding of our world lies with each of us respectively, we must be aware of the disparities of purchasing power in the world as well as the great gap in accessing information and knowledge. Those from developing countries might not always have the option to access the very knowledge, the very books and resources that might support them in finding solutions for growth in their communities. One certain way to open the path to change is to allow the same kind of resources for people in Africa, be they professionals or students or communities-at-large.

STATISTICS OF DESPAIR, STATISTICS OF HOPE

When we work on HIV/AIDS or when we read about it, the most striking thing is the incredible but sad statistics that we crunch out; so many orphans, so many dead, so many infected—that many more to die, this many more to be orphaned. We have come to the stage of having acronyms for children orphaned by AIDS: OVCs (orphans and other vulnerable children). By the end of 2007, sub-Saharan Africa accounted over 65% of the world of people living with HIV. Even though the region holds only a little more than 10% of the world's populations, it is the region most affected by HIV and AIDS, with approximately 22 million people living with HIV. By the end of this same year, the world counted approximately 15 million children orphaned by AIDS, most of whom were also African children.[9]

It seems that we are so caught up in statistics, yet the statistics we calculate often only tell us what is not going right. Wouldn't it be good to also have equally available and widespread statistics about what is going right, what kind of progress has been made, and how the work on the ground is changing the future for the better? Yes, at the turn of the millennium, the projection was that by 2010 there will be 25 million children without parents in Africa. But what are we doing about it now and today? Is it another meeting or conference, or rather another pilot project for 1, 2, or 3 years? These are lives and each life counts. For us, it has become numbers and numbers have no soul.

Statistics about Africa are widely circulated, and often paint a terrible

[9] UNAIDS Report on the Global AIDS Epidemic.

picture of life on the continent. Most of the problems revolve around poverty, epidemics, health, armed conflicts, migrations, food insecurity and water sanitation. According to the World Bank African Development Indicators (ADI) 2008, only 5% of the population has access to improved sanitation facilities in Eritrea; in Sierra Leone nearly 3 children out of 10 die before they reach the age of seven. While South Africa has 84 mobile phones per 100 persons, Ethiopia only has 1 mobile phone per 100 persons; in Liberia nearly no one has internet access, 0.03 access points per 100 persons.[10] With an overall population of about 780 million, life expectancy on the continent averages about 50 years old; infant mortality at birth is still among the highest in the world with 90 losses per 1000 births. In 1996 alone, 14 of the 53 African nations were afflicted by armed conflict;[11] 30 wars have occurred in Africa since 1970.[12] These same conflicts have not only taken the lives of almost 10 million, but have destroyed the social fabric and infrastructure, and most of all taken away peace from the region.

But statistics can also describe hope for the continent. It is true that Africa is the only continent that has been experiencing digressing development, but it is also the continent that is least populated, despite widespread perception to the contrary. Africa is most associated with harsh living conditions, widespread poverty, and war and armed conflicts. Despite all of the above challenges, the continent is endowed with immense natural resources, an abundant wildlife, a wealth of social and cultural heritage... just to name a few and each of most of these resources count as the untapped potential for economic development. Even though some parts of Africa are still struggling to get internet connectivity and mobile communication, overall, Africa was the first continent to go completely wireless in the 21st century when mobile lines took over fixed lines at the turn of the millennium.[13] Africa holds 9.4% of the world's proven oil and gas reserves; it is estimated that 25% of the United States' oil imports will be from Africa by 2015.[14] In terms of mineral resources, while the discovery of minerals has led

[10] World Bank. African Development Indicators 2008

[11] http://www.un.org/ecosocdev/geninfo/afrec/subjindx/121confl.htm

[12] Ibid.

[13] Ali Mufuriki – TED Conference Presentation in Arusha, Tanzania, June 2007.

[14] Ibid.

countries such as DRC, Sierra Leone and Liberia into brutal civil wars, other countries such as Botswana, Zambia, South Africa, Namibia, Tanzania, and others have been building steady and growing mineral-based industries.[15] It is not that minerals are a curse to African states, but rather that leadership has defined the impact of the mineral resources on the countries.[16] It's about leadership, about governance and about the electorate demanding accountability from those they voted into office. Accountability includes all sectors and all aspects of the social welfare system; knowing how natural resources are exploited and demanding that it is done in a way that serves the communities is part of the basic right that comes with democracy. African mineral production supplies a substantive portion to the global market: Gold 21%, Diamonds 27%, Platinum 78%, Bauxite 43%, Uranium 38%, and Iron Ore 17%, to name just a few.[17] The African market offers a large market of potentially 800 million customers, and it is yet to be tapped.

It is undisputable that there is potential for the African continent not only to develop, but to grow in industry, trade, and private investment initiatives. What is stopping us from doing that? There are complex yet basic issues to be addressed, such as infrastructures, human rights, peace, and food security, as well as basic health and education to reach all communities on the continent. And while government bodies and policymakers might be the first groups of society that we think of when speaking of development, we have to also see that each African has his or her role to play to not only support our governments to achieve economic growth but also to engage and initiate innovative and creative programs ourselves.

The continent is on the tipping point whereby the next decade will define whether the peoples of the continent manage to overcome the challenges and move to an industrious era, or whether we remain in an economically challenging state, perpetually dependent on external aid. An effective, sustainable, and organic way to support the change opportunity at hand might be to find means to mobilize change agents across the continent and create a platform for exchange, for co-creation and collaboration. This

---

[15] Ibid.
[16] Ibid.
[17] Ibid.

would allow us to have a field of creation and a field of emergence for a new reality. One challenge in making such a field of creation happen is the fact that many Africans who are in fact able to substantively contribute to the continent's development often leave the continent for better opportunities elsewhere in the world, to survive internal conflicts or run away from being killed. There is severe brain drain that is eroding the human resources base that could be tapped to make the necessary changes in favor of building stronger economies and livelihood opportunities.

THE GRASS IS GREEN ON THIS SIDE, TOO: WHY AFRICANS EMIGRATE, AND WHY THEY RETURN HOME

In Africa, despite the negative perceptions and images of Africa that are presented by the media or imagined by people who have never been here, people are humane.[18] When you cry in Africa, we cry with you or at least share your sorrow emphatically. When you laugh, we laugh with you. We celebrate together. We mourn together, no matter what country in Africa. There is heart in Africa. There is culture and tradition. We respect our elders and raise our young together. No child belongs only to his or her parents—children belong to the community. When we count family, we include even far relations, because the links are tight.

Nevertheless, life looks so much easier and kinder abroad—given a choice, on the average many African men and women would leave their countries to go settle abroad. This is true not only of Africans, but also of many people in the third world. This desire to leave the country is often based only on economic choices, that is, choices that have to be made to find a better livelihood.

In most African nations, employment is often hard to secure. But even before we can talk of employment, it is a fact that even education is hard to access. Apart from education, health care is not always available, and health issues such as HIV and malaria decimate populations. For a man or woman born in an average family, there is little likelihood of making it to be educated and employed with a decent income, while having decent health care.

[18] The atrocities we see on the news, to my mind, are a result of the stress in the environment due to poverty, lack of hope, and manipulation by arms traders.

One of the core roots for this dilemma is the fact that; we experience severe migration toward the West, hoping and looking and dreaming for better chances for life.

It is in search of these dreams of a better life that many leave the continent. Some leave legitimately, others are more clandestine. But, whether it is legitimate or clandestine, the reason for leaving is the same: a search for a better life or security. Many who are in the communities throughout the African continent think that the solutions for their lives are outside their countries or the continent. They think of Europe or America or the Middle East, or anywhere else envisioning the comfort and better living conditions if only one could leave and go settle abroad.

When I first tried to move back to Ethiopia in the late eighties, many friends would just wonder what in the world was wrong with me. How could I leave the life I had in Europe or in the United States and want to come back home? In fact, one time I was stuck in an elevator with an older gentleman in the Ministry of Lands. He bombarded me with questions about everything and especially about what I was doing. I told this man, who was possibly the age of my Grandfather, that I have come back to live here, to be close to my family and to apply what I have learned in my country. He laughed hard and said: "yeah, right...you probably dropped out of school or could not manage life out there. That's why you're back. You young people will say anything just to look good. All liars! All just a bunch of liars!" I was stunned by what he said. I felt tied by our culture that dictates that we have to be respectful of older members of the community and I was stuck on the opposite side of the elevator with a stuck door. I said nothing for the next few minutes until someone came to let us out.

Everyone seems to think that life is better abroad. We are so convinced about this truth we have built up, that it blinds our community from seeing the opportunities that are right there in our own countries. In most of the African countries I have visited, this same belief that life is better abroad applies. But as we attempt to go abroad, we often forget to consider that even though the earning may be higher, the cost of living is just as comparatively high as well. We often fail to see that the financial security we long for is often an illusion as it is made up of credit as opposed to true liquidity.

In my own experience, I have learned that one of the factors that hold we Africans back from returning home (other than a situation of conflict/war in the home country) is often the debt and the financial burdens accrued in order to keep up with living abroad (loans to buy a home, credit card debt, school loans, medical bills, etc.). Sometimes, when and if we decide to return home, we may have only debt to show. Financial constraints make it difficult to return because we are not always in a position to come back with enough liquidity to help the members of our community or even invest our earnings to build something at home. Of course, this is not the rule, and there are many Africans who return home with enough personal worth to build, invest, and get involved on the home territory—but this is not true for the majority.

How many times have we seen friends and family members so eager to leave the country and enthusiastically pack up to go abroad after gaining an ever elusive Travel Visa? But as soon as the high of the travel, departure and arrival fades away and the new routine kicks in, the picture looks different. In a very short time we realize that the quality of life we expected does not compare to what we may have had at home. In fact, before we even realize it, we end up trapped in the systems governing life abroad (the rent, insurance, taxes, medical costs, etc.). Sometimes, before we know it, we reach a stage where we can hardly afford to buy a ticket to fly back home. Even if we fly back home, we worry about what we can afford to bring back with us as gifts for the family and friends who await us, thinking that we are living so large. This is just one of the factors deterring many from returning home. Other key factors such as being able to have security, opportunities for work, health, and education play an equally important role in our decision not to head back to our home countries.

Many intelligent, able, and willing educated African men and women attempt to come back to their countries to work and build a life. Many make the difficult choices of leaving hard-earned careers and comforts abroad to return and settle in their home countries. Such men and women, returning with an education earned in a Western school and paid for in hard currency represent people who come with new ideas for investment, innovative concepts for development, and enthusiasm for working at home.

However, returnees are rarely given incentives or opportunities to make a smooth transition. Instead, often those who return are faced with intricate and complicated bureaucracies as well as with completely different social communities and a different society than the one they left. This makes it hard to come back. It makes it hard to re-integrate into the system as the person we have evolved to becoming. Sometimes, our communities want us to fit back into the character they once knew. This makes it also difficult. We have all changed in different ways, our societies have changed and our cities and countries morphed into new shapes. Within all this, most of us still hold in our hearts the image of the community we knew before we left. And when we can't find it, because things have changed, it takes renewed courage and resilience to still choose to stay and work it through. In my case, returning to Ethiopia was quite a learning experience. Once I spoke about it with a girlfriend of mine, Consolata Bakareke and she said to me "In my opinion, you were very young when you left and I wonder if the image you have is not one you created with your mind rather than the one with which you left. Unless it is the one you had in your family." Maybe the image I had of my country was one that I established itself in my mind through the years I lived outside Ethiopia; maybe it's an image that I have made up from the stories I was told; maybe it's truly an image that reflected what the country was when I left – I am not sure, maybe it is a combination of all of the above. The fact remains that for me and many of my peers returning back attracts us and at the same time, we are conscious of how challenging it can be.

The transition or the returning process can be difficult and very frustrating, and very few countries ever facilitated the return of those who would want to come back. Simple things such as support in securing a place to live or maybe even land to build a home would help greatly, but are not offered. It seems that Rwanda might be facilitating such things for the Diaspora; it might have to do with the mindset and the commitment of government in place. Based on my own experience, coming back home seems to be an upward struggle. One wonders why one would fight to return, even if life is tougher abroad, and even if our capacities and skills could be used to greatly contribute to our respective countries and common continent? Why would we go to all the trouble? Would it not be easier to just continue living life disconnected from our homes and our communities? Would it be better to remain abroad living anonymously among those who will always ask us: "Where are you from?" The "where are you from" question is a subtle way of telling us that we are not from "here." We don't belong. We are just visitors. I had this conversation with Consolata many times and she always said that the question of "where are you from" is asked everywhere and that the only way to stop it would be that everyone stays at home – but this is incompatible with the trends of globalization. Yet, one thing is for sure, we cannot stay outside and expect things to change back home. Again, the argument is that we cannot go home, leave the careers, jobs and opportunities that we have to feed our families and raise our children to go home to our countries where nothing is in place for us to sustain our lives. While we cannot remain disconnected and expect to have a say in how things are done, it's obvious that it will take a common effort both from the side of the policy makers in country and that of those living outside to come to terms with it as our common commitment for development and progress that should be the beacon that determines our actions and defines our decisions.

In Sierra Leone, the returning people are referred to as "JCs" (for Just Come Backs), and the local communities do not look always look favorably on this group. As in most other African countries, there are two sides to this. On the one hand, there are those who want to come back for a short while, just to see the folks at home, cruise around town in fancy cars, and insist on making sure that they are better than those who stayed behind. There are also those who truly come back to re-establish themselves at home. Unfortunately, in most cases, all those who return are categorized in the same box. The local communities think of them as arrogant, disconnected show-offs, which might be indeed the case in some instances. But what happens then is that those who want to genuinely return with a commitment to work and to contribute are also seen in this same light until they each individually prove that "they" are different. The result is that those returning to truly work find themselves neither fish nor fowl. They are not part of the local community anymore, and they are not part of the returnees either.

In my own case, I found myself in a similar situation when I returned to

Ethiopia. I could see how others who had returned were behaving, and it was not pretty. Some were pretending that they had forgotten our language, even though they left the country as adolescents or young adults; others were discarding local traditions and ethics in favor of the behaviors they had learned in the West. Some would even speak very loudly with heavy, newly acquired foreign accents (this was especially true for those coming back from the United States); this behavior, would of course, only alienate the local people.

There is work to be done on both sides of this dynamic. Those returning home to work might have to abandon the illusion that coming home will be like a honeymoon, something easy. It is important to know that it is not easy and it will require a lot of work until the person is fully integrated back into the society. Our respective governments might have to pay attention to the opportunities that such people would bring back with them, and support those who return as best as possible, to facilitate their integration, both professionally and socially. While governments are aware that thousands of citizens leave the country to go abroad, there is not much they are doing to change that, as to encourage people to stay rather than to leave. There are severe opportunity costs related to the brain drain, and it is the responsibility of not only the community, but also the governments to work toward retaining the capable people that can contribute development in the country. This goal could be accomplished by making available opportunities for work and education as well as social welfare, similar to the opportunities that these people would get abroad.

However, the current reality is that many people hope to leave Africa in search of better opportunities, in search of a better life, and who can blame them for that? Would we not do the same if we were confined to the lack of food, lack of health, lack of education, and lack of a proper livelihood that many are faced with? Among the saddest stories of those who so desperately want to leave the continent are the clandestine migrants. We hear in the news regularly how men, women, and children drown in the Atlantic Ocean or in the Mediterranean Sea as they attempt to reach the coasts of southern Europe. The desire to leave is so prevalent, based on the belief that life is better outside of Africa. Getting a visa to go to a foreign country is equivalent to getting a ticket to heaven. But is this really the case or is this rather wishful thinking? Life in Europe or the United States or elsewhere in industrial countries can be hard and employment is often not open to Africans or foreigners in general, who often lack the networks to be integrated into the system. Of those who manage to be successful in the West, very few return home, mainly because at home they cannot get the jobs and the salaries they can earn abroad. I have known many African men and women who, upon their return back home, behave in ways that are even more "foreign," more "colonial," and more "expatriate" than some of the expatriates. They are arrogant and have often lost the respect for their own culture, and in cases they behave in such intolerant ways that it is difficult to bear. They shout at their house help, they mistreat their co-workers and just behave in ways that is so foreign to the basic culture of hospitality and of household management of most African nations.

But regardless of whether the behavior is pro-Africa or against, whether individuals behave with basic ethics and manners or whether they behave in ways more colonial than the colonials themselves—the main idea to remember is that it is the responsibility of the majority in the society and the communities to be tolerant, inclusive, and compassionate in order to attract people to return, and once they return, to encourage a behavior that is constructive and conducive for development.

HOPING FOR CHANGE

Now is the time to look into the future and realize that unless some of us are willing to come home and continue building our future together with the civil society, the public and private sector, then in a few years, there might not be a home to come to – a home where we feel at home. Unless some of us are willing to come back, are willing to take on the responsibility to do our due share and contribute to build our nations and communities, and to support the efforts already in place in the best way we can—we have to realize that we are not being constructive by just remaining on the sidelines, abroad somewhere commenting or criticizing the situation in our countries.

In order to come back, it is necessary to try and see beyond the challenges on the surface. It is important to be able to look deeper and gauge the opportunities that exist in our countries despite the poverty, despite the governance challenges, despite the fact that returning home might not be an easy exercise. It is our commitment and our presence here, on the ground, that will in time create a different reality, one that offers us the chance to raise our children in peace, to see our investments yield profits, to know that we are safe and secure, and can enjoy the rule of law in our home countries. Unless we demand such a reality, it may never come. Unless we see the opportunities at home and unless we are willing to commit to long-term development, we may have to continue to leave our communities and countries. I am not saying that it is possible to see the opportunities everywhere and at all times, because there are situations of conflict and war that will certainly force us to leave. But outside of that, it is our responsibility to work collectively toward building nations where families can live in peace, where we can be treated with dignity and justice.

Such change can be brought in by empowering enlightened leaders at all levels. Such leaders do exist — often we need not look further than ourselves or the person next to us to identify such type of exceptional personalities within our working environment, our families and our communities. It is our willingness to take on responsibility and enroll others in our vision that will unfold a better future for all communities across Africa.

Despite the challenges of life in Africa, going away is not the answer. In any major Western city, you will find various ethnic neighborhoods, because people need to get together with their own kin. We miss home. We miss home, traditional cuisine, stories from home, even a bit of drama from home. The dilemma is that we might be miserable to stay abroad and be similarly miserable to go home.

How can we be channels for change and transformation if our paradigm is locked in a paradox without answers? It is a paradox that for me is so poisonous and toxic because it has contributed to the loss of our dream that one day Africa will be a place with the same living standards as any other region of the world. There are days I often witness how men and women around me, across various communities, have lost faith and stopped believing that one day things will be fine and in order in Africa. We tend to look toward the outside, instead of focusing on what's within our reach right here in our countries, focusing on our personal inner world and how we can mobilize ourselves to create the space that we want. We tend to think that the answer lies outside. We may perpetually look outside our borders, our boundaries, and our world—yet, it is not outside we should look. Maybe, just maybe, the answers to the complexities we face is right here within our reach, within our communities and our boundaries. Maybe we need to reposition our perspectives to get that particular angle where the solutions become apparent.

CHAPTER TWO

Differences in Perception: "Solutions" and Their Problems

There are a countless lenses through which a myriad of actors engage the work we call "human and economic development." It is like having a thousand cooks from a thousand places and asking them to cook a new meal, based on recipes collected from afar. As such, it is very hard to communicate and harmonize efforts in a way that is inclusive, comprehensive and participatory. Part of the difficulty emerges from the differences in perceptions, in levels of consciousness, in educational background, in maturity, and often, differences in the level of experience not only in this work, but really in life in general.

A PROBLEM OF TIME

In my own experience, one of the challenges that I constantly faced was that of the limited time allocated for the various programs to be implemented and to produce results within a limited and given time frame. Change is time-specific — it is in combination with time that we can see the fruits of the change emerging. If we are unable to perceive with our senses that the change has taken root, we may become discouraged and want to give up. Public or civil society communication campaigns for behavioral change are a great example of this dynamic. Whether the campaign is for the prevention of HIV/AIDS or for the use of mosquito nets for malaria prevention, it is not easy to see at the early stages of the campaign that the population is in fact listening to the messages being delivered. And the process of engaging and adopting these new behaviors takes time. At times, the leaders and managers of such programs are not persistent enough. Often they lack the necessary endurance, leading to such kind of programs being interrupted at too early of stages and/or budget allocations not being sufficient. But we need sufficient time to see the outcome of our efforts. Sometimes, the simpler the change we want, the harder it is to see. In parallel, campaigns calling for military mobilization produce immediately perceptible results, as do campaigns for radical change or responses to an immediate call.

There is a serious difference between a project's life cycle and the time it takes to actually see the results and outcomes of the work. When we work in projects for human development or to improve the livelihood of communities, it is unwise to think in the short term. No matter how many resources are committed, it will be necessary to have mid- and long-term perspectives and objectives in order to see true change taking place and eventually witness transformation. However, in reality, we are often confined to projects with a lifetime of 3 to 5 years, which is not enough to see deeply rooted and durable change — by the time a project really gets started, it is often time to think of wrapping up or handing over and already closing down. For example, if we speak of HIV/AIDS projects, it is difficult to see behavior and value changes quickly taking place. So, we need time, yet time is not always available, because funding dries out or it is only earmarked for a specific, limited period of time.

I would like to demonstrate this dilemma in the example of everyONE, an organization I worked on almost a decade ago and established in 2003.

When I wrote the initial proposal stating the purpose and aims of the organization, I did so with a good ten years of experience working on HIV/AIDS. I was convinced that an innovative and effective approach to the issue of HIV/AIDS would be to have a radio talk show, presenting true stories from the communities, during which the listeners would have a chance to call in and take on the role of the person in the story.

So, for example, within the theme of HIV testing and the debate as to whether or not an employer can require an employee to be tested, we told the true story of a man called Samuel. Samuel's employer requested an HIV test and his doctor revealed the sero-positive results to his employer without Samuel's consent, therefore violating his basic rights. Samuel was therefore faced with possibly losing his job, and was certainly looking at discrimination from his colleagues and facing even more trouble at home. As the listeners called in, they had to call in saying, "I am Samuel, and I feel ______ etc." — men and women of all ages called, and they all spoke as Samuel.

We started getting calls from all over Ethiopia, and the show became very popular; we started out broadcasting once a week in the evening for 90 minutes, and the show later moved to Saturday mornings for 120 minutes. We were able to raise issues that were difficult to bring up in public or to be presented through conventional publications. We spoke through stories, and through these stories, it was in a way our own collective story that we started talking about without fear and shame. Conversations became alive and people were listening. Our aim with this kind of talk show was to avoid preaching about HIV/AIDS, and instead to plant seeds of reflection. We were hoping that people would start questioning their behaviors, their attitudes and values. We hoped that this questioning would open the way for change. And in my opinion, I feel that it did.

Now to come back to the funding issue, our funding was for only three years. The radio show did excellently, beyond our and other's expectations, but at the same time, even though in any country such a program would be considered a public service, in the Ethiopian context we ended up paying the greater part of our budget to keep the show going. To make matters worse, at the height of the program's success, the money ran out — and it was essentially impossible to raise the kind of money we actually needed to continue the program. Our main donor had adopted a new strategic direction, which did not include programs such as ours. The end of the game was that we were faced with having to interrupt a program that was actually working perfectly well, before we could even reach a level where we could show the changes and transformation it brought about. As such, we lost a valuable opportunity and momentum.

However, had the funding been available for a longer period of times, such as 7–10 years, and even had the funds been disbursed in phases, it would have allowed everyone to focus on the programs rather than obsessing about finding funding or spending undue time for writing reports to meet the whims of alternative donors. Most donor organizations talk of partnership with civil society, when in fact the relationship is flawed from the get-go. It is a "giver and receiver" relationship which can never truly be a partnership because the parties do not stand on the same level ground. There is an inherent vicious circle in this story that has to be broken. And it is in fact this widespread dilemma that exists within small local humanitarian organizations with limited in-house capacities to raise funds and put together reports, which puts them in a comparative disadvantage to access external funding successfully.

This particular experience and many others I have had in my career reflect the problem of time that plagues development projects and the challenge of funding them for local organizations and entities in this globalized world. Because of the focus on producing outputs and results in very short periods of time, projects are hamstrung before they are even begun

However, there are different ways and concepts to relate to time. Westerners and conventional thoughts teach that time is money, time is precious, time is finite, and so on. Time is also intangible and acquires its value from the recounting of our achievements or lack of the same within that set period.

It is interesting to realize that most African settings do not hold this same relationship to time. For most Africans instead, time exists not as fragmented by seconds, minutes, days, but as an endless and continuous line emerging from eternity and going forward into eternity. Time is endless and time is an unfolding of our lives. Often, in most African communities and settings, people make appointments or declare plans, and end the sentence with *insh'Allah* (God willing), meaning, "We shall see." Humans plan and God executes or allows the execution of our plans. Time belongs to God and we are merely graced with it, for as long as 'He' the Almighty will allow us. This is true no matter the level of consciousness, worldview, or education.

In my nearly twenty years in international development work, I have not seen many occasions allocated for reflection. I have not seen value attributed to the long-term impact (positive or negative) of our work, outside that which we can see at our own gross level. Group vision-sharing or goal-setting may be a common retreat exercise, but in a more-or-less shallow way. There are individuals or rare organizations who actually do create occasions for true and deep reflection about what is ahead, but most just participants go forward without deeply scanning the terrain.

I think of time in possibly a Western way, while I also relate to it in a more African pattern. I realize that tomorrow will come and that today I must work in order to achieve my personal objectives or be where I need to be when tomorrow rolls around. My desire to advocate for a longer time-frame for development projects is an outgrowth of my African perspective on time. In order to have strong and lasting change, it is important to look at time and its relationship to our action. This remains true in our policy formulation, our legislations, our political structures, our education systems, and even in the examples we set for our children.

The tragic result of this problem, of the short time-lines in development work, is that when our assignment is finished or our project closes down, not much is seen that can be directly correlated with the sweat and heart equity we have put into the work. In disregard of our endless hours of work, the indicators in the logical frameworks that we have defined as targets in our so-called consultative processes do not take into consideration the intangible human- and soul-level benefits. Which donor would accept happiness or peace of mind among the beneficiaries as a measure of achievement of the funds being spent? Which donor would accept inner balance and new perspective as a measure of achievement? Yet, many programs have achieved such intangibles as happiness, balance, peace of mind, etc. — and those changes often bear in fact more tangible results, but only when viewed over time and from another perspective. The requirement to come up with tangible measures of success is when the complexities arise.

THE PROBLEM OF THE SHADOW SIDE: INDIVIDUAL MOTIVATIONS AND CAPACITIES

When it comes to Africa, standards of research — ethically and scientifically — become blurred with the researcher's personal capacities or limitations. This is a difficult truth that I learned the hard way.

In Addis Ababa in 1998, when I was working as a Communication Advisor for MSF, we hired a consultant to evaluate our program. We wanted an external evaluation to give us a sense of what had or had not been achieved. The consultant prepared a whole outline of how she would conduct the work. Along with that outline, she prepared a long list of questions to use in her study. In reading the questions, I felt spiritually pushed around. I felt that the questions did not relate to the women as human beings, but rather as sex traders and cold-blooded prostitutes you might find in criminal or violent movies (creatures without humanity). At an early stage, it became very clear that the consultant categorized the women were working solely from a perspective where she saw them as prostitutes and nothing else. I can't say that this is solely a Western perspective, because I had seen people within the country entertain a similar perspective. Maybe we can say that it is the perspective of people who lost the humanity in their heart and are unable to use their heart to relate to others. At one point, I found a question that I will never forget. The question asked: "How many times does the client come in and out of you before his climax?" I told the consultant that this question was not relevant to the study we were commissioning, and that if she were anywhere else in Africa, she would not ask such intrusive questions.

Both, my boss at the time and the consultant replied that this was public health and that my knowledge of public health research was not sufficient to understand this research and its methodology. Such questions as asking how many times the client goes in and out of the woman (the project beneficiary) until ejaculation are such a violation of human dignity, yet this type of treatment happens regularly because the poor beneficiaries have no sense of their rights. The NGO workers/consultants/researchers might even be convinced that their work is for the greater good. In this case, I objected, naming it as an unethical or improper question with no relevance to the study—very quickly, I was told that I did not know how research is conducted and that this was a necessary question. I was not in a position to object further. In favor of my boss at the time I have to say that he had always stood behind my positions for the women, because we could both see the situation of the women in the same heart. During this incident, I believe he was caught between the pressure from the authorities to have the project evaluated, and at the same time the consultant, who at the time was a good twenty years older than both of us, misled his judgment .

This incident marked one of the key moments that eventually led me to resign my post with MSF-Belgium, and it raised my awareness of the impact of a person's shadow side on their actions.

Although one cannot generalize across the board, I have to say that I often wonder about so-called Non-Governmental (NGO) workers/development volunteers coming into developing countries, especially to African countries, with an invasive and disrespectful attitude?

Most international workers certainly come to support and help, but I have to say that in my twenty-some years, I have seen too many who come merely looking for adventure, or sometimes just out of curiosity. I have seen too many examples of people taking the opportunity to practice what they just learned in college and filling their CVs with some kind of experience abroad, before starting proper professional careers in their home countries. Or there are the ones who are just hunting for glorious fodder to add thrilling points to their storytelling and conversation at tea/coffee parties or cocktail events. As a consequence, the volunteers or international workers, who come merely looking for some of the things mentioned above, make it very difficult for those who truly come with serious intentions to genuinely contribute to development. It makes it hard because government officials and communities as well as the members of the local civil society end up thinking that "all" Western or International NGO workers come to our communities not to work per se, but to have an adventure, drive their big cars and enjoy the night life, sometimes even with the same so called women in prostitution, which might be the beneficiaries of some of their projects. Although this is true for some expatriates, it is only fair to say that it is certainly not true for all of them. Yet, this negative perception ends up being costly to all the NGO workers as well as the possible communities/projects they would have come to work in.

The core defining factor is the intention with which volunteers and international experts come. Are they coming to share their knowledge and are they open as well to learn from the counterparts in their host countries? Or do they behave like in an open laboratory where they can try out what they have learned in college, or just seeking a new thrill? Is a job in an NGO the Western World's answer to unemployment and on the job training for their future aid experts? Or do volunteers indeed come to truly help, and if so, can they also see where they themselves might need assistance from their local counterparts? It is true that all around Africa poverty in monetary terms is widespread, while their wealth of wisdom, tradition, culture, and traditional knowledge is not being recognized. Are the volunteers aware of that wealth? Are they prepared to learn and remain open to the realities that await them? Have they been adequately prepared and briefed about what to expect when they arrive and what is expected of them once they start working in the projects? It seems that very little preparation is provided for the myriad of experts and volunteers; in addition, international experts more often than not think that they already know all they need to know and come out of place attitude of "know it all". It is very rare to see any expatriate expressing their doubts or uncertainties on any given situation, as this could easily take them out of business. It is like they are "god" and "god knows it all".

The level of consciousness from which a person operates defines their behavior. This level of consciousness is defined by how all other aspects of the person have developed. This would include their different lines of development, such as ethical, cognitive, moral, emotional, etc. My own experience shows me that those individuals with more highly developed moral, ethical, and emotional lines are more apt to deal productively with the issue of development and can work better in humanitarian organizations. I have realized my own effectiveness growing as my development in these different areas continued. Cognitive intelligence then becomes almost a side issue — if the person is deficient in the emotional, moral, and ethical lines, then no matter how good their intentions, their contribution is be tainted by the shadows they inevitably carry with them.

In countless conversations with civil servants in various African countries as well as with Africans working in international organizations, I have seen that many consider international development workers as full of arrogance. There is a sense of entitlement which most expatriates carry themselves with. Many just come into a room without honoring the space they are entering; they come with the assumptions that they know more and have their pre-fabricated solutions ready at hand. It is like we Africans owe them something, as if we have to be grateful. It is true that they bring with them aid and funding, which is often direly needed in our countries, but they often forget to see that through this aid they also, personally, get employment and often a livelihood that they could not afford in their own home countries. At times, it is something we can laugh about and leave to the side, but often such behavior is just simply revolting. The most revolting aspect is that little is done to change the situation; as many expatriates come and go for their respective terms of employment, the behavior remains. And we just sit and watch them come and go. My friend Consolata often says that it is only the African colleagues of these expatriates that can change by committing themselves to results, to excellence and to refusing to accept any kind of patronizing behavior from their expatriate colleagues. Often, expatriates are not even aware that they are being observed – as Africans would be if they entered a small community in Europe for example. Expatriates hardly realize that the neighborhood and the community either know them or know of them through the grapevine.

In 2008, a North American came to work as a volunteer in Sierra Leone. I met her a day after she had arrived. This tall twenty-something young lady was walking around town with the shortest shorts and a little top. Her attire was nothing that would raise eyebrows in Europe or the United States; it was hot, so she wore short shorts and a top — for her, it all made sense. Except, she did not take into consideration the environment into which she was entering. She was not aware of the space around her. She spoke with a loud voice, and even worse, she laughed extremely loud. This might be a sign of self-confidence or self-assurance in the Western world, but in most African cultures, being loud is not looked upon favorably. I was wondering how I could tell her that she cannot behave this way. We had met in a restaurant, and I tried to tell her, but she could not hear my words or message or catch the subtle signs I made to indicate that her behavior was not ok — I suppose she was not sensitive enough to take in that information. To this day, many refer to her as "that woman with the short pants!" The sad part is that this young woman was really coming to work and with serious intentions. She came with a lot of knowledge and was ready to roll up her sleeves and get the work done. But her attire was completely wrong, and even though it is a minor detail when you look at it from the perspective of the work she accomplished, this small detail took away so much from her experience, because it colored the way local people perceived her. One could argue that maybe the people around should have been more tolerant and taken her for who she was and how she was. Yes, it's a valid argument. Maybe instead of being judged for what she wore, it might have been better to judge her on her performance. Yes, it's a valid argument. But it did not happen. While it is true that there may be some level of intolerance in Africa when it comes to women's attires, it is also our common responsibility to inform visiting volunteers, expatriates and also returning Africans about appropriate dress codes. Being appropriate is only a sign of mutual respect.

Incidents of a comparable cultural/ethical discrepancy or gap happen often. Let me describe a further situation, an incidence with a friend of mine who came to help with our organization in Ethiopia. He came along with his wife who was also very nice, and we happily received them both. However, the following story reflects the need for emotional, moral, and ethical development almost in preference to cognitive intelligence

My friend's wife was very kind and caring, with a northern American worldview; he, on the other side, was very sensitive to the cultural realities of Ethiopia, but unfortunately, she was not. One day, just a day or two after they had arrived, we had a team meeting around the conference table in my office. My friend participated in the meeting as a way of learning more about what we do so that he could be in a position to advise us. At the same time, his wife sat at my desk to read. What she did not know is that our organization had moved into my father's old office space. I used his very office to work, and hence also his desk. The desk, made of heavy old wood and leather, is about the same age as I am; and for us, it holds history, it holds memories and most of all it is like the heart of our Fort. It had for me and all of us in that office a life of its own. So, as the meeting is going on, I looked up her way and only to find to my surprise, that she had her feet (with shoes) crossed, resting on the desk, and was quietly reading her book without any reservations at all. I remember some of my colleagues looked at me and I looked back at them.

Having worked and lived in both Europe and the North America for a substantial part of my life, I know that there are differences in culture. But I don't know of any culture where it is okay to put one's feet on the desk of one's host! One could think that she was just simply rude, but I know for a fact she is not rude per se. It was more of an attitude issue. It might be that since it is Africa, maybe she thought you can just do anything you want – it's really an issue of perception and how she saw us.

All of us in that office that day could only see a combination of ignorance and arrogance, and lack of manners. I asked her to move her feet off, politely. I could not bring myself to express the outrage I felt in words. From that moment on, I have to admit that something in me shut down the potential relationship I could have built with her. I knew my friend came to visit us with the most noble intentions, I knew that. I also knew that his wife was a great person, but her lack of sensitivity to the prevailing culture was like ice water pouring on my head — it cooled off and froze any possible relationship, conversation, or whatever else may have emerged from her visit.

In that moment, the level of consciousness from which my friend's wife was operating was completely out of line. What made her think that she could behave this way? Is it because it is some African country? Or is it that in her mind, we may be seen as wild and simple people without culture, values and norms. She might not have know better, but how did she fail to feel the consternation in the room? In my opinion, she lacked the emotional intelligence to navigate the cultural differences with awareness of the need for her to be sensitive and adapt her behavior to local conditions.

I am still pondering the case of the consultant whom we hired in MSF, the woman who was so disrespectful to the women in my program. I still don't understand what may have led her to put such dehumanizing and humiliating questions in her interviews. Was it because the women were selling sex, because they were poor, because they were African, or because this was somewhere other than in Europe or the United States? Did this consultant really think that her questions about the intricate details of how the women handle their clients would bring key information to evaluate our program? It all leaves me intrigued and speechless, when reflecting on the situation. It also leaves me appalled and revolted, because I know that had this questionnaire been made elsewhere, some kind of ethical standard would have been used.

When young NGO workers come to Africa from Europe or North America or another donor nation, many might come with noble intentions of doing serious humanitarian work; sometimes I would even say that they also come with very romantic and idealistic outlooks and imaginations of Africa. However, it is also true in my experience that some come expecting to save "poor Africa," others looking for an escapade, a chance to explore the "dark" continent and to do fun things. Others might come to practice what they have learned in school before heading into multilateral organizations. There would be no harm in all this, except that we are dealing with local communities, we are dealing with lives, families, and people. The comfort of coming with an organization allows the NGO workers to go straight into the lives of people. But this needs to follow, in my opinion, a respectable approach. People are first of all human beings that deserve the best we can offer. Because a community or a person is poor, it doesn't make it ok for someone else to come along and patronize them. Let us take an organization working on reproductive health and family planning. What would you think if a local nurse or social worker comes along with a young international volunteer and off they go with their questioning about the most private and intimate aspects of their lives? The women can't pull out of the situation they find themselves in, but often they have to go exactly through such type of interrogations to gain in the best way some meager benefit for their families. And the conversation continue, while the social worker translates the conversation in English for the international expert, who is taking notes and asks even more questions about the women's lives, about their husbands, about their sexuality, just about very intimate questions. Often it all happens at the doorstep of the homes – with little privacy or none at all.

Seemingly most expatriates do not have enough or any type of preparation to deal with the prevalent culture in their host countries. Many travel to various destinations in Africa without honestly seeing the potential of the men and women they come to help and work with. At times it seems that they just come to download and apply their knowledge and standard procedures and off they charge to the next destination. This is difficult to accept as it has a negative impact in various ways: in terms of lost opportunity to exchange and learn together, in terms of human relationship, in terms of emotional exchange and a chance to build a long term link and a culture of trust and mutual understanding, just to mention a few.

Others might be so over-confident that they end up in dangerous situations, like a young volunteer I once met who ended up getting detained by local authorities in the Ogaden Region of Ethiopia.

In 1998, a young French woman came to evaluate some projects being carried out in the Ogaden Region of Ethiopia for one of the International NGOs operating in that region. This region has been an unstable place due to a consistent conflict between the Ethiopian government and the Somali communities, which started already much before people started talking about the war against terrorism. This young expert was told to stay within the project area, but she decided to discard those directions and do as she pleased to do. The trouble started when she walked off and went into restricted areas, where she was stopped by local authorities. When she was asked her to show her identity papers, she refused to follow the instructions. She instead told the men that they did not have the right to ask her such kind of questions. The result was that they took her to their duty station, where she was detained. It took a number of days and a lot of administrative trouble and negotiations to get her released. Had she been caught by the rebels, it may have possibly cost her life, but she was just too caught up with herself to realize that it was in fact her irresponsible behavior that let to this situation.

This problem of the individual shadow side is not just limited to Westerners in Africa. For example, at times the maladjustment creates Africans who reject their heritage and adopt rather a more European, American, or Western way of life. Many times I have witnessed Africans behaving in ways that were demeaning toward other Africans. Whether it is to show that "they" are educated, or that "they" have money, or that "they" are just better than the rest, such people treat other Africans with more arrogance than what might be expected of the worse colonials. This often applies to housewives who make their domestic employees work as pseudo-slaves, or those who treat people with disdain, like being contemptuous toward beggars or being haughty and snooty to the average person. Such Africans consciously ignore the social cultures of respecting elders, and forget that shouting is not really an accepted way of treating employees. For me, it is painful to witness these moments, since such type of behavior creates dissonance within the community. It is painful, not only because of the shame and humiliation such people subject their victims to, but also because their behavior is a direct reflection of how much disharmony might exist in their souls and beings.

I have met many Africans who have so completely abandoned their heritage. For many years, I was very intolerant of such people, because I could not understand why someone would abandon their roots. It revolted me to see people who did not want to have anything to do with their roots, their history and their cultural heritage. I just could not understand. In time, I have learned to understand that there may be different ways we can each show up and be counted. Some might want to remain as authentic as possible, and some others might want to emerge as more integrated with the rest of the world – meaning with not so much ethnicity – which can be fine as well. It does not really matter. We all have experienced a different way of upbringing, which reflects in our behaviors; each way is equally valid. It is our capacity to be tolerant of others that will actually allow us as a people from one continent, to push forward and join the rest of the world in the Global Village.

We are all different, and in our difference, we all have our own ways of expressing ourselves and carrying our respective burdens. We all have different levels of consciousness and different concerns.[19]

Through his research on human psychology, Dr. Clare Graves speaks of value systems and levels of consciousness, and how the different levels of human consciousness development may define how we each think and behave. Following the research of Dr. Graves, Don Beck and Chris Cowen introduced a spiral overview illustrating how, at each stage of development, human societies adopt various value systems.[19]

[19] Spiral Dynamics, Mastering Values, Leadership and Change (Don Beck and Christopher Cowan, 1996).

According to Graves,[20] everyone has a right to be at the level of development of where they are; there should be no pressure to evolve further if the circumstances do not call for it. So, whether some Africans remain completely committed to Africa or whether some are rather elusive about it and associate more with other parts of the world, does not matter. It is just the way that each expresses their values and beings in the world. And even though, in my opinion, when one abandons ones' heritage for another acquired one, it is like walking with a pair of borrowed shoes, it may work for some, even though it is often unnatural and odd. What is important is that each one of us in Africa is inclusive of others; is tolerant of others; and most of all is not judgmental of how others are expressing themselves. It is true that much of the internal conflicts and wars that plagued the continent result from the lack or even absence of tolerance; still there is hope that tolerance can find its day with not only more education but also with having access to more role models that reflect this tolerance. At a regional level, even though there have been various pan-African movements during the past as well as in present times, I believe that we still have a long way to go, in order to better understand each other and to work for common goals.

I have also witnessed the opposite of this tolerance in the form of African men and women, who returning home with a radical rejection of the rest of the world. They go to the other extreme of exerting severe racism toward all other non-Africans that live in their countries. We get so wrapped up about "our" Africa that we forget to see our role as world citizens. We might then forget that as much as Africa is our home, it is also part of the world, and that our aim must be to find ways to live harmoniously with each other, while at the same time being inclusive of the rest of the world.

There is a story I want to share to illustrate the above.

In December 2008, my husband Matthias, my children, and I were at the airport in Addis Ababa to catch a flight to Ghana. We had spent the

[20] Clare W. Graves, an American Professor in Psychology is the person behind the research and development of Spiral Dynamics. Spiral Dynamics, now, further developed by Don Beck and Chris Cowan, speaks about societal and human development levels and how these levels define the paradigms in which we respectively operate. See: Spiral Dynamics – Don Beck & Christopher C. Cowan.

Christmas holidays with family in Ethiopia and were headed back home to Sierra Leone. It was very early in the morning, with the usual airport hustle and bustle. As we waited in line to go through security, one Ethiopian man was aggressively pushing his cart in the line, and eventually pushed into my two daughters and me. So, my husband asked him if he would step back and wait patiently for his turn. The man just exploded without any warning, shouting back at my husband the following: "I am in my country here and you can't (f...cking) tell me what to do...you (f...cking racist) and then on and on with the (F... you and F...this and that)." On and on he went, insulting and ranting and shouting, it was so disgraceful. From the way that he spoke and the way that he appeared it was obvious that he was someone living in the United States and had probably come back to visit family. Before my husband could answer back, I stepped in to firmly tell the man that "it is you who is "the" racist in this case. Pushing your cart into two small children and shouting was rude to say the least, as well as disrespectful and shameful." However, the guy did not want to listen, and continued shouting until security interfered.

Matthias is a humble person who fell in love with Africa long before I met him, and who has spent a good part of his life working in the African countryside with the rural communities – communities where most Africans living in the Western world would not even go to, as they would consider the people there as backward and primitive. But because this guy at the airport assumed that all white people were racist, he felt that he could shout all he wanted, making accusations and insinuations. It was upsetting, but to apply an Integral perspective, if this man's level of consciousness is at this stage, well, then it is exactly at this stage and he would not be able to see a different reality other than that which actually appears to him. For this man, it is a deeply rooted fact that all whites are racist. Nothing will make him change, unless he himself is open to evolve his perception of others, his surroundings and his environment. In this case, Matthias could instead have come to the conclusion that Africans are rude and racists. It is up to us to be more tolerant and more firm at the same time, to be able to constructively deal with individuals of such kind as described above.

By the same token, I would like to share another airport story to illustrate the point I am making about levels of consciousness and human development.

In 2005, I was waiting in the transit lounge in Nairobi International Airport working on my laptop, when an older white man approached me. He had a camera with him and acted like he was on some discovery trip. Then he asked me if he could take my picture. When I asked him why, he replied "when I go home to Germany, I want to show my family that I have seen an African using a laptop." Can you imagine how I felt hearing such kind of nonsense? I think this must have been his first trip to Africa and maybe he came to Kenya for making a safari. But one thing was sure, this man had no idea what he was actually talking about. For a short moment, I was speechless. Then I looked up and told him that if he even dared to take my picture, he would be in more trouble than he ever could imagine. He spoke back to someone traveling with him making derogatory comments (in German). Of course, he had no idea that I spoke German. I told him in German that I would call the Airport Police on him if he continued to make such insulting statements about me. The episode ended there.

Should I be upset because this man is uneducated, clueless, and possibly rude? Or, should I conclude that all Germans are like him? No, it is his level of development, his value systems that makes him behave this way. I cannot change this one man; it is the value systems that we have to understand in order to find the leverage points to make systemic change happen. The onus is on each one of us to try to have as comprehensive an outlook as possible, to avoid falling victim to ordinary yet sad incidents that might veil our perspective on life.

THE PROBLEM OF THE SHADOW SIDE: ORGANIZATIONAL BEHAVIOR

By their very name, NGOs are non-government organizations, yet I personally consider the larger international NGOs with substantial funding as international organizations that also execute the policies of their respective countries under the name of support to the civil society.

I find that the "non-entity" connotation is passive-aggressive and misleading. Under the mask of being non-governmental, such organizations and their employees come with own rules and framework as to the governance of our bubbles of existence. In many instances such organizations are more loyal to their own organizational dogma or policies than they are to working to benefit the local population. This is especially true in faith-based organizations.

Speaking of non-governmental organizations brings me to share some additional thoughts on so-called "volunteers", which I have mentioned earlier on several occasions. The expatriates working for volunteer organizations are classified as such, because on a western scale their compensations are very modest as compared to the average income in their host countries. But why do they do volunteer work and what does it mean for themselves? Is the work truly selfless, or is there something that they want to have in exchange? Is it even healthy to work for nothing in exchange for the time invested in work? Would it not be demeaning to the other side not to demand some kind of compensation, even if it is just the experience one gathers? Not wanting something back for our work would be like saying that one is willing to give but not willing to receive, because there is nothing the other could give in exchange that would be of value. The need to think carefully about volunteerism was brought home to me in a very personal way.

In 2004, I attended a Spiral Dynamics Workshop outside of Seattle. As I presented my work, someone asked me what my compensation was for all the work, and I responded that I did not get any compensation. And the woman said to me very casually: "oh, so you are another Jesus wanna-be, martyr of 'I just wanna help' crap!"

I could not believe she said that. Hearing her was like being shocked awake from my sleep — and indeed, she hit a serious blind spot and shadow I had been carrying with me for a long time.

Since then, I have worked on being clear about my intentions, about why I want to do something, and what I have to offer as well as what I have to gain from whatever I engage in. It has been a hard path to travel because it is so much easier to hide behind nebulous intentions, but I have learned from this process that the clearer our intentions and our reasons for engagement, the more powerful our work and the results we yield.

It is important to bring light to our true motivations on both sides:

the Western side as well as the African side. I have often heard expatriates complain that their African colleagues have no motivation to work. One of the reasons for low motivation among the African counterparts of international NGOs might be that the international staffs have chosen to come to work here in Africa for their own personal reasons and choice. This choice is often made not from a standpoint of survival or from needing a job, but rather to have a different experience, to contribute, to put into practice the knowledge acquired in school, possibly to learn more and to serve. So for them the job is more than just employment – it is rather a process to achieve the objectives that led them to come in the first place. But on the African side, in most cases, the job is first of all a job; it is about having employment that allows us to feed our families and to take care of our basic needs for life. As such, volunteerism is a luxury and we need to be clear about that. In fact, the expatriates who come as volunteers often earn more than professional Africans hired in the same organizations save for some very few exceptions. One could argue that the education level between the expatriates and their local counterparts are not comparable; but that to me remains just an argument that sustains the vicious circle of lack of access to education, hence lack of access to professional opportunities, which leads to low purchasing power, etc. In most African countries, where the average working person has to support not only their immediate families but also a number of relatives and extended family, a job is vital for survival.

The living conditions, the employment opportunities, and the social welfare systems are not yet so evolved enough to allow Africans to engage in volunteerism rather than working for full pay. For African nationals, NGO jobs are often quite attractive and well paid as compared to the public or private sector employment opportunities. However, African employees usually do not benefit sufficiently from the benefit schemes that international NGOs offer to their expatriate staff.

Interestingly enough, many of the approaches of international charity NGOs in Africa focus on the strengthening of already existing social welfare systems of African societies, where families help each other, create support systems within the communities and as such create somewhat of a social welfare safety net.

As a sum, the differences in our intentions to engage in humanitarian or development work, as well as the level of consciousness from which we operate, create a complex organizational ground that demands astute and sensitive leadership in order to make the organization work, and to achieve the objectives set. In some cases, inadequate leadership can foster unnecessary problems.

I remember in Ethiopia, when I was working for MSF, *there was a very sad incident whereby a new and young volunteer almost lost his life. He was in charge of a program near the Somali border, and as he drove back to Addis Ababa with his driver, their car was ambushed by rebels and they were shot at. The driver died, and the volunteer ended up severely injured and eventually paralyzed for life. There is a bit of a discrepancy between the official story and the story that is known on the ground. While officially the incident was associated with an attack from rebels, local sources say that the volunteer had been publicly reprimanding one of the drivers for either being late and/or for carrying unauthorized passengers. Some suspect that there may not have been any problem had my colleague instead taken the driver into his office to speak to him in person about their differences. But instead, some of those who worked in the project during that time mentioned that he shouted at the driver and humiliated him in front of other colleagues. In a culture where honor and respect come first, such a humiliating behavior can easily lead to retaliation from the community. This case shows that no matter which level of authority the organizational hierarchy might give, in some cultures real authority is rather earned from the community through character, the level of respect, age and wisdom. In this example, if in fact the story on the ground holds true, then maybe the volunteer committed a great error in so reprimanding the driver in such a way. He surely did not take the time to understand the role that is driver might have had in the local community context. He may not have taken his time to see how shouting is considered in the culture. The question of what might be the consequences of humiliating someone in public never occurred to him. But these are all questions that would not even have to be asked if the development worker in question was operating from a place of mutual respect.*

The leadership capacity of the person heading development projects very much defines the direction and success of an intervention. When MSF started as an organization, it was founded by European physicians – one of the founders Bernard Kouchner is now the French Foreign Minister – who wanted to give their time and know-how to situations of humanitarian crisis due to wars and/or natural disasters around the world. In time, the mandate of the organization changed from addressing solely crisis situations to addressing development issues as well. As the organization grew in size, in the number of projects and in its presence in the world, I think somewhere along the line the convictions and commitment of the founders and early members of the organizations might have not been as vivid in the minds of the newer members of the organization. More than a means of providing support for destitute communities, MSF became a great brand to have on one's career path. This subtle and possible change in the convictions of those working for the organization might have led to the situation where a number of volunteers did not always understand the subtle issues in development or maybe did not even care to know. Joining MSF has its own excitement — one feels great in the headquarters offices and there is a sense of being sent out save the world. There is a sense of youthful invincibility and also a certain level of self-importance. There is a sense of community and self-confidence that often blurs our common sense about the rest of the world; it is MSF , and then the other NGOs.

I suspect that there was a disparity between how the program manager in this tragic incident saw the situation and how the situation was viewed by the local community. It is these subtle gaps in how we see and act in the environment that can lead to life-threatening situations. I think it is legitimate to raise the questions on how much of the spirit of MSF's founders do the new volunteers still live, and how much of that spirit do they carry with them. How much of the leadership of the founders do the new volunteers understand and/or even possess? What does it mean to drive around in a car branded with the logo of the organization? Is there a basic benchmark for ethics and behavior for volunteers to comply with and a minimum level of responsibility and capacity to integrate into a local society that is needed to make the job?

We have to give due consideration to exploring how leadership is exercised in such organizations. Stories like the above illustrate the need to bring about leadership competence in synch with the local context in order to benefit the work and the communities the organization sets out to serve.

"SOLUTIONS" THAT CONTRADICT LOCAL CULTURE

Many times we have tried to duplicate social programs such as gender-rights or women's programs, imported from industrial countries to African countries. But these efforts often fail, because the programs do not take into consideration the culture and traditions of our people. Gender programs, for example, often portray men as the enemy. However, men should be partners of women and gender-oriented programs must go in this line—to encourage partnership and deepen understanding. Unfortunately, this goal is not attractive enough for many of the front-women behind many gender campaigns who subconsciously want to share their personal disappointments. But we have to recognize that not each man is per se bad, while confessing that not all women are good; there is a balance to be respected.

Similar biases also affect programs on HIV/AIDS. Although it might have changed by now, at the onset of many of the HIV prevention programs in the early nineties men were generally portrayed in a negative light. My sense is that such biases may have seriously hindered the progress that could have been made at that time in reducing the infection rates.

In Addis Ababa in the 1990s, the average cost of sex work was about 30 ETB for local clients and about 100–150 ETB for foreigner (1 US dollar was about 8 ETB during that time). The girls looked beautiful so work was always available, except that for every client they took on they lost a chunk of their soul with the transaction. I felt revolted that the 4–5 USD I could spend on a snack, a magazine, or a glass of wine is the same amount of money that human beings will trade to give up their most intimate self and at the same time risk their lives. In the late 1990s, a serology study in the Arada area in Addis Ababa found out that of the 378 sex workers tested for HIV, 78% brought a sero-positive result. This means that 78% of their clients ran the risk of having also taken this infection home to their wives.

At the same time, the nature of the culture and prevailing religion (most mainly Christian-Orthodox and Muslim) was as such that sexuality was not a topic of conversation. As if ignoring an elephant in the room, we continued (and continue to this day) to refuse to come to terms with the existence of sexuality in the light of our traditions. It is easier to leave it in the dark. Despite all of the death and suffering through sexually transmitted diseases and infections like HIV/AIDS, rape, abuse, and infidelity were not among the topics displayed on our official dashboard at MSF.

A young girl told me that she spent the night in jail because a client picked her up and accused her of stealing his watch. He promised not to report her if she agreed to anal sex free of charge; otherwise, he would drive her straight to the police station. This girl said to me that she preferred to be beaten and abused by the police than be abused by this client who was most likely HIV-positive and would certainly not use a condom. It is important to note that his owning a car was not the norm and meant that he was most likely middle or upper class — by the way of the same classes of people that are responsible for the functioning of the public and private sector that keep the country going. Men from the middle and upper classes can use their position of power to bargain for anal sex, knowing very well the other person has no safe way out.

One day I called my grandmother, whom I often called to talk with and get guidance on my work. I was frustrated that day, and I said to her that if you know that HIV is transmitted through blood or bodily fluids, then why are people not careful? She just sighed and said to me that we communicate the wrong message. Being in a monogamous one-to-one relationship or using protection is fine, she said, but please stop preaching about abstinence. She said that after a certain age, sexual activity is as primary a need as food or sleep, and that our messages of abstinence confuse people and put them in a difficult position. "The agencies will find out in time that this message is not appropriate. I just hope there will still be people alive then," she concluded. What she said made sense to me, but it would be hard to defend in my workplace.

As the HIV/AIDS programs were often designed by international NGO-workers or Africans with a Western education, we failed to link our programs to the prevailing culture and traditional realities. We assumed that the women we targeted had the liberties that women in developed countries had, and that the women we targeted had the same legal or even cultural rights about their sexuality. As long as development organizations are making such assumptions, while failing to work with the local culture and local reality, efforts to create change cannot be as successful as they could possibly be.

EGOCENTRIC DECISION-MAKING

Another hindrance to the success of development work is egocentric decision-making by countless managers and development workers.

There was a time when I played a substantive role in helping raise over 5 million US dollars to buy antiretroviral drugs for approximately 5,980 AIDS patients. All we needed to do to finalize the funding was to prepare a letter from our organization (at the time I was working for a United Nations agency) stating that our office would contribute a minimal amount toward administrative fees. I discussed the matter with my superior and he told me that he was ready to support the initiative and that the organization would provide the minimal financial support (enough to hire a local social worker and provide transport allowances). I drafted and submitted the letter to my boss for his signature. To my great disappointment, the letter remained in his in-box for about five weeks. He was aware that the signature was needed urgently. He was also aware that the letter was drafted and waited for his signature. Despite that, the letter remained unsigned for five weeks, which meant that the funding for the drugs was also delayed for another five weeks.

It is a bitter pill to swallow when we see how a person can view certain lives as more (or less) important than others. Would my boss have delayed signing such a letter if he had not been covered by his health insurance package or if he had not had the privilege of his personal financial safety net in place? Why did he not see the importance and the impact of his signature? Would he have given it as a matter of priority if he knew that he was HIV positive himself? What is it that made him so laid back as to not sign a letter that could potentially improve the lives of almost 6,000 people? What was it? I could not understand, and still don't understand his reasons to this day.

In 2003, I was part of a United Nations Development Program (UNDP) mission to Kinshasa, where we were sent from Addis Ababa to explore grounds of collaboration with the UNDP *Country Office in Democratic Republic of Congo (*DRC*) and also engage in a dialogue with other multilateral and bilateral organizations in the country. I was the most junior team member in the three-person mission, and I was very willing to defer to the other two, and remained open to learning and gaining experience from my colleagues.*

To my surprise, during one of the meetings with a senior official of the World Bank, one of my colleagues tried to send me a note on a piece of paper, but the other colleague intercepted and kept my note. I was in the middle of the presentation and did not understand whether I was going off track in my presentation or whether I had forgotten an important aspect that had to be included. So I continued my presentation. A bit later, my cell phone rang and I apologized and answered (earlier, I had informed them that I was expecting a call from New York and had left the ringer on).

Well, the call was not from New York as I assumed — no, it was from the hallway! It was actually the colleague who wrote me the note that called. I thought something really bad had happened to him and, concerned as I was, I asked if he was ok. He was fine. I asked if there was a problem; there was no problem. Finally, he said to me that I should wrap up my presentation quickly, because he did not want to miss lunch. I glanced at my watch and it was only 11:55. As I learned later, my colleague, by the way a national from an African country, neither had diabetes or another illness that would have forced him to eat at a certain time. He also did not have an appointment for lunch; no, he just simply did not want to miss his lunch and left our meeting room while we were presenting our respective line of work and basically doing the work we were sent to do.

I cannot put in words the kind of disappointment I felt. He was actually a Harvard Graduate and UN *permanent staff who was supposedly committed and concerned about the topic and reason for our mission to* DRC*. And now he was telling me to wrap up so that he would not miss lunch. Can you imagine my level of disappointment and anger inside?*

It is not unusual to hear associations being made between the low development in Africa and the fact that there might not be enough qualified, educated, and able individuals to do the work. It is also not unusual to hear issues of corruption that diminish the modest progress being done. But, in the situation that I described, it was neither corruption nor incompetence that prevented my colleague of actively participating in our meeting. On the contrary, he had all qualifications one would expect is needed to effectively get this type of work done. He was not just a college graduate, he was a Harvard graduate. He was not just anyone, he was among the seniors UN staff within our team. He was not just starting out in his career, but had been working for over 20 years within the UN system and I had often found myself going to him for guidance, advice and learning. Was it possible I was clueless about how work is being sometimes done in international and/or multilateral organizations? It seems unlikely to me that anyone could agree to the unacceptable behavior of my colleague. Isn't it indeed unacceptable that while somebody wants to wrap up an important meeting, his/her colleague prefers going instead for an early lunch, while knowing that the conclusion of our meeting could potentially unearth opportunities for collaboration and in service of the civil society organizations and communities in the DRC? Everyone has a right to be mediocre, but if this is the choice of that person, then it would be better to stay out of the UN system and rather leave the space for others with more commitment to their work – people who could leverage the opportunities of the post they occupy so that necessary programs for improvement of lives can be implemented and executed. I realize that what I say sounds a bit too righteous, but I really wonder when we will actually stand up to criticize such type of behavior and stop promoting such kind of people.

Where do we put ethics in this case? The resources to sustain such a post might be USD 150,000 to 200,000 a year and the operational budget for such a position might be a multiple of this sum. It is time to stop such type of conference and seminar tourism for people who are only interested to increase their own income, while showing no concern about the theme to be worked on. I believe that the project beneficiaries in our host countries deserve more than that. Shall we continue being quiet about those, or isn't it time to ask for more accountability of UN personnel, keeping in mind that their level of Daily Subsistence Allowance is well beyond half of the annual income of millions of people being trapped in poverty in developing countries?

Knowing that at that time four out of ten Africans[21] were barely surviving with less than a dollar a day, it seems perverse that we, the so-called development practitioners and workers, would not fully engage in our mission. And should we as Africans working within the UN system do an extra effort, proportional to both, what we were costing our organizations and the extreme living conditions that we knew our African country mates are subjected to, to contribute to real development and progress in our countries. Maybe it helps to reflect on how we actually define daily subsistence? How do we relate to our missions and the expected results from the missions? Is it all about report writing through copy/paste exercises and making them shiny with graphics and colorful photos, or does it actually matter what we do when we are sent on mission with a business class airplane ticket? If we are at all responsible for the resources expended to sustain us in a post, shouldn't such responsibility be reflected in the quality of our work and the ethical standards we abide by?

Either through regular self-reflection or coaching, development practitioners, regardless of whether they are Africans or Westerners, need to have more clarity about the purpose of their assignments. They need to have clarity regarding what it is they commit to when they assume the post, and eventually, organizations need to make sure that it is those people with a commitment and purpose aligned with the overall direction and objectives of the programs. If it is just about having a well-paid job and having the privilege to enjoy the financial and social benefits of our privileged contracts, then I think we are missing the point. We need to be clear about our intentions and our motivations, and also have a solid commitment to translate our skills and capacities to benefit the communities our jobs and organizations try to serve. This clarity of purpose requires internal assessment, but also requires successful communication across the cultural differences between Africa and the West. And such type of commitment must first of all come from the Africans themselves, before blaming the expatriate community working in our countries for their performance in similar assign-

[21] KY Amoako, Speech 1999 - http://www.africaaction.org/docs99/eca9910.htm

ments. A certain level of self-criticism and self-reflection seems to be timely in the current situation, where we are at risk in failing to achieve almost any of the Millennium Development Goals (MDG) by 2015.

WESTERN IDEAS OF AFRICA: COMMUNICATING ACROSS CULTURES

For development workers, as much as we are concerned for the welfare of the people of the nations of Africa, it is important to have the humility and modesty to learn about the culture and the traditions of the communities before marching in with our own formulated solutions to solve problems that we may not fully appreciate and/or understand. There is actually often a lack of understanding on both sides of the cultural divide between the West and Africa, and such misunderstandings impact development work in a number of ways.

Possibly because of shadow-side issues and projections, many Western development workers do not recognize the professional capacity of Africans; mediocrity is the perceived norm, and if someone is successful then he or she is seen as an exception. (Interestingly to note that, according to my experience, Western development workers are not scrutinized in the same way). Unfortunately, it is more often the case that the consistency in work and the motivations to continue working for seemingly far-fetched results might not be prevalent in Africa. However, potential lack of motivation or willingness to work is not due to a lack in intellectual capacity, but rather to the circumstances under which African men and women live. Educational and professional development opportunities are lacking, and something as simple as taking leave to rest, a so-called vacation, does not exist, which contributes to the possibility of burn-out.

Another factor adding to how African workers or communities are negatively perceived is communication capacities both in oral and written form. International NGO workers coming from donor countries are often young college graduates. Often they are from cultures of direct communication, of looking into someone's eyes straight on as they speak, of calling things as they see them, without leaving any room or space for the conversations to expand. Such communication is great and very target oriented, but at times it can be too clear and too succinct, diminishing any chance to emerge subtle matters or issues that need to be brought into the light. In parallel, most local NGO workers in Africa are soaked in the local culture of communication, which is not always so overt and snappy; there is room left for whatever may want to emerge. Speaking succinctly is seen as putting people against the wall, as closing any chances for negotiations, for clearing up misunderstandings, and for allowing learning and synergy. Within prevailing African cultures we don't always say everything all at once; there is a time for everything and the timing to unpack the conversation is an art. Some will argue that the way that conversation unfolds in this way is a waste of time and that it is more of a problem, rather than a quality; and that it might be an attitude that has to change for Africans to be part of the global exchange. It is arguable.

The result of these differences in communication styles is that often Western development workers misunderstand their African counterparts and underestimate their capacities. This cultural communication difference is particularly apparent in report writing or in making presentations: what a Westerner might put in a report as a personal achievement, an African might omit because of perceiving the content as being boastful.

As much as it takes training to be able to communicate clearly and positively, it also takes training to understand cross-cultural communication and learn to appreciate the ways we each express ourselves. There are many other factors, of course, that encroach on Western and African colleagues within the field of development and especially in humanitarian organizations, but the main challenges are the attitudes with which some young Western international workers come to Africa and the disparity in how communication is practiced on either side.

Often, during discussion with my Western friends and colleagues on issues such as conflict resolution, leadership capacity building, personal development, access to education, access to technology, etc., I have felt like my voice has landed on compassionate ears. But somehow I don't feel that my colleagues have really understood what I am talking about. It is like trying to describe and explain what an airplane is to someone that has not even seen a car, a basically impossible endeavor.

The realities I discussed and issues that I brought up in such conversations with my Western colleagues remained often strange and barely understood by them as they might have never seen or experienced in their own lives. Often, they may not have been able to relate because what I was talking about were subtleties of another world. How can one possibly understand subtleties if one has not even been close to the tangible realities of this other world? For example, when we talked of ethnic-based conflict, it was hard to explain to them the foundation of the conflicts. To my colleagues, I was talking about Africa and it seems that most of them perceived it as one place. I am not saying that they did not know that I was talking about several countries, but I am not sure that they were aware of how different the cultures and traditions and realities can be from one place to another, while at the same time there are underlying commonalities that distinguish the continent from other regions in the world. I felt my colleagues had not always understood what I was talking about because they just did not understand the dynamics at play and the realities at place in Africa, beyond what they knew from being portrayed by the media. At times, it has been very frustrating to not have been able to explain myself in a way that I felt understood by my European or American counterparts.

In Ethiopia, the saying goes that "foreigners"[22] don't understand the concept of holding one's mouth shut, or in other words they don't know when to be quiet. This is to say that they are very likely to repeat to another anything they hear. They cannot make the distinction between what is to be talked about in public and what is to be kept to themselves. This is especially true when it comes to name dropping. In my pursuit of my own projects (see Chapter Six), I have sometimes been able to obtain support from senior African Leaders or institutions, but whatever support I could secure was based on the personal relationship I had, rather than on just the concept of the project. Often the initial support was verbal, enough for me to know that I would have the necessary backing in due time. Yet our team would want to be very accurate about the names, positions, and con-

[22] Foreigners are referred to as "Ferenjoch". This is the plural of Ferenj which would mean Foreigner. By Ferenj we are always referring to a "white/Caucasian" Foreigner. Africans are referred to as "Africanoch," Indians would be Hindoch, etc.

tact details of the people who extended their support; this made me very uncomfortable, because I did not know where the information would end up. Verbal support such as I received is often an encouragement, nothing more than saying that in due time I can return to concretize the support — such verbal support is not at all something to wave on a virtual flag. But it was a big challenge to explain my reticence to my colleagues and our group that were working so hard in putting together the program. Dropping those names would have helped in our quest for funding, but would not have been culturally appropriate and may have jeopardized that support. If we simply said we had the support of Senior Africans, would the sources of funding we sought understand our situation, or would they need to have everything written in black and white? It was a big dilemma for me and a source of a substantial degree of frustration.

As I look back now, this tension between the African and the Western ways of using names might be related to the fact that in most African traditions people don't feel compelled to present their entire inventory of knowledge. It is okay to know and not necessarily speak of what we know. In fact, it is those who speak the least who often know a lot more than those who unravel their heart's content to anyone willing to listen.

I can understand why the possible funders would want to know all the individuals backing a certain program before funds were made available for it. However, when we talk of a program aiming to bring change and transformation, would it not be worthwhile to explore other indications of validity, such as the number of people signed up or the names of the possible lecturers? Such a program might require a certain level of discretion as it is being set up, especially at the early stages. It is like an unborn child, and in the same way that one should not speak of bearing a child at the early stages of the pregnancy when all is still so vulnerable, so it is with programs that have to be set up and designed. At the onset, discretion, quiet commitment, and a steady path are the best means of concretizing the program.

As far as our program was concerned, we were fortunate to have it endorsed and supported by several former African Heads of States and many very senior elder leaders. But, their support was due to a couple of things: 1) the quality of my relationship with them and, 2) mostly the vision of the program I presented. It was really about the technical aspects of the program per se. I chose not to explain this fact to my colleagues, because I thought it would be misunderstood, possibly sounding somewhat conceited on my part, so I was never really able to explain to them how I had secured the support. In a way, and in retrospect, I realize now that rather than making assumptions about my colleagues' perceptions, I should have been more outspoken about all the subtle matters that existed in launching the program we had in mind.

It was a mistake not to speak up, because my colleagues used to mention the names of these leaders at any occasion without adequate diplomacy. It made me very uncomfortable, because the support I had gained from the elders was such a gift and not really something we could take for granted in this way. All this may be due to the fact that in the Western world it is okay to pride yourself on who was on board and which well known personality supported the initiatives. In contrast, the way that I was raised the more prominent the names of those supporting an initiative, the more quiet one was expected to be. Africans are expected to be a lot more subtle, in a way not to "jinx" things, and in a way to leave room for the support to establish solid roots. Those renowned persons who stand to support an initiative will be introduced in due time, and until such time it is not necessary to talk about or advertise it. My reluctance in explaining all this to my colleagues eventually brought cracks to the process, and these cracks marked the beginning of the end for that iteration of the program.

In my heart, a growing dissonance started creating a rift between our group and me. On one side, there was my perception of Africa, its needs, and how our program should be designed in order to address these perceived needs. I did realize that those needs were perceived through my lens and through my own biases, regardless of how valid or questionable they may be. On the other side, there was my colleagues' perception of the continent and of what the program would look like based on their understanding of the situation and also of the depth of Integral Theory (see Chapters Four and Five) that they each knew and wanted to apply in service of the vision I had shared with them. I often deferred to my colleagues, not giving space to my own equally valid understanding of the Integral theories and practices.

Even though I noticed that there was often quite a remarkable difference between what my colleagues knew theoretically about Integral and what they in fact practiced in their lives and work, I failed to bring myself to say something about that or to call them on the discrepancies I saw between what they claimed to know and practice and what I saw the reality to be in their behaviors and application of their understanding of the theories into their daily lives. At the same time I realize now that not speaking up at the time when I should have is a reflection of where I was in my own practice and reality. It is not that they were wrong and I was right, but rather that all of us did not always "walk our talk" in one way or another.

Time has allowed perspective and room to deepen reflection; given that, I can say that the way my colleagues/friends perceived or understood the issues impeding the development efforts for the continent was not allowing space for transformation, our own transformation and also the transformation of the environments we hoped to engage with. As much as it is common parlance to refer to *Africans* as an entity or a group, and I do it as well, it is a slippery term to use. It can only make sense if and when the person using the term is also conscious of the wide range of cultures and identities that exist within this so-called Africa, and of the underlying commonalities that allow us to refer to the communities of this continent as "Africans." When my colleagues spoke of the "Africans," however, I did not feel that they were making the distinction that I just discussed. I was not sure whether they were conscious that one can't really refer to the "*the* Africans" in the same way someone might speak of Europeans or Americans. It is important that we remain aware that there is no such thing as Africans. Africa is a myriad of nations and a multitude of civilization, societies, norms, languages, and diversity, to name just some of the barometers of distinction. At times, actually more often than not, I felt inside of me that the Africa that we referred to in our documents and discussions was that which was portrayed in the news or known in the mainstream (poor, dirty, diseased, etc.).

Finding a common ground of understanding among people is not always easy. Gaining understanding is not easy to achieve, and it is even harder to achieve this among people from different cultures and communities. In my case, I had a difficult time reaching this point of understanding with the friends and colleagues that I worked with in the United States to set up Integral Africa (see Chapter Six). Sometimes it was undue modesty on my part that got in the way, sometimes it was my reluctance to engage in confrontations or debates about the issues we dealt with, and sometimes it may have been the eagerness I had in me to start the program. I thought that things would smooth out in time, but I was wrong, and this is one of the greatest lessons I have learned.

I have learned the importance of speaking up and expressing my arguments, even if that means losing support and making some people unhappy. I was raised — I can even say programmed — through my culture and upbringing that confrontation, conflict, and arguments are not acceptable. The better way is to be anointed with patience, allowing those we work and live with enough room for them to experience a turn-around about the issues at hand, in their own time. This is a good system, which inherits a lot of respect for each other, but seemingly it only works among people who share the same cultural and traditional foundation. In an international working environment, where each person comes with their own cultures, traditions, and ways of communicating and working together, maintaining the culture of patience and conflict averseness can be a source of further frustrations and complications.

A good friend of mine who lives in Seattle, Washington, once said to me: "Yene, just get a real job and get paid for your education/knowledge." And then he asked "What are you doing in Africa anyway?" He could not understand why I spent so much time and effort working in Africa. Given my educational background, I could probably build a lofty career for myself in any Western country. But for me it was not about making a lofty career, it was about being there and being counted among those who stood for the development of this continent with so much untapped potential. Africa is in my heart and even though there is so much lacking and in despair, at the same time, one can find so much of love, compassion, wisdom, hospitality, and laughter. Of course this may be perceived as an idealized vision of Africa and it is possible to argue that this image of Africa no longer holds true given all the internal conflicts and wars. But despite the conflicts, I still feel that we can agree that one common denominator across the continent is community and hospitality among the people. Personally, the African continent represents the one region where I feel a sense of inner peace. During one of our conversation, he later told me that to him the image that he has of Africa is one a dark and chaotic place. He could only envision the diseases and the wars as broadcasted by the mainstream US TV stations. While I was surprised and also saddened in a way at how he perceived this continent, I also appreciated what he said, because it was his honest truth and his own perspective. The description of Africa that he gave me was how he saw this far away continent from where he lived in Seattle. I also appreciated his candid comment, because many would have bottled up their opinions just to be polite. He could just not understand why I chose to spend so much time in Africa, this kind of hopeless place with myriads of problems and continuous humanitarian crisis. And from his perspective he is right: why would anyone want to be there? For many of us, the picture is different, even though we also see what Roy sees and know the existence of all the challenges, we also see the other side of the picture – the side that is full of possibilities and untapped potentials, the side that is full of opportunities and the side that is open for change.

Part of the challenge in gaining understanding is the knowledge of our respective cultures and ways of being. How does one interpret silence in a conversation or what can be interpreted as trespassing the boundaries of good manners? It all depends on the culture.

After a seminar in Boulder, Colorada, I returned to Seattle and, as usual, I stayed with my dear friend Dana Carman[23] *and his wife Sarah Keenan. It had become almost tradition that Dana dropped me at the airport on my way back home to Lusaka (I lived in Zambia at the time). And during the long drive to the airport, we had come to develop a habit of talking about*

[23] Dana Carman is a Principal of Pacific Integral. My relationship with Dana was and still is very special. He became like a brother to me and often we had heated conversations about various issues. He and his family have become like family to me and my own greater family (my parents, my aunts and my grandmother) consider him as part of us. When he came to visit us in Ethiopia, on a trip to discuss Integral Africa with possible institutional partners, Dana blended into the society with such ease that one would have thought that he either had some Ethiopian heritage or must have lived as an Ethiopian in a previous life.

what had been achieved with my Integral Africa project so far, and what was to be done until my next trip. So, enthusiastically, I told him my plans for developing the program curriculum. I expected the same kind of enthusiasm from him. Instead his answer was, "Don't be so arrogant!"

I was shocked and did not understand from which spaceship that answer came. What arrogance was my friend referring to? I remained silent for a while. I did not answer back. We were getting close to the airport, so I thought it best to just leave this comment in the parking lot and take time to address it at a better time. I think that Dana must have been the one person that I can think of that might have been even more excited about Integral Africa than me. I loved him dearly as a friend and respected him highly as a teacher – so his comment blew me away. In my upbringing we are raised to defer to the hierarchy of age and or knowledge. I figured it would be best for me to think this over before I reacted. Many thoughts flooded my mind, including wondering about how this friend saw me. Was it that I just passively wait until the curriculum is designed or was it that he thought I did not know enough to express my thoughts and contribute to the development and design of the program?

I did not feel the need to swiftly reply. I did not think it would be wise to do so, so I remained quiet.

My "not responding" may have led Dana to misunderstand my reaction — just because I did not reply back, it does not mean I did not react or have a reaction to him. In most, if not all Western circumstances, reactions are expected to be verbal and articulated. A reaction of silence may be understood as giving in or as defeat. It is not so in the African way: silence is silence and by no means should this be interpreted as giving up or defeat. It is just silence, a pause to let things settle and a time to wait for clarity for the next step. There is saying in Ethiopia that refers to re-grounding in times of conflict or turmoil before one reacts back, "Only when the sand settles back down can we be in a position to look to the horizon again."

I bring this point up not to speak of an old story, but to illustrate how many Africans are so very often deeply misunderstood by their Western counterparts because we just communicate differently and we may not always jump to answer back. We take more time to assess the situation and our answers are not always as pointed. In fact, intuitively we use several lenses and perspectives to look at a situation. Some may argue that we have to learn to communicate and interact in whatever way is needed to be understood and get over our cultural or traditional ways. This might be possible for some; for me, I have difficulty in changing who I am or how I am in order to be heard. It's a challenge. When discussing this topic with my friend Consolata she told me that in her country Rwanda there is a saying that goes as follows: "If you go to a country where they eat flies, learn how to swallow them alive". At the end of the day, it's about overcoming our limitations, overcoming our habits to be heard and to be counted.

In the particular case with Dana, I was thinking both about my way of looking at reality and his. I was wondering why he might have said that in relation to me, to the program, to himself, to the theories that we had in the curriculum, to how he related to African development and to how we were intending to take Integral Theory there.

This experience was a great moment of learning. I remained silent. Throughout the trip back home to Zambia of almost 33 hours, I spent time contemplating, reflecting on the entire program of Integral Africa. I thought about the partnerships that were supposed to take place to launch the program. I thought of how we might overcome the challenges of intercultural and multilingual communication situations. I realized at this stage that the program of Integral Africa might not be understood in the same way by all who were involved in it. I realized that we all had our individual agendas and thoughts about it and that until we found an opportunity to bring those personal priorities to the surface, we would keep on stalling.

Once I arrived in Lusaka and took some days to settle down, I wrote a long letter to Dana about our conversation in the car and emailed it to him. He called me back immediately. He did not even realize what he had said, and had absolutely not intended to blow me away in that way. We discussed how we really needed to be mindful about the words we use and the ways we choose to communicate. The language that we use may be the same (in this case English), but the meaning that we associate with the words and comments can be completely different. To me the word "arrogant" was loaded. It would have meant to me that I had fallen out of sync with the education my parents and grandparents had bestowed on me. Among the most strongly discouraged things in my family were arrogance, lacking clarity, lacking the capacity to pace ourselves, etc. So Dana's comment went straight into the depth of who I am, without his intention. The comment hit me in this way, because Dana was not an outsider to me, he was in my inner circle and was part of those I count as beloved friends and family.

Such are the challenges of attempting to gain understanding across cultures. As much as development is a complex issue, and as much as immense amounts of financial and nonfinancial resources have been poured into it, there is one simple truth — development is directly linked to the goodwill of the leadership and collective commitment for change both from within the African nations and also from the Western nations that maintain their links, through bilateral and multi-lateral cooperation with the continent. This is how I see it. If we have the commitment and goodwill at the highest level of leadership, then development is not as complex. It may even be quite straightforward. However, because there are so many tangible and subtle issues tied to it, ranging from the geopolitical influences at a regional and country level to economic factors of purely personal interest, development becomes very complex.

In the face of this complexity, it is of course foolish to think that one can come up with a solution. Wouldn't all the people, organizations, and institutions that have spent decades working on development see the way out? What would possibly make me think that I can offer a valid and worthy contribution? I can stay with this question and remain, like many, sitting on the side benches, choosing not to participate. Or, I can also choose to go out on the playing field and do what I can. It might be that this "do what I can" behavior was the trigger that could be perceived as arrogance — arrogance in the face of the curriculum development, arrogance in standing in to say that I might have something worth exploring, arrogance in refusing to accept that what we have today is the best we could achieve, etc. Our willingness and commitment to get involved, in whatever capacity, is what will bring change. It takes the efforts of a large number of men and women, a critical mass of people, to start the process of transformation of our current reality into the future we want to see emerge.

Differences in cross-cultural perceptions can be a source of challenge and a source of strength, depending on how much awareness we bring to the communication. In the same vein of conversation about perceptions and about how thorny it can get, I want to share a couple of further stories.

Priscilla Banda, a lady who was helping us with the house while we lived in Lusaka, Zambia, asked me if God liked white people better. Her argument was that it seems that white people have everything and that they are never in need. It seems that they get the money, the jobs, and all the advantages of life they want. I told her that God might even love us more, since we are still around and living in spite of the living conditions, epidemics, conflicts, and lack of social welfare.

It was her perception of the world, my perception, and our common willingness to share our thoughts that allowed growth and learning for each one of us. From where she stood, from the perspective of her life, it seemed to her that God loved white people more. She had not considered that God loves us equally or maybe even more, since we are still around despite all the developmental complications we endure. From where I stood, I thought that it might be possible that we are more graced by God, because despite all the terrible conditions so common to many African countries, the communities still live and still manage to go on to the next day. I think this is afforded to us only through grace.

This conversation with Priscilla took place in 2004, and I know that her perception has changed. Before we left Lusaka, we were fortunate to find a job for Priscilla at the DED – Zambia main office. She started as a cleaner and went up the ranks to the point that she is now an HIV/AIDS focal person, that drives to visit clients and communities. The last I heard of Priscilla, she was being sent to Namibia for further training. I am certain that the perspective that God only loves white people has changed. The quality of life is both a result of opportunity, commitment and hard work.

Similarly, there is a story on perspectives.

At a gathering in Addis Ababa in the late nineties, I met a woman working as a development volunteer. She was from one of the Scandinavian countries. In the conversation my husband told her that we hoped to go to Europe in the summer. She then turned right away and enthusiastically asked if I was excited to finally go to see Europe this summer. In her world and perspective, she assumed that any African who goes to Europe must be thankful to the Gods, and possibly such a lucky African would not intend on ever coming back.

I was surprised at the stereotyping. In Ethiopia we say that no matter what the situation, you have to behave as you have been raised and always know that your behavior reflects on the entire family's honor. So, instead of giving her a hard answer highlighting how ignorant I thought she was, I just told her, "Yes, I am so excited! I just can't wait to go!" What else could I say? I could not tell her that I might possibly know more of Europe, its history and culture than she did. I could not tell her how ridiculous I thought she was to make such simple assumptions. I just tried to understand that her assumptions were based on some truth that there is a lot of immigration to Europe, that most people in Africa and developing countries can't wait to leave for Europe and that those leaving Africa rarely come back.

As human beings, one of our common limitations might be the lack of capacity to take several perspectives and a corresponding lack of ability to entertain multiple realities. At the same time, it is within our reach to question what we see and not mistake our assumptions for the final facts, a practice that can lead us to be aware of our blind spots and potential oversights.

My life takes me back and forth between the United States, Europe, and Africa; sometimes it is for work, sometimes family, or sometimes for school. Each time I enter one space coming from another, there is a moment of hesitance and refocusing my senses to acknowledge where I am. At the very gate of each world and space, there lays my choice to come in fully as the person imbued with the world I just left, or to enter with a blank slate in my mind and heart. When the change is between north and south, the main angle of change is wealth-related, or rules and regulations related.

Sometimes it seems that the most vivid changes happen within Africa as I go back and forth between areas of absolute poverty and areas of full-blown surplus. This going back and forth between worlds, between languages and cultures, can be complex to understand and is at times very tiring, especially when you try to make sense of it from the brain instead of the heart. In the midst of the inquiry that arises, I had to learn to let go, to allow myself to be taken with the flow, and not force conclusions about how to make sense of it all.

CHAPTER THREE

Understanding Change and Transformation

There is still tremendous potential on the African continent, with immense opportunities lying below the surface of poverty, conflict, and other development challenges. To bring out the potential of the African nations, I believe that there must be a critical mass of change agents who will be ready to assume the role of leaders in all sectors and at all levels. This leadership development refers to all levels: the individual who is in the role of leader, her or his actions in this role of leading, and the context in which the role is played out and the actions taken (Volkman, 2009). Accordingly, the key to building a critical mass of change agents is not only in gathering a number of individuals to lead, but also in establishing distinctions within the concept of leadership among these individuals, to fine-tune the mechanics of transformation and sustainable change.

A South African friend of mine, Paul Cohen, says that South Africans were blessed to have Nelson Mandela as a leader. Paul told me that during his years in prison, Nelson Mandela sat in meditation for 27 years, years that allowed him to find the wisdom, insights, and direction that saved the country from collapse.

Paul and I met in April 2008, when he made a presentation at the Integral Without Borders conference in Istanbul, Turkey. I stood to make a comment on his presentation, intending to encourage him about the work he is doing in sustainable ecological communities. But, instead of making my comment, I ended up speaking about his country. I wanted to tell him about the moment my perspective on South Africa changed, the day I heard President Thabo Mbeki speak not 20 meters away from me. At that moment I knew what was meant by "Rainbow Nation," and realized it had been my own limitations that did not allow me to understand what Rainbow Nation could mean.

As I stood to speak of this moment and share my thoughts, I felt my heart fragment into pieces of grace, because now I saw that Rainbow Nation in Paul. I could do nothing but sob and laugh as well. "They have succeeded! They have succeeded!" was the voice I could hear in my heart—managed to overcome the odds, managed to move past the hurdles they could have been limited by, and managed to reach something beautiful and remarkable.

I believe that there must be a way to bring change agents together in order to create an organic collaborative circle. If God grants me the years, I hope to see change for Africa before I die. I believe we will see change in the next twenty or thirty years, and it is to this change and transformation that we, all, ought to contribute all of our capacities—we, Africans; we, development workers and volunteers; we, people of the World. Even though, one might also say that we must also be mindful that some countries' situations have been worsening with the years rather than improving; overall, I trust that things will improve.

MY VISION OF CHANGE AND TRANSFORMATION FOR AFRICA

There are two stories that I want to share with you, for you to keep in mind through the next chapters. The first story, of caterpillars and butterflies, I heard from the author and activist, Lynne Twist.[24] She talked of a cell in a caterpillar called an ***imaginal.***

The "imaginal" are cells that live within the caterpillar. At some point in their lives, they are activated and start looking for other "imaginal cells" in

[24] Lynne Twist is the author of a number of books on The Soul of Money, http://www.soulofmoney.org/.

order to connect and form a network.

Once the network of "imaginal cells" is formed, this association then will enable the body of the caterpillar to change and transform into a butterfly.

However, if the "imaginal cells" are not able to connect, the change does not occur.

The story of the imaginal is like a parable speaking of the potential for change agents coming together to create change in Africa. Unless the change agents' collectives come together with shared vision and harmonized efforts, then change will not occur—it will be like spinning our wheels in vain. Personally, I know how much the various individuals I have met and recognized as change agents have contributed to the work that I try to initiate. And, I believe that I have also already made a modest contribution towards this.

I am trying to explore what would happen if 100, 500, or even 5,000 change agents came together with a joined vision for a better African future. What would happen in terms of development? Would we be bold enough to make a request to ourselves and each other to work towards change, a request to each other to work towards transforming life from the way it is to how we wish life would be? Would we also be bold enough to expect a positive outcome? Would we be bold enough to stand up and be counted? Would we assume our individual responsibility for the collective and each do our part?

The second story is about Japanese Samurais, who are said to never miss their targets because they can envision the target in their mind's eye constantly. When the target overlaps that bull's eye, they shoot. It is precise, it is the harmony between vision and action, between now and the line of Time. It is knowing and being aware of the unknown, and trusting that we will know all that we need to know when we come to the moment of action. It is about awareness and remaining at the ready while we are also just being.

For me, Lynne's story was not about butterflies or caterpillars—it was a parable for talking about transformation, a parable holding my own dreams and hopes for Africa. What will it take to change our continent? Unless the imaginal cells (change agents and leaders with a new consciousness) come together, we may never see the butterfly come to life. Unless, like the Samurai, we maintain our target in our mind's eye, we may never be precise enough in our aim to attain it.

To create change and transformation for Africa, we need a combination of both mind's eye focus on the target we aim for (collectively) and a movement to bring this collective of imaginal cells together. Imaginal cells for Africa are the individuals within our communities who can link up, join wires, and redirect the flow of energy. However, change is not only about creating networks, it is also about having a shared vision and shared eagerness to witness good prevail.

I am conscious that this may sound naïve, but it is far from being naïve. The Universe is good; it is intelligent and compassionate. Regardless of religious inclinations, we have within ourselves the power to continuously create and evolve, if we operate from the spiritual level rather than from within the constraints of the flesh and blood visible to the naked eye. I trust that change can happen and that we can individually and collectively induce the mechanism to bring change, even though some of it will need time to take root or manifest. What we need is a critical mass of men and women that can take the lead to shift the paradigm.

Lynne Twist's story could be a model of our own lives. Unless we, too, connect to one another and create the butterfly for the future that we want, the opportunity may pass us by, and we may remain forever as caterpillars crawling aimlessly in different directions.

I generally believe that each one of us is an imaginal cell. Our challenge is to connect with one another to make a positive difference in the future of Africa. It is in the effort of emerging as a connector and as a catalyst for change that this book came to be, as a way to open the gates for change and a way for transformation to take root.

There are thousands of intelligent, committed, and knowledgeable change agents around the continent. But one of the common challenges we face is that we don't know each other. And, if we don't know each other, we cannot possibly work together. Even before we speak about work we would not be able to have a peer support platform for advice, guidance, and encouragement unless we put in systems to network. And, if we don't know each other, we cannot possibly encourage others or be of support to one another. We therefore need to create a ground, a kind of a platform and mechanism to systematically allow men and women from all parts of Africa to meet and exchange their experiences, ideas, and visions. This is, in my opinion, the most promising way forward, to evolve our mindset, to progress leadership, and ultimately to bring development to Mother Africa.

When the day comes that we can finally bring together change agents from all over the world, focusing their attention on how to holistically, comprehensively, and systematically bring transformation to Africa, then we have a chance to succeed. When development work can start to be done free of ego, free of self-interest, and free of greed, then we can be ready to see change take place. We will then witness change agents who can work harmoniously, in sync with each other, and who can be selfless enough to birth synergies.

CHANGE AND TRANSFORMATION: HOW TO CREATE THEM

The challenge of change is that it requires of us a clear vision of what it is we want to change — where is it we want to go (from where, to where), and what new reality do we want to create? In addition, we need to understand the dynamics of change — how change happens and does not happen. The details of how to get there or what it will take to get there are not as important as the commitment to travel the journey. How much do you want this change? What is at stake and how much are you willing to invest in it? What are the tools that you can use, and what strategies and approaches would be most effective? These are the fundamentally important questions.

For many of us, life circumstances oblige us to stand by the crossroads of choice. We find ourselves with the choice to change, or not to change. If we choose change, we find ourselves at another bifurcation regarding the mode of change and how we are going to carry out this change to make it durable. In my own life, when we uprooted from Ethiopia in the mid-1970s and moved to Europe due to the political situation, I "had" to change to adapt to new environments to survive — change was not an option, but a necessary step for survival.

When change becomes a requirement for survival, then our inner intelligence takes over to engage the process for the sake of survival. However, when change is only an option, then we must gather enough motivation to make it through the process in order to witness transformation. When change is not an obligation, then we are left to our own capacity, will, and determination to see the process through.

Making change occur and be sustainable (i.e., creating a state of transformed new reality) is not as hard as it appears. Change is a precise moment in time. It is a decision and the execution of the decision. Once the change fully integrates in our reality, then we are in a position to witness the transformation that arises from that one incident of change. The key is to try and experience, in slow motion, the subtle and sacred moments between the instant we are confronted with the thought of change, the split second right before that, and the split second right after we have accepted the change, in order to feel the texture of the dynamics involved in changing and transforming.

What is it that pushes us humans to change—is it discomfort with our current reality and circumstances, or is it our ability to envision another future? In my own life, change has often emerged because of a shrinking or expansion of my world. At moments of change, I felt as if my world had shrunk on me, like it was a set of clothes that had shrunk in the laundry, oddly tight and no longer fitting well. Often frustration arises as I struggle to articulate that which is precisely uncomfortable. The fact that things are not quite the same anymore can be due to an internal and subjective factor or to an external and objective one. It could also be due to something in my own personal and individual realm or something related to the collective realm of which I am part.

Knowing and feeling the core source of that too-tight feeling and discomfort is what allows any of us to actually put into motion the effort for change and to ultimately transform our reality. In a simple example, when my clothes get too tight, it is either that I have put on weight or that they have shrunk through washing. When I realize I have put on weight, and this excess impacts on how I feel or don't feel, that realization is the trigger that puts in motion the thought of doing something about it. My reality is becoming uncomfortable, so I shift towards wanting to change. The next step is mainly knowing to "what" I want to change, the "how" and "when" will follow. In this example, I first identify the core reasons that have caused my weight gain. Then I must either change a habit that emerged and caused the weight gain or re-establish my nutrition and exercise program. The core reasons for weight gain can be something as simple as overeating, especially around the holiday season, or they can be something on a deeper psychic level—it is up to me to uncover the source of the matter. Once the cause of the situation is known, then finding the solution to the problem becomes a lot simpler. Once the solution is envisioned, then it is only a matter of following through so that I can see the change and eventually benefit from the transformation.

This same process applies to larger-scale or more complex change. Complexities arise with change on a larger scale because at that level there are many people and institutions that have to be involved in the process of change. Each person's or each institution's level of consciousness, their willingness or lack of willingness to collaborate, and the need to secure the resources for the change are all factors that increase the challenge of making large-scale changes happen. While change on a larger scale might come with difficulties, the process is similar to that of bringing change in the life of one person: identify the situation, the core reasons for the situation, the solution or desired outcome, and ways to reach that outcome, and then follow through.

Sometimes, there are instances where radical change takes place, when we are fed up with a situation and some inner inspiration and strength pushes us to manifest incredible change. Radical change can be experienced by chain smokers who one day just drop the habit overnight because they are fed up with the cigarettes or realize the harm they cause. Similarly, on a greater scale, revolutions happen when the collective is just fed up with the existing structures and decides to rise up. When the injustices are too much to bear, when societal balance is lost and reality is skewed to one side, the collective finds the spark to rise up and stand for change.

Whether change comes as a process of reflection or radically as a reaction to dissonance in the current reality, change happens and is very possible, both at the individual and collective levels. Change is a process that emanates from a Time-specific action—the relationship of change to "Time" is what will eventually lead to transformation. The process of change remains constant regardless of what we want to change: whether we want to change our own lives or that of our families,' whether we want to change a community or a nation. It is about vision. It is about persistence. It is about faith, courage, and resources. Most of all, it is about innovation and creativity that allow one to home in on results. In this process of change, Time plays an important role, and can be either an ally or a saboteur.

THE RELATIONSHIP BETWEEN CHANGE AND TIME

Using Time as I refer to it means looking at a situation in the context of eternity, knowing that our short lives restrict us to relatively few things we can do in the greater scheme of things. At the same time, there is a tremendous process of change that we can initiate, even if we may not be alive to see the fruition of the process. Martin Luther once said: *"...And, even if I knew today that tomorrow would be the end of my life, I would still plant an apple tree."*[25] We must be compassionate enough to plant an apple tree, to "plant" our thoughts and aspirations, even if we know we may not be here tomorrow. When we can see Time in its divinity, then we can surrender, knowing the Universe will give us a tailwind to execute our visions.

How we handle conflict, be it trivial conflict in the office or a greater conflict at the organizational level, can be highly influenced by how we relate to Time. When someone has wronged us, it is easy to attack that person verbally or psychologically. But when we are conscious of Time and the repercussions of our words in the life and Time of this person on this planet, then we slow down and choose our words carefully in order not to create undue toxicity.

Knowing Time is both endless and impermanent makes us slow down; slowing down in our thoughts and actions allows us to make true and firm steps forward in our lives. Knowing Time opens the path for wisdom and divine insights. Knowing Time will allow us to make changes that last and

---

[25] This well-known quote can be found on http://www.brainyquote.com/quotes/authors/m/martin_luther.html

morph into eternal transformation, sort of a reconfiguration back to the essence of the being that is within each of us. Acting from our essence is one of the keys in accessing a new paradigm of existence. Addressing this matter would be even more important during our times, where climate change challenges world societies to redefine patterns of growth and development in a more holistic and sustainable way. This challenge lies ahead of African nations and each and every country in the rest of the world. Understanding change and Time, we, as people of all nations, can stand within the laser beam of eternity in order to be part of those who will collectively rebirth what Africa has always been — a land of heart, wisdom, and truth.

Accepting a different perception of Time is in most societies a real challenge. I once told my sister Fofi, who was really pressed for time, that it would all happen in God's Time, and she became so upset with me. She said: "Yeah, except that He works on the scale of Eternity, and that I need this thing, like, yesterday!" Time is a challenge for change and transformation, because I believe change and transformation are founded on knowing Time and knowing that we must make Time an ally and a part of the equation. If someone cannot envision the future and put into the equation how today's actions will define tomorrow's reality, then it is difficult to persuade such a person to take the necessary steps to change.

Change happens in a Time-specific mode, where transformation is triggered by the Time-specific change and is manifest through the process of living this change in our lives. Transformation is the result of the change we have applied and chosen to execute. Change might be easy, but transformation asks for persistence. Change is the adoption of a new path for the journey, and vision is like the compass that keeps us directed toward the horizons we want to reach. Transformation is the actual walking of the path in order to reach the horizon and is fully influenced by the direction we maintain or change.

All actions and all behaviors in the entire spectrum of Time impact and influence realities right in the moment, as well as through the very spectrum of Time. The consequences of our actions are not always measurable within our level of thinking. Sometimes, and even often, decisions taken in service of a mindset or policy come to be known as detrimental later on in Time.

To me, one of the most important and tragic illustrations of the consequences of the choices leaders make is the story of Rwanda, a country known mainly for its horrific genocide of 1994. I have included a short excerpt of Kapuscinski's (1998) account of the history of Rwanda.

> Unlike many African countries that count several tribes and ethnic groups, Rwanda only has one tribe, the Banyarwanda divided into three caste groups.[26] Historically, the Tutsi cattle owners (14%), the Hutu farmers (85%), and the Twa laborers (1%) made up the population (Kapuscinski, 1998).[27] The kingdom of the Banyarwanda existed for hundreds of years and was ruled by a monarch called Mwami, who was Tutsi (Kapuscinski, 1998). The country was closed, it did not try to expand its territories nor did it allow foreigners to enter. The Tutsis were the lord and owners of the cattle, whereas the Hutu were the farmers, such as vassals in the feudal systems. At some point conflict emerges between the two castes. The Tutsi need more and more grazing land for their cattle and the Hutus find themselves cramped for land to cultivate. It is around this time that the Belgians come into the picture. Although Belgium was not very active in this colony, it had been working through the Monarch to manage their colony. In the mid fifties, at a time where many African nations fought for independence, Rwanda also made its demand to Belgium. Brussels had no game plan, so they adopted a strategy of only delaying the response, but also of abandoning the Tutsi relationship and engaging with the Hutu population, inciting them to rebel against the monarchy. A peasant revolt erupted in 1959. The Hutu population moved against the Tutsi Lords and Cattle owners, armed with spears, machetes, and hoes and a great massacre took place. The Hutus massacred both the Tutsis and their cattle. Many Tutsis fled to neighboring countries. This revolt marked the end of the monarchy and feudalism. The Tutsi caste lost its' dominant position and the country entered into a vicious cycle of conflict and hatred that led to a number of genocides,

[26] It seems that many Rwandan do not think that it is only one tribe, hence the 1994 killers who would throw Tutsis in the Nyabarongo river saying "go back to your "origins..."

[27] These statistics might be considered fabricated and fake according to some Rwandans.

> the most famous one being that of 1994.
>
> This strategy addressed the immediate priority of the Belgian government, which might have been to buy time in the face of the demand of the Mwami. However, in the long run, the hatred seeded in the 1950s, added to the emergent issue of land distribution among the Tutsi cattle owners and Hutu farmers, led to the tragic atrocities of genocide committed in the sixties, the seventies, and eventually that which the world witnessed in 1994 in Rwanda.[28]

In the 1950s, the Belgian government was at a crossroads regarding how to handle their colonies. In the background of this crossroad, Rwanda was experiencing a severe land shortage that brought tension between the Tutsi cattle-owners and the Hutu farmers. As did most Western countries with colonies in that time, Belgium chose one way over the other possible options. Belgium chose change: a change of discourse, a change of strategy. The result was a transformation of the reality for the people of that small country. Sadly, the choices made opened the way for a reality in which millions of men, women, and children endured unimaginable losses and suffering.

Transformation is not always beneficial to all, nor is it always positive. The story of Rwanda is an example of how we humans can misguide the future and fall out of sync with the Universe. One could argue that violence is part of the Universe and that is why it is prevalent, but I believe that violence occurs when we fall out of sync with the ethical code we use to define what is appropriate for our universe. In the end, Belgium's choice, this transformation of the trajectory of the country, led millions to be subjected to atrocious death and trauma. Similar choices are made throughout the world every day, sometimes in the confines of our private lives and sometimes at the scale of regional or even global impact.

Another experience that illustrates choice and its impact happened in my own country, Ethiopia, in the early 1990s, after the change of government from a Communist regime to the new democratic government. Eritrea had been fighting for independence from Ethiopia for years. The core

[28] Ryszard Kapuscinski, The Shadow of the Sun (New York: Vintage International, 2001).

reasons for wanting independence were linked to how our Emperor Haile Selassie, had dealt with the Italian occupation and colonization attempts.

In 1896, the Italian troops attempted to enter Ethiopia with the intention of occupying the country as a colony. To their surprise, they were defeated at the battle of Adwa by the then Emperor Menelik II. A few decades later, in 1935/1936, the Italians, under Mussolini, attempted again to invade Ethiopia in order to make it an Italian colony, but could not manage to take over the country due to both the military strategies of our leaders and the endurance and commitment of our soldiers, as well as the fact that the Ethiopian troops were more familiar with the mountainous landscape of the country. Eventually, Italy returned with an array of artillery, which was beyond what our people were able to oppose during that time, and Italy managed to occupy Ethiopia for a total of five years. During this time, our Emperor, from his exile, called on the League of Nations to find some solution to free the country from Italian occupation. An arrangement was made that Italy could take the region of Eritrea as a protectorate and retreat from the rest of the country. After the end of the protectorate, when Italy withdrew from the country, Eritrea wanted to transform to an independent state. But Ethiopia was not willing to agree, neither under the reinstalled Emperor Haile Selassie nor under the succeeding Communist regime. This situation consequently escalated to a civil war and resistance that lasted close to 30 years.

In the early 1990s when our new democratic government took office, it came with a policy of federating the nation and allowing any constituency the choice of possible independence. This, of course, gave a choice to Eritrea to be independent or remain attached to Ethiopia through a referendum. There was a lot of jubilation around this time. I was in Ethiopia during those years working with MSF Belgium. As per the result of the referendum, Eritrea became an independent state. Soon after this referendum, there was a falling out between the leaders of Eritrea and Ethiopia. As a result, the two countries decided to deport the citizens who were living or working in the other country — when the sun came down and the wind started to blow, and the relationship between the two countries changed for the worse, the populations of both countries were torn apart.

Coming from a very old Ethiopian family, it was very difficult for me being in Ethiopia during that time to witness what happened. I was unable to understand the rationale for the changes taking place, tearing apart a once great nation, including local communities with very strong family bonds between each other. In the following, I give a short description of one of my experiences:

Addis Ababa, Ethiopia, Fall 1998. *I usually went to the office very early to get there before everyone came in. It helped me start my day quietly. On my way, I saw people escorted out of their homes, wearing the* Gabi *(traditional shawl). It was sad to witness this situation. Some people in the office talked with excitement about a new market that had opened to buy goods, houses, and vehicles from evicted Eritreans, saying things like, "Someone told me that they have the best deals because we can really press the price down." One of my colleagues was Eritrean, a wonderful man called Eyassu. He spoke many languages (English, French, Italian, Amharic, Tigrigna, and some Somali). People in the office were teasing him about being picked up by the police, and as the days passed, he looked just worse and worse. I was leaving on vacation, and I was sure I would not see him again.*

But when I returned, I found him as he boarded the shuttle. He looked so good; to me, it was like finding a brother in the midst of challenge, but through the challenge finding this brother with the essence of resilience. Resilience shines. I cried when I saw him, but I was not really sad — my tears rather flowed, because of the power of resilience that I witnessed. Despite the insults, the teasing, the stress of being picked up or not, the stress of not knowing how to manage his children and deal with all other uncertainties — there he was, standing tall and at peace. These were the tears that come from the depth of my heart and that flow from the well of the paradox of ultimate evil and ultimate goodness.

Later on, we had an office celebration for New Year's and we rented buses to take everyone to Lake Langano, a common recreation place for the better-off citizens and the expatriate community in Addis Ababa. We brought tents, food, music, and drinks with us, and very few people slept at all due to their excitement and their party mood. It just went on the whole weekend through. We laughed and danced, cried, and laughed and danced some more.

The management team of MSF *had a special way of tightening bonds among colleagues and to build a good team spirit among its employees. Most of those present were to become in one way or another very close friends and allies in my work. This gathering was a sort of grouping of souls before the wind blew us to the four corners of the world.*

A week later, the office was quiet. I was getting my coffee when I heard a whisper. It was Eyassu — he had been finally picked up. My heart went flat. The sky was heavy on me and I felt like my blood had changed to soda water and the bubbles were rising up to my throat. My tears were never too far and always looked for a reason to flow, and so they did. Again, it was from that well, the well that is not of today, but that is timeless and carries the sorrows of sad stories or women crying for men. I called my aunt, and she said to me that the first thing I needed to do in order to help was to stop crying. "You are not helping anyone this way. You are only going to get yourself in trouble," she said. I dropped the coffee and went to find Eyassu, I tried to find the place where he was detained.

It was hard to get in. The usual Kebele[29] *had turned into a detention center, where Eritrean detainees would be kept until they were dispatched to the border. However, I managed my way in, and there were plenty of the new detainees. All of them were wearing the* Gabi. *I tried to find Eyassu, but could not see him. He was standing right in front of me, but I did not see him, almost as if I was ignoring him so that I didn't have to deal with the reality. There was only a bench between us and it was enough to demarcate us. This little wooden bench was like heavy metal bars. It was demarcating us clearly, and we kept to our sides. If I stretched my hands out with the palms facing him and my fingers pointing to the sky, I thought that maybe we could touch through the glass—but there was no glass, no wire mesh at all.*

My mind was going in a thousand directions. When you look into someone's eyes and you both know that this may be the last time, the gaze lingers. Our gaze carried out a PowerPoint presentation of what we had lived through

---

[29] Established by the Communist regime, a *Kebele* is the smallest administrative unit of Ethiopia, similar to a ward or neighborhood. The houses used to serve as *Kebeles* were often nationalized homes with large compounds and enough rooms to be used as office space. At times the *Kebeles* became detention centers, as in this case.

and experienced together. So, once in a while a smile cracked my straight lips. At times, a sour knot grabbed my throat and my eyes fought not to let out the tears, and I smiled again, but this time from surrender. Such is life!

They say that the texture of life is the moments of intensity we live. Buddhists say that pain is a fact, but suffering is optional. So, like the spectrum of colors, the spectrum of life experiences serves us a range of colors and textures where our soul's palate is offered a myriad of flavors and tones. The best thing to do is to surrender and allow, allow the wave of emotions to run its course that we may die in peace one day.

So I stood in the Kebele *and I looked at him standing on the other side of the bench and wondered, how did he end up there?*

The change in the life of this one man and all those deported during this time between the two countries, occurred as a consequence of a series of choices made through Time, each leading to the next.

Seeing the changes that took place from Eyassu's perspective, he saw himself caught behind this bench in his *Gabi* as a result of the historical changes that took place during that time in Ethiopia and which manifested themselves in his personal life. He had spent his entire life in Ethiopia and did not really have family in Eritrea. It is like a strange movie with a weird turn of story. How does somebody leave everything they built behind, all the relationships, the memories, the life, everything, and just leave with one bag of clothes or some personal belongings? Eyassu's wife had to stay behind to sell their household goods and pay the utilities before leaving. His children were young and had no idea what was going on.

Similar deportations happened on the other side of the border where Ethiopians were deported out of Eritrea. The deportation process was not easy. It is one thing when we think of it as a policy or a political decision; it is another thing on the ground, when each affected person has to pack up and go. How do we tell our children what happened? How do we explain to them that we could not find other solutions?

My grandmother was very sad about all this. One day she sat in her living room with the United Nations (UN) Under-Secretary and Executive Secretary of the United Nations Economic Commission for Africa (UNECA), Mr. Amoako, who is a family friend, who had come to visit. In a conversation about the Ethiopian-Eritrean conflict, I remember that she told him that the following: "the story of Ethiopia and Eritrea is nothing that could not have been solved sitting around a table with elders. Now, we, the people of both countries, have to pay a dear price," she sighed.

Around the same time, war broke out between our two nations. It was a war that left bitter wounds on both sides. So many soldiers died on both sides, they were lost in a meaningless war. So many brothers killed each other. So many mothers and wives cried. The irony is that many of these soldiers may have been related and would have celebrated together if they had met in a different time, at a different place, with a beer or a cup of coffee to share at the end of one afternoon somewhere in town.

At that time, I worked with MSF, and Fantu was one of the first women who joined our program to support women surviving from prostitution. She had worked in the red light district of Addis Ababa earlier, but now she was just trying to raise her children (one son and three daughters). She was affected by the Eritrea-Ethiopian conflict as well, as her son was drafted to fight in the war. I think she did not really understand the implications of her son being drafted to the front line, and I also believe that she did not understand the structures and workings of military systems. So she came to see me one day with the following idea in her mind.

Fantu came to see me in the office, and told me that she had come to say goodbye. I asked where she was going and she replied that she was going to bring her son some Atmit (a special, warm, oats-based food, often prepared for children or people who need to recover from illness). She said that her son could not sleep unless he drank Atmit before going to bed, and that she wanted to find him at his posting to give him enough Atmit while he was on duty.

I could not really understand what was going on. He was drafted to go to war. He was drafted as an adult and there would be no way for her to find him easily. It was another aspect of the war. It was a mother looking for her son and wanting to give him food to take him through his days. It was a mother wanting to ignore the fact that the son might not come back or might even have already been shot dead. But I could not discourage her from her plans, but rather tried to contribute some money to cover at least the expenses she had to carry for her bus fare. She went looking for him, and by some miracle, found him. She came back to tell us the story of how she had found him and how she had left him at his base. He made it alive out of the war and is today living with her in Addis Ababa.

This story struck me, because in this war that tore our countries apart, families, mothers, and friends cried on both sides. I understand that our leaders have to make hard decisions to protect the sovereignty of the state, but I still wonder if there is not another way to protect sovereignty — through dialogue and negotiations instead of senseless bloodshed.

Sometimes, it seems that we may not be as conscious as we should be about the impact of current affairs on the history of our lives and the history of the world — how today's policy might actually define tomorrow's reality. At the same time, as much as this sounds intangible, these policies and high-level decisions clearly affect our individual lives a lot more than we think. It might help a great deal if the people in leadership positions could in fact be truly aware of how close our individual lives are to the policies — this would, in effect, lead to more humane management of our countries and development programs.

But for such awareness to take place, we must first start with understanding ourselves, knowing who we are in order to have clarity about where we are trying to go and how we plan to get there. It is just so essential to also understand the circumstances in which we live and operate, so that we can work in a way that would be compatible with the system in place. Otherwise, the system is bound to eject us very quickly. I say this to really emphasize the need to understand ourselves, and secondly to understand the mechanisms that allow us to personally change and transform in order to become agents of change and transformation on a greater scale.

EMERGING TRANSFORMATION

Transformation emerges from a change we make in a specific moment. It is the change we make in a precise Time and place, and our ability to remain with this new way of being that results in a transformed state of being and allows the emergence of a new paradigm.

Our sustained commitment to the act and unfolding of change results in a transformed reality. This transformation has a slightly different anatomy based on whether it happens at the individual level or at the collective level.

True transformation is divine. True transformation asks for sincerity and surrender. It is when we come naked in all of our strength, all of our misery, all of our power and beauty, that transformation is possible. It is when we come as we truly are with all of our "selves." When we come with that self that is afraid, that self that is courageous and outrageous, that self that is a child of history and an ancestor of the future — then the ground we stand on changes to the platform and field open to transformation. It is only in truth that we can be channels of change and transformation. To be a channel, a true one through which the souls and spirits can whisper their wisdom, it is necessary to decompose like compost and emerge as clean as a baby leaf that aims to rise to a great Shola tree one day.

Individually speaking, it seems that we may be left to our personal visions, hopes, and aspirations to engage the process of change. My ability to envision myself in 5, 10, and 15 years from now will be the catalyst to engage the journey toward this vision. The vision is like the horizon and the closer I get to it, the further it will look. One must remain on the path trusting and knowing that the process of the journey is that which will bestow in me the life, the sparkles of the vision I held out. No matter what happens, once one has engaged the path, even one step later, one is no longer a part of the reality where one started. One is at *reality + 1 step.*

Collectively speaking, this same process of change applies. However, this time, we would need to have a collective consensus on the direction in which we want to go or a shared vision of the future we aspire to allow. Extending this concept to economic and human development work, the question is how can we as a collective bring the reality of a healthy and prosperous future to the countries and continent that today stand destitute and well below the lines of poverty?

When looking at the situation of Sub-Saharan African nations or the region as a whole, the economic and human development indicators paint a picture of disaster and imminent collapse. Yet, we in Africa, the majority of Africans, and in particular those of lesser means, continue to exist one day at a time. My friend, Roger Jover, who was the headmaster of the French International School in Lusaka from 2002–2007, always said that Africans must be the most optimistic people in the world — especially in the context of all the challenges they are confronted with each day, because if they were not, they would not be able to wake up the next day.

Again, it comes back to the role of Time. In most African countries and for the majority of people, Time is not pressing, and our ways of living do not reflect that we are in fact conscious of Time. We cannot think of planning today for something in six months or a year. We live day to day. At the same time, this living from one day to the next one is the grace that God has afforded us so that we can actually wake up in the morning and have the strength to go on with our day, despite all the challenges and obstacles we face. It would not be possible for the average person in Africa to wake up and go on, if they were consciously aware of how precarious life in Africa is, and if we did not have the ability to go on day by day, one step at a time.

There are so many individuals here in Africa and beyond, who are ready and able to invest themselves in developing the various aspects and levels of the economies and livelihoods of our people. But where do we start to bring out the change and the transformation that we may see collectively? When we speak of change and transformation, by default the topic of leadership comes into the picture, because it is through leadership that it is possible to form the collective and give it one mouth/one heart to speak from and through.

Will we ever witness the day of a prosperous Africa with the same opportunities for livelihood available to men and women in other parts of the world? Does economic and human development in African nations only depend on what governments and multilateral and bilateral aid organizations can provide, or is there something that we, ordinary citizens, can do to contribute?

If we can start from the premise that the change we look for in Africa is not solely the responsibility of our various government bodies, or Western donors, but that it is in fact the responsibility of each one of us as individuals and caring citizens of the continent — then, individual contribution is possible. Through such contribution, it is possible to move towards a changed future, towards a transformed Africa. So, what are the steps to be taken and how would we have to proceed? What systems and structures would be needed to allow everyone's involvement? What would it take to mobilize a critical mass of men and women to shift the current paradigm to one that would allow us to actually change the future? Such are the questions that have led me to look into what we Africans, and our allies who share our concern for Africa, can do for this continent.

I personally believe that we urgently need to create more action-oriented platforms of communication and discussion, more opportunities for exchanging knowledge, information, and technical approaches, and sharing innovative and creative development practices. We should start collaborating, start trading across our shared borders, across nations, and throughout the continent. Right now, one of the biggest challenges is that the African men and women who are committed to making these kinds of contributions and leading the process of change often do not know each other and have no way of meeting systematically. In these days where communication can be so easily and effectively done through the Internet, the starting point may have to be the Internet, followed by actual organized meeting opportunities where learning, sharing, and exchanging can happen with the aim of inducing change in all sectors.

This platform or program will begin with conversations around the issues that are raised in this book. This will be followed by discussions that will inspire others to come with their concerns and the issues they want to raise. The change will become a story at a time, one person at a time, and one conversation at a time; this approach may seem to take much longer, but I feel that the best approach is to slow down in our actions that will push us further and faster forward, as each step we will make will be a step towards change.

CHANGING LIVES, ONE AT A TIME

Over the past two decades working in Africa, I realized that change really happens only over time. Even though it is costly in terms of resources to bring about such changes, the most sustainable changes are those that are targeted to one life at a time, maybe one community at a time. Every single action we take affects lives, our lives and possibly many other lives. Each of us is a potential resource person to create change. The choices we make along with the action define the kind of reality we create.

I once met a wonderful woman named Elsa. I had been invited to be part of an NGO panel on Ethiopian Christmas Day at the University of Addis Ababa, to offer a meal for children orphaned by AIDS. At the panel, Elsa and I casually exchanged phone numbers and for months it stayed at that. One day, she called me and asked if she could give her children my cell number, because she said, the doctors had told her that she might have a few more days to live, a week at the most. I told her it would be ok to give them my cell number and that her kids could call me whenever they felt like talking to me. However, I also told her that, if she could postpone her departure from this world for a few months, we could really use her help in the office. I still remember her voice on the phone — she sort of stopped for a moment, and I think in those moments of pause, she may have traveled into the world of Spirit, into the other side of consciousness, where she may have reconfigured the next days of her life. She said, "Ok, I will come to the office." A year later, I reminded her that it had been a year now, and asked whether she was still planning to leave us. It ended up in laughter—because she had decided to live.

Sometimes the options we have appear quite clearly. In the case of Elsa, the story tells us that there is much more to human resilience in the face of terminal illness (and by the same token, in the face of severe living conditions) than medically and scientifically supported facts would highlight. The human spirit, when aroused, has the capacity to bypass what we know empirically and manifest outcomes that we as humans can only relate to as miracles. The same kind of story came with Meaza.

Meaza was in bed being paralyzed. She was about the same age as I and about the same height. She must have weighed only around 40 kg, but in no case more than 45 kg. Her mother told us that it would be better for Meaza to die, because she could not bear to carry Meaza anymore and could not help her to go to the bathroom and wash herself. I was called to go to Meaza's house by my Aunt Koky, who had known Meaza at church. And, because she knew Meaza was suffering from AIDS, she thought that I might be able to help her either through my organization or through the network of people I knew who worked in the field of HIV/AIDS.

Meaza and her mother lived at the time near the railway station in Addis Ababa. We called the area "Legehar." (The name is derived from "La Gare," *the French term for train station. The French had built the railroad to connect Djibouti with the new Ethiopian capital Addis Ababa). Their house was very small. When we walked in, it was unexpectedly clean and tidy. Meaza's mother had snow-white, smooth hair cut very short to the skull. She looked beautiful even though the hardship of life had taken its toll on her. The TV in the room had been covered by a nice crochet piece, and all around the room there were pictures of the archangels hanging on the walls, which were plastered with newspaper and magazine paper. On the side of the room there was a bed, and in that bed, Meaza lay, hardly moving. She just sighed once in a while and only her eyes were roaming around the room. She had lost so much weight that her cheeks had sunk in and her lips were hanging on her teeth. I did not know what to say. I did not know what to do.*

We had the usual greeting conversation, and Meaza made an effort to speak; she murmured some sounds, and her mother took over the conversation, while Meaza fell back in the state she was in before we walked in—laying there with eyes rolling around as if scanning the ceiling for something. Then she jumped back into the conversation and told us she was ok, but that she had painful sores from lying on her back all day. Her mother was moving around the room trying to tidy up what was already so clean. Once in a while, she would glance at us and then glance back to the Archangels with their armor and swords killing the dragons and the serpents. All the Archangels, Kidus *Mikael,*[30] *the chief of all the Archangels,* Kidus *Giorgis,*[31] *on his horse slashing the Dragon, and* Kidus *Gebrel,*[32] *coming with his Avatar flowing in the wind—they were all alive on the walls of this tiny home. And as the mother was talking to us, she would also address these Archangels one by one, asking them when they would relieve her of this life. She said to us that if Meaza died, then she would go to a monastery and stay there until the end of her life.*

[30] Saint Michael.

[31] Saint George

[32] Saint Gabriel

It is difficult to be in a situation where you know that the odds are just so against you. I so wanted to help, but knew there was not much I could do. The work on HIV/AIDS is often heartbreaking, because at times there is only so little we can do to help. When we work on prevention, we hope that the people listen, and when we work on care and support we hope the money doesn't run out to buy the drugs. In this case it was neither about prevention nor about care and support. It was about a desperate situation.

At one point, and I don't really know how or why to this day, I told Meaza that I could not give her money, because I had none, but I could give her a job. I remember her eyes when I said that. They bugged out and stared at me as if I had said the most foolish thing ever. She sort of smiled and said to me, "Are you joking? I am paralyzed! How will I work?"

I explained to her that she could write and that her job could be writing stories. She would be free to write her own stories or whatever she wanted to write, but the deal would be that every Friday we would come to collect the stories and every month we would send her salary.

She was quiet for a moment but then when it sunk in, she was so excited, she could hardly stay still. I told her that she was free to do what she wanted with her salary, whether she wanted to buy Anti-Retroviral (ARV) Drugs or coffee for her family, to me it did not matter. Just because she was working for an organization working on HIV/AIDS, I did not want her to feel obliged to buy ARVs.

We had to find a name for her position. She would be our first Home Writer, and this is how the Home Writer Program came about.

Within days the news went around the neighborhood—even though Meaza was ill and bed-ridden, she was working. Neighbors started coming to visit and the discrimination stopped. Within months she lost her paralysis and started coming to the office, with the responsibility of managing the Home Writers Program within our organization, which was called everyONE.[33]

Meaza started the program for 10 more Home Writers. It was not about them earning money or not dying, but about the quality of life in the days they had left. Because she had a job, she now had access to purchasing power,

[33] http://www.everyonesworld.org

and this purchasing power bought her a place in the society.

Meaza stayed in our organization and is still working with us as a social worker, as of the writing of this book. She is well, she is healthy, she is helping and supporting her mother, and the life that she had before her recovery is set aside as an episode to be forgotten. Yet, at the same time, she often brings it up and speaks of how much the turn of her life has amazed her and all those around her. She has become an inspiration to her community. She certainly has become my mascot for hope. Who would have ever thought that such a transformation would be possible?

As much as I love to think of this example of transformation, I am also often frustrated that our authorities did not really allow us to continue the Home Writer Programs, because, they said, they were not founded on proper public health research. So, I wonder how innovation can take place, if the only programs allowed to be implemented are the ones done through the classical and often noncreative public health foundations. Unfortunately, our effort to enroll the authorities in support of this program did not succeed. The Ethiopian authorities did not allow any program not proven through public health research to be implemented, which eventually forced us to stop the Home Writer Program.

To me, this sad ending to the Home Writer Program story is a reflection of how very few people are willing to take the risk to try something new, even if this new way of doing things proves its benefits. To my knowledge, there are no other such programs in Ethiopia or elsewhere; care for AIDS patients is limited to providing them aid in acquiring drugs and food security. In my opinion, this option is neither empowering nor does it re-energize people living with AIDS. It is important to have a job, to have a responsibility, and to have something that we are accountable for because it adds to having a purpose to live, a reason to wake up in the morning, a place to go in the day, and people to see for a professional reason. We all need a purpose to wake up to. This is the key to life. One of my mentors, Mr. Abdul Rahman Turay,[34] once said to me that there is always hope as long as

[34] Mr. Abdul Rahman Turay, a seasoned economist, is the Principal Advisor to the President of Sierra Leone and head of the Strategic Policy Unit at State House, as of the writing of this book.

we are alive; we go to bed at night because we trust and hope that we will still be alive tomorrow. In addition to the hope of being alive the next day, it is about having a cause to wake up to. The lack of a reason to wake up, the lack of feeling responsible for something and needed by someone or some organization — this lack takes away our ability to long for the next day. And it is this longing for the next day that keeps us alive, and that improves the quality of life of AIDS patients.

There is another story that I want to share, in line with the importance of a job, a reason to wake up, and a need to be accountable in the context of personal transformation. The story is about a man called Fike, an amazing man with an inspiring story of change and transformation.

When Fike contracted polio, he was 6 years old. As if to add salt to the wound, he also contracted leprosy around the same time. By the time he was 8 he had to leave his village in the north of Ethiopia to come to the capital, Addis Ababa, and join the hundreds of mostly physically handicapped beggars. He lived in the sewage system, because he had no other place to live. He only came out to beg and find food. Before heading back to the sewer, he would stop by the local bars and either buy Tej, the local honey wine, or get himself a glass from the last bit left from each customer's glass. The alcohol helped him get knocked out and spend a quiet night. At one point, as he continued begging, his body became severely affected by leprosy. He lost most of his fingers, and his face became quite scarred. Because of polio, he also could not walk. So, he had a wide board made into some bizarre and sad version of a skateboard.

When things got really bad, he went to the hospital where they treat all leprosy patients, and tried to get treatment. The standard option was to amputate his legs, but for some reason the doctor refused and wanted to give surgery a chance. The doctor thought that maybe they could save Fike's legs. After a series of operations, and many years of treatment, Fike still has both legs, walks straight up, and has also been treated to stop the impact of leprosy.

I met Fike a few years after his operations. By the time we met, he did not live in the sewer anymore, but in a plastic house. He was not a beggar anymore. He had joined a Church and started serving the Church and its community. He was part of the prayer team.

When I met Fike, I was going through my own set of challenges, and he soon became my spiritual teacher. I would leave my office—at the time I was with United Nations Development Program (UNDP)—and would go sit with Fike during my lunch hour or right after work. His place was right in the neighborhood where all the people affected with leprosy lived. In the beginning, the other people who lived in the area could not understand what I was doing there, because the neighborhood was almost closed off and reserved just for people with leprosy.

Being with Fike and his community gave me a chance to breathe and rest. It allowed me time to introspect and pray. Fike's prayers were powerful, and his guidance helped me deal with my work in the office and with my private life. Eventually, my visits became so normal and regular that his friends would notice if I did not come by for one reason or another. They would often ask me if all was well with me and why I did not come to visit.

Once I set up the organization everyONE, we hired Fike as a community worker, and he was responsible for the community of people with leprosy. In the office, I tried to have a habit of weekly meetings where all team members would be present. We would have to present what happened in that week, what to expect for the following week, and how all that fit in the greater plan of the organization.

The miracle of Fike happened when I told everyone at the meeting that if they missed submitting their report by Friday, they would be fired on the second Friday they missed. Fike raised his hands and said it was not fair since he could not write, as he did not have fingers. He called me Mimi, and he said, "Mimi, that is not fair, how should I manage this?" I replied, "However you decided to manage this, it is your decision, and not mine." I replied this way, not because I did not empathize with him, but because the reply came blurting out of my mouth. I was shocked by myself that I could answer this way, but later realized that this answer came from a deep place in my heart, a place that stood for Fike and his potential, a place where I felt that discrimination (positive or negative) is not always empowering for the person. I wanted to see Fike come out of his circumstances and work free of his physical limitations.

The precise moment when my answer reached his ears, I witnessed some-

thing I had never before seen. It was a moment of things just totally turning around. Fike was literally shocked that I replied the way I did, and everyone around the table was equally shocked (I was shocked myself, but could not take my words back). The entire team was appalled that I would lose my manners so quickly. We all stared at each other, and back at Fike. Then, a second later, Fike's energy changed and he had the biggest smile on his face.

What happened was that I was not discriminating against him, negatively or positively. I told him that he was free to pay or charm someone into writing his report (that was his call), but on my side I just wanted to see that report. My stand gave him the green light to go; it gave him the recognition that, despite his disability, he had as many opportunities as anyone else. Despite the fact that throughout his life, he was considered useless and hopeless, that day he felt, he knew, that it was not true. The truth was that he could take on his physical challenges and overcome them in order to access the kind of life he wanted. In the end, I believe Fike had someone work with him to write his report; he would dictate and the other person would note down what he said.

From that day on, Fike was so motivated; he would walk miles from his home to our office and back. He would carry a laptop bag and tilt his body to reflect the weight of the machine in there, even if it was imaginary. He said, "One day, you'll find me owner of a 'lafftoff.'"

These three stories of Elsa, Meaza, and Fike illustrate that each one of us is a potential change agent. As of the writing of this book, Meaza is well and healthy, living in Addis and working with us as a social worker. Elsa left our organization, but she is alive and healthy, raising her children and continuing her work as an activist for HIV/AIDS. Fike is also in Addis; he works hard with his community, has built a brick house, and last I heard, had gotten married and had a baby! All these stories are just a snippet of so many other ones that take place each day around the world and in Africa. So, change is possible. Change is attainable and transformation is within our reach.

Our ability to convey the possibilities we see in others is a powerful means to bring such people into new possibilities and facilitate or inspire change paradigms. It is our capacity to see the potential in others that can lead us to support the communities and people around us to progress, change, and transform their lives. But in order to do that, we need to first see the potential in ourselves and allow our dreams to exist. It is about compassion and, at the same time, it is about courage to accept what might be considered the norm around us and still go beyond that norm despite the odds. It is about daring to follow our hearts and listen to our intuition and translate that into actionable items.

In a nutshell, it is about challenging, responding, and reacting to the reality that surrounds us with the voice of the child that is within all of us: questioning, inquiring, and examining what else can be possible. When I asked Elsa if she would possibly postpone her death and die next year so she could help us work, that question did not come from my adult self, but from the child that is still within me. It is a legitimate question to ask if someone would be willing to wait another few months before they call it quits. If we tap into our "all-ness," our essence, I really trust that we can come up with solutions that will surpass those that we formulate just using our minds. This is the approach we need to transform Africa.

CHAPTER 4

Integral Theory: A Better Tool for Creating Change

> "What if we took literally everything that all the various cultures have to tell us about human potential — about spiritual growth, psychological growth, social growth — and put it all on the table? What if we attempted to find the critical essential keys to human growth, based on the sum total of the human knowledge now open to us? That is we attempted, based on extensive cross cultural study, to use all the world's great traditions to create a composite map, a comprehensive map, an all-inclusive map that included the best elements from all of them?"
>
> –Ken Wilber[35]

When I worked briefly for United Nations Development Program (UNDP), with the task of providing support to 14 country offices within Eastern and Central Africa on HIV/AIDS programs, the focus of my assignment was to introduce leadership development and transformation models in order to address the issue of HIV/AIDS. It was a turning point for me. At one of the first events I attended, Dr. Monica Sharma and Dr. Moustapha Gueye from the UNDP New York office came to Addis Ababa and talked relentlessly about the "Wilber Model." I had not heard of this model before and, to me, it sounded like yet another model-in-vogue, with the same lim-

[35] Wilber, K. (2007). *The Integral Vision: A Very Short Introduction to the Revolutionary Integral Approach to Life, God, the Universe, and Everything.* Boston, MA, Shambhala, p, 16.

ited lifespan of a few years of popularity and then total obscurity.

Just because there was such a craze around the so-called Wilber Model, it turned me off at first. For some reason, I am repelled by anything that is fashionable or the hype of the day; my sisters often joke with me and tell me that one day the fashion police will arrest me, because I am never with the times in terms of clothes. But this is not just limited to clothes — I just don't manage to follow the hype. I tend to go only with what works for me, and I shy away from raging crowds, whether their excitement is for fashion, art, work, church, or whatever. So, true to my nature, I remained on the margins of the workshop and just watched the various speakers deliciously present Integral nibbles, flavors and scents, and little bites for us to chew on about Wilber and his model. I remained reluctant to take part in the conversations and new flavors presented. But, eventually, I realized that it would be best to engage in this new Wilber thing, because the essence of my new job entailed that I become one of the preachers of this material.

I had not known of this Wilber theory or Integral Theory[36] before, and I approached it very skeptically. This Wilber model spoke of the interior and exterior, and the individual and collective quadrants (see figure 1). It was a map to locate ourselves, our realities, and understand the leverage points. The theory talked about systems, about human systems and about uncovering the leverage points for change, for transformation, and for impact. I was skeptical, but in order to deliver on the job I had accepted, I had to learn it ("one more darn thing," I cursed) and at least give it a chance. I am very grateful for that pressure, because in time, I came to see the Integral Theory model as the best hope for Africa.

INTEGRAL THEORY CONCEPTS USED HERE

The Integral approach is basically the use of a holistic lens to examine reality and grasp its various levels and subtleties, and deepen our understanding of reality in a comprehensive manner. This map is just a map; it is not the territory (see figure 1 for a very simplified version of the Integral

[36] The Integral Community has grown around the practitioners of the Integral Theories and Praxis. See Ken Wilber, Integral Institute, Pacific Integral, Integral Leadership Review, Integral World, Integral Review, some universities, etc.

map). The use of the map allows us to truly see the reality we face from multiple perspectives and multiple levels. The vertical columns consider the internal versus the external perspective, and the horizontal rows consider the individual versus the collective perspective. The map thus generates four quadrants: internal/individual, external/individual, internal/collective, and external/collective.

Figure 1 – Simple Illustration of Integral Theory's Four Quadrant Map.

	INTERNAL	EXTERNAL
INDIVIDUAL	**Personal Values** Attitudes and Beliefs All that is on the inside, but can't be seen on the outside	**Individual Behavior** Individual's Biology All that is seen from the outside Individual
COLLECTIVE	**Cultures and Traditions** Our Norms and Collective Values All the collective worldviews and values that define and distinguish a living entity— group, organization, community, society, country, etc.	**Systems and Structures** Rules and Regulations Government structures and established social systems All that might be concrete and tangible, seen in terms of what makes a society, a group, an organization, what it is.

This map has implications for understanding reality, which in itself is the foundation of creating change. From a personal perspective, the use of this map as a tool to examine reality allows us to explore our internal and external environment. We may explore our values, our attitudes in relation to our external behavior. The quadrants offer us an opportunity to assess whether our personal values and attitudes are in line with the collective. Are we in line or do we stick out like a sore thumb? From a collective perspective, the use of this map allows us to see what the prevalent culture is and how this culture relates to our external systems and structures, which include the objective behavior of that which we collectively value.

Frequently, it is change agents, meaning individuals with minds and visions ahead of their own times, that are needed to move a community, a society, or even a nation forward, so that it may operate from levels of consciousness that are more evolved than the dominant or mainstream consciousness. Change agents are individuals who will have to be patient, wise, and resilient, as the community will often resist their pull. It is therefore vital that there be a platform or a way to bring change agents together, in order to allow them to support each other in their efforts toward evolving the circumstances of their respective communities, societies, and nations.

One of the main attractions of this model is that it surfaces all the aspects of a situation, putting them out on the table in plain view. As an example, there are many gender equality programs or programs for stopping violence against women. In many cases, such types of programs either do not last very long or take a tremendous amount of time to really get anchored and sustained. Mapping such programs into the four quadrants surfaces several possible reasons that could explain the causes for their failure (figure 2). In Ethiopia, the many organizations working against violence against women (including beating, rape, excision, etc.) aim all of their activities at communicating messages to the communities or to the government bodies — messages that usually target the Upper Right Quadrant. But only very few organizations or programs look at the other three perspectives, meaning the other three quadrants of the model and the issues mentioned within.

This is just one practical example for the use of this model, even though this might be a rather simple one. However, the complexity and value of this tool can be best appreciated in the books and publications dedicated to it. I touch upon it here to bring to your attention the importance of having a comprehensive and holistic view of what reality is or might be, in order to formulate and create innovative approaches for sustainable, durable, and humane solutions for development.

Figure 2: Applying the Wilber Model to Assess Programs to Stop Violence against Women.

	INTERNAL	EXTERNAL
INDIVIDUAL	**Personal Values:** Did we take the time to see what the personal values, attitudes, and beliefs are among men, and among women? Do women think it is right to be beaten? Do men think they have a right to beat their wives or partners? Where does the acceptance of violence start? Do we learn it from our parents? Were we beaten as children? All that is on the inside, but can't always be seen on the outside	**Behaviors:** Communication Programs to stop violence against women Use of Media, Advertising, Workshops, etc. All that is seen on the outside Individual
COLLECTIVE	**Cultures and Traditions:** Our norms and collective values: how does society look upon violence against women, or violence in general? Does the community react when they witness (hear or see) someone being beaten? Are there elders who can be involved? What measures do we as a society have to council, advise, and if needed, reprimand one who commits violence against women? All that defines and distinguishes a living entity (group, organization, community, society, country, etc.) to be what it is.	**Structures and Systems in Place:** Lobbying and advocacy work Rules and Regulations: are the laws changing to punish those committing the violence against women? Government structures and established social systems: Are there safe-houses built and available for women looking for shelter? All that might be concrete and tangible, seen in terms of what makes a society, a group, or an organization what it is.

The Integral approach has generated a number of useful theories that interact with it, and the concept of Spiral Dynamics could be of particular interest in the African context. Spiral Dynamics[37] represents a way of looking at reality that takes into consideration the society's and individuals' levels of development. To describe a complex theory in a few words, Beck and Cowan talk of levels of societal evolution: accordingly, individuals and societies evolve through different stages. Each stage has its own ways of being, its own rules and regulations, and its own way of making sense to its members. As a society moves from the earlier stages of existence to the later stages, we can see the emergence of a more complex society. It is like human evolution — we transcend our stages to the next stage, while at the same time we keep the previous stage. Ken Wilber refers to this process as *transcend and include*.

TESTING INTEGRAL THEORY ON MYSELF

I am unable to preach something I do not believe in, even if it is required for a job I have to do. I was therefore faced with having to understand this model and even find a reason to believe in it, in order to do the work I was hired to do at UNDP. I thought it would be a good approach to try the model on myself, before I could persuade anybody else of its usefulness. The presenters said that this model could help us address any problem, at any scale, so I figured I would try it out on something simple and ordinary, such as changing habits. Since we were attempting to apply the model to improving the situation with HIV/AIDS, which in essence is about changing habits, I thought that if I could use the model to quit smoking myself, then I would be able to apply it in community mobilization for HIV/AIDS.

I had made many attempts to quit smoking, and each time I did not manage or I relapsed back into it within months (at the longest). Considering my smoking habits, I mapped out my four quadrants (figure 3), and very quickly, I had a glimpse of the various options applicable to me. I could literally see the reasons for my frequent failures by putting together the missing pieces that had triggered my repeated failures. For years, even though I valued healthy living habits and attempted to be smoke-free, my behavior was not in line with those values. In addition to that, because I smoked, I was in contradiction with my family norms and societal norms that de-

[37] See, e.g., Don Edward Beck and Christopher C. Cowan's *Spiral Dynamics: Mastering Values, Leadership, and Change* (Malden, MA: Blackwell, 1996).

cent women should not smoke. My social surroundings did not offer any structures or systems to overcome my addiction to nicotine, so I had to find these structures myself or even create them. Rather than rebelling against the societal norms that looked down upon women who smoked, I had to understand that in this particular society (and in my case, in a conservative Ethiopian family/society), that was just the norm, and it was OK. In freeing myself from the judgments of society and also my ability to create a means to let go of cigarettes, within a short period of time, I was able to get rid of the addiction.

Figure 3: Application of the Wilber Model to My Desire to Quit Smoking.

	INTERNAL	EXTERNAL
INDIVIDUAL	**Personal Values:** Healthy living Living within the norms of my culture	**Behaviors:** Smoking Individual
COLLECTIVE	**Cultures and Traditions:** Judgment of women who smoke Good people are free of bad habits Good women should try to emulate the Virgin Mary	**Structures and Systems in Place:** Lack of support to quit smoking Rejection of women who don't aim to be like the Virgin Mary Collective

What became apparent to me, as I mapped my habits in the model, was the fact that there was a great contradiction between my internal values and attitudes toward healthy living and my external behavior of being caught up in an addiction to cigarettes. In my culture, women who smoked were almost by default seen as women with low character, and to some extent as women who were of questionable background. Yet, my background was that of a conservative/Christian family and I was far from having a low character. I knew that none of the judgments society placed on women who smoked applied to me; I knew smoking did not turn me into a bad person. It is a habit like any other, which is of course bad for your health, but just because I smoked, it did not mean that I was a person with a doubtful character. It was apparent for me that one of the tensions I was caught in was the fact, that, on one hand, I wanted to live up to my family's and society's expectations, while on the other hand, I had this habit I did not know how to get rid of, and through this tension, I added more stress and anxiety to myself.

The first step in giving up smoking was to clearly see that whatever judgment others had about women who smoked, those were their own judgments, and I had to realize that I should not carry others' projections. I had to almost neutralize and distance myself from the impact of the way society looked on women who smoked. This created space for me to come out of the tension I had been stuck in for years, and to think of my own values in relation to my external behavior. Once I got rid of society's judgment, I was able to empower myself to engage the path of changing behavior. I managed to do that, because I literally had to weigh out what I value most: is it my own wish to have a healthy lifestyle or is it the cigarettes? This threshold brought me to a decision point of acknowledging that I valued a healthy lifestyle more than having cigarettes as part of my life. From then on, it was about accepting the fact that there would be some few days of discomfort whereby my body would still be asking for nicotine, but that sticking to my decision would eventually wean me off the dependence on nicotine.

The mapping of my smoking habits did not only allow me to become a non-smoker, but also made me better understand the potential of this tool in making any changes that a person or a community might wish to make. I figured that if I could quit smoking with support of this model, then maybe I should look into it further. So I ordered some of the books Ken Wilber wrote about the subject, and something else happened when I read about his concepts of "Holons," which I will describe in the next chapter.

ANOTHER IMPORTANT ASPECT OF THE INTEGRAL THEORY: HOLONS

The theory says that Holons refer to the fact that all things are whole unto themselves and are also part of something else; Wilber says that all things are "Holons." The Holon concept — simultaneous whole-ness and part-ness — allowed me to understand another important concept.

We each are whole and a part of that whole. In regard to my smoking and my community, I realized that I am my own person with my own values, but, in addition, I am also part of the society which has its own value system. Sometimes the values we have and that our society or community has might be the same, sometimes they might be different. In either case, it is our ability to remain simultaneously "whole" and "part" of the greater whole, and our ability to hold that balance, that will permit us to stay balanced and sustained in the system. Any time we give more attention to the greater whole, we erode our own sovereign existence, and likewise, any time we give more weight to our own individual self against the society, we end up in dissonance with the system. Whether it is in respect to society, to a community, or to our families, the concept of Holon remains the same. It is our ability to recognize and understand this concept, which can allow us to deepen our understanding of the systems which we are part of. It is therefore our ability to be fully a whole unto ourselves, with due recognition of our own boundaries and being, and at the same time our consciousness of being part of a greater whole, which will allow us to achieve equilibrium in our being and find an optimum reality from which to operate.

Therefore, in my work place I am "Me", an individual, but I am also part of the Team. Alternatively, one can say that I am the TEAM, and that TEAM is also part of the whole, in this case the organization. In the greater perspective, as an individual, I am both one and part of the greater one, be it in my community, in my country, in Africa, in the world, or the universe. Knowing, understanding, and being able to completely accept the environments we live in as a Holon, with a multitude of Holons at differing levels of analysis, all related to one another, is a major step in being able to apply the tools of Integral Theory effectively.

As a development practitioner, my ability to see myself as part of the community in which I work, as part of the organization in which I operate, and my ability to recognize and honor my "own whole" self — this will give me the right to create, innovate, and share the ideas, concepts, and knowledge that can emerge from my unique position. At the same time, knowing that I am part of the community and the organization, allows me to remain open, sensitive, and receptive to what the community or organization might exchange with me in terms of knowledge, wisdom, and insight. I can also then receive the questions and the demands, and be aware of the true needs on the ground. All of this awareness of my roles would be one of the Holons of my life.

In our work as development practitioners, we often lack this knowledge of our Holons, and we come as outsiders, the same as a guest surgeon with a sharp scalpel who conducts surgery without fully understanding or knowing anything about the patient lying on the table. When we come as disconnected outsiders, we fall prey to ego-based work. We lose the chance to connect with the souls of the community we have come to support. We lose the chance to understand, to learn, to grow, and subsequently we also lose the chance to do good work. So, we stay a few years and we write our final report on the work conducted, and then we go off to the next post! I believe we can and should do better for the sake of a better world.

I am not saying that development work always takes place in this manner. But rarely have we taken the chance to be open to the situation, to be open in a way that respects our own selves and parameters, and to appreciate the complex environments and circumstances we have entered. It is like when you drive uphill in a car with a stick shift — when you can stop without using the brakes, just by playing with the gear box, then you have attained the balance of give and take. It is this particular kind of balance that understanding Holons can offer us. It is this precise balance that can allow us to perform beyond what is expected, because in this balance we exist not from our ego self, but from the deep divine self that we are, and we are open to all the divinity around us — this is when magic happens!

APPLYING INTEGRAL THEORY TO MY WORK

To my absolute surprise, I soon warmed up to Integral theory and recognized it's potential. I realized how it could be used as a catalyst for change, not only in the field of HIV/AIDS, but also in the field of economic development as a whole. The more I saw the potential of this practice and approach, the more I envisioned what else one could do with it to benefit our communities and countries as a whole. The more this conversation played on in my mind, the more restless I became. This was also the time when I quit smoking and I left my job. I then decided to learn more about this theory and to follow through with my dream to launch an organization that would function along these principals. I realize that I am lucky and very fortunate, because some people cannot afford to leave a job for studies due to personal responsibilities that the job allows them to handle.

From 2004 to 2005, I participated in a two-year seminar program called Generating Transformative Change (GTC) in Human Systems, offered by the Pacific Integral Institute.[38] The program focused on teaching the application of Integral theory and an Integral approach to the working environment. The format of the GTC program appealed to me, because it allowed participants to resource themselves through regular online learning and face-to-face intensive seminars. It also focused on the applications of Integral theory in business, consulting, and all professions in general.

When I first learned about the GTC course, I signed up intuitively, even though I had no exact idea of what I was signing up for. When the course organizers sent me the details of the course, including the choices for accommodations and transportation to the retreat area, I was reluctant to share that information with my family. It sounded too esoteric in both language and content. The brochure talked about the "intentions" of the seminars, about methods of teaching, with which I was not very familiar, and I had absolutely no idea of the location they wanted me to come to. We were to meet in Mosswood Hallow, somewhere outside Seattle. They gave us the option to sleep in a "Yurt," and I had no idea what a "Yurt" was. My sister thought I might be heading into a sect.

But, I bravely reached Seattle and met up with the person who was supposed to pick me up. As I came up the escalator at the airport arrival area, Kim stood there holding a sign with my name. She was very tall, slim, and very pretty, with salt-and-pepper hair. As I approached her to greet her, she gave me a huge hug and the warmest welcome; I would later learn that Kim is the epitome of a big heart. I was supposed to stay with her for the duration of the course. Each day we drove from Seattle all the way out to Mosswood Hallow (about one hour and thirty minutes), and each night we drove back.

---

[38] www.pacificintegral.com

In these five days of driving back and forth together, Kim and I became very close. I met her family — her children, her parents, her brothers, and her sister — and they welcomed me into their home. Over the next few sessions, I even grew fond of her dog Brio, who joined the family in later months. I am in contact with Kim to this day; in fact, I know that I can call on her whenever I may want, and she knows that she can call on me for anything that is on her mind.

Similar friendships developed with all the other participants. Of course, there may be a varying degree of closeness, but I can say today that it is always a pleasure to hear from any one of the participants of my cohort, or even hear from others who were part of the later cohorts. Our cohort was the first one, and we all felt a bit of a pinch when we heard of other cohorts coming; a childish part of us wanted to keep the program like it was, and keep the group as it was. We still joke about it, but the joke is close to the truth. There was such closeness that we were, almost all of us, reluctant to see other cohorts join. The organizers of GTC were such a source of inspiration and learning that part of us did not want to share them with anyone.

At that time, I was mostly focused on consulting work, and I participated in the program by traveling back and forth to the United States from either Ethiopia or Zambia. I was committed to learning about Integral ideas and practices, and it was at GTC that I absorbed the potential of Integral theories in African development. The GTC program birthed a wonderful network of Integral practitioners working in various fields including organizational development, education, health, communication, politics, and environmental issues. Our cohort had participants from all corners of the world. Some were working on peace programs between Israel and Palestine; some were working on Women's Right, others were Health Care Industry experts. We had business people, spiritual teachers, and environmentalists, and as we sat together, it was possible to find most regions of the world represented among us and through our presence. This diversity of participants allowed us to delve into discussions and debates as we tried to see how the theories and tools could be applied in our respective contexts and programs.

In May 2005, I had the opportunity to attend a seminar at the Integral

Institute in Boulder, Colorado, where I learned more about the Integral Transformative Practice (ITP), taught by Terry Patten.[39] The Integral Transformative Practice, now renamed Integral Life Practice, is a practice that allows one to grow and evolve into one's fullest self. It involves working on the different lines that are part of our lives, such as cognitive, physical, emotional, spiritual, psychological, and so on. Through this practice, one attempts to increase the level of development of each line. Working the different lines allows the practitioner to evolve to higher stages on the development line. For example, in terms of increasing the cognitive line, the practitioner might consider various learning programs to increase their knowledge base; for the emotional line, the practitioner might consider having emotional work done either with a coach or a therapist; for the spiritual line, the practitioner might consider various meditation programs. There are numerous lines that we can work on, and there are equally as many practices that we can do in order to evolve through the developmental stages.

Although I knew little about ITP at the beginning of the seminar, by the end I understood the value of ITP and the role it could play in the process of transformation at the personal as well as at the collective level. ITP is a way of integrating all the aspects of our lives so that we can live more fully, more energetically, and more consciously. It allows a person to have various practices in the many lines of development, which then leads to becoming a more holistic/wholesome individual. As such, it is a comprehensive integrated practice that aims to touch all aspects of our life and being.

In this same seminar, I also learned about Polarity Management, taught by Beena Sharma,[40] which I also found to be an incredibly useful method. Polarity Management actually makes explicit what we often do intuitively in African settings: when things do not work or a problem persists, sometimes we choose to just *manage* it until an appropriate solution is found. Polarity Management deals with unsolvable problems and offers tools to

---

[39] Terry Patten is a co-author of *Integral Life Practice* (Ken Wilber, Terry Patten, Adam Leonard, Marco Morelli; Boston: Shambala, 2008). Terry and his wife Deborah Boyar have been for me a source of inspiration and encouragement through all the ups and downs of the Integral Africa journey (see Chapter Six). Deborah was our first major benefactor and her contributions allowed us to advance Integral Africa from concept to being an actual program.

deal with such types of problems in a way that finds alternative solutions to the problem, while complementing our problem solving skills. It's about managing problems even if that means not instantly finding direct solutions to solve them. Polarity Management allows the user to choose not to be faced with the full burden of the problems, and gives the user space to work on other fronts until appropriate solutions can be found for the particular problem faced. I was excited and amazed that there was in fact a tool that verbalized and made tangible a problem management capacity I knew as part of the African tradition. I was happy because this tool would help me express of lot of what I learned from our elders and communities in Africa in a language that would make sense to my colleagues and team-mates. Through this Integral tool, African managers and leaders can have a language and a process that will allow them to objectively account to Westerners for their decision of non-action (i.e., managing the problem and giving time for a solution to appear).

As these highlights illustrate, I was drawn to the Integral approach, because I believe that it offers the most comprehensive instruments, approaches, and mapping tools to understand the reality we live in. It has allowed me to understand my reality in ways that can relieve me from the pain of not understanding, and the frustration of feeling stuck in a room with no windows. Integral theory and its application give me glimpses of hope for better understanding and addressing the challenges we have been facing in Africa and other parts of the world. The entire approach allows us as practitioners to speak out and tangibly explain what has always been subtle.

For example, in my work on HIV/AIDS, I encountered considerable frustration from not understanding why it took so much money, energy, and effort to run our campaigns when the message was so simple: Technically speaking, HIV is transmitted through body fluids, so, people should use the necessary precautions not to have an exchange of fluids. We preached the ABC's (as we used to refer to Abstinence, Being faithful, or Condom use).

---

[40] Beena Sharma is trained in Polarity Management and teaches it during seminars. Polarity Management is about knowing that some problems may not have an immediate solution and part of the solution is managing the problem, as opposed to trying to resolve it.

We preached this day and night, but I personally saw very little behavior change. As I outlined earlier, my grandmother had once explained to me that our abstinence messages were creating confusion among the communities. She spoke softly and told me: "you must know that after a certain age, food, shelter, and sexuality come as the basic needs for a human being." She then asked me: "how do you expect full grown men to choose abstinence? They are not monks or recluses; please be reasonable and come up with a better message." Although I was surprised about her opinion, because I was too caught up with our own messages, I accepted her guidance. I understood what she said, but I was unable to explain it to others, and was even less able to convince my colleagues to make changes based on this idea. The Integral approach gave me the language to explain my grandmother's wisdom and other non-tangible understandings to my colleagues in terms and in a logic that they could understand.

From a Spiral Dynamics perspective, my grandmother was saying that at the main population's level of consciousness, it was not possible to understand abstinence. And, in a sense she was right —sexuality plays an important role in the earlier stages of development and is also carried through to the later stages, as are needs for food and shelter. At the same time, in order to completely grasp the meaning and benefit of abstinence in the absence of a monogamous relationship or the use of condoms, the societal development has to be at a level of consciousness that accommodates such behavior.

If we look at HIV/AIDS through the Integral lens, we can see that our policies and structures are not in accord with what we say we want to accomplish, which is to enable the community to respond to the epidemic efficiently. We can even go as far as saying that the cultures are also not conducive to bringing on a change. If rape is rampant, how do the laws treat the rapists? Do the established structures make it easy for the victim to get help? Does the culture condemn the victim or the rapist? We speak of marital abuse, but when it comes to that, where can a woman go when her husband becomes abusive?

Integral and its application can help us find the whole in our systems. It can allow us to gain both a microscopic view and a macro/meta view of how things are interrelated. That knowledge then allows the construction of programs that are much more likely to succeed.

After I became familiar with Integral theory, I resigned my assignment with UNDP. I had finished my contract and was waiting for a renewal, but between my boss, who took his time, and his assistants, who dragged out the process, I decided to just tell them that I would not come back. I was happy to be free and be able to fully commit to doing something that I had conviction about. And, I am grateful that my family environment and economic circumstances allowed me to take this path.

I chose to resign in order to focus on two activities. First, I wanted to start another organization called everyONE[41] where we would work using Integral concepts and models, and promote an awareness-raising among the communities. The goal of the organization would be to encourage people to make a conscious and informed decision about their lives, and find a means to formulate their own responses to their living circumstances as opposed to handing them "our" solutions for "their" problems. My commitment was to avoid preaching and, instead, to focus efforts on creating opportunities for reflection, for awareness-raising, and for responsibility. The second reason for my new-found freedom was to take time to learn more about this theory and about leadership and transformation in human systems, so I enrolled in a doctoral program in humanities, focusing on exactly that: transformative inquiry.

In our organization, everyONE, we worked with communities to address HIV/AIDS, but decided not to preach the usual message of prevention, abstinence, or monogamy. What we did instead was to level with all members of the communities (often very destitute communities) to bring clarity to the life options they held in their hands, and also to ask them to take on the responsibility for the decisions in their lives. Through this approach, which was to me a common-sense approach and one with compassion and respect, we were able to see miracles taking place.

Our aim was to mobilize the communities at the grassroots level, and to encourage exchange, discussions, and debates about their concerns. We also wanted to use the National Radio to broadcast a talk show that would tell

[41] www.everyonesworld.org

one story on local concerns each week. As discussed in Chapter Two, as we broadcast the stories, people called in to speak as the person in the story we were telling. At the height of the program, we had an estimated coverage reaching several million listeners. According to the Radio Station Manager, listeners were calling from all parts of Ethiopia.

One day we told the story of a secretary who needed her boss's permission to attend a training abroad. When she asked him for permission, he told her he would only allow her to go if she had sex with him. As the woman was married, and committed to her family and husband, she refused the offer and let the chance for training pass by. Later, out of spite, the boss asked her to stay late for work and used the situation to assault and rape her in the office. When the victim returned home, she chose not to tell her husband for fear of his reaction, and she also decided not to have any relations with her husband, until she found out her HIV status. Meanwhile, the husband got suspicious, thinking that she might be having an affair, and started beating her up. The woman found herself in a bind. If she told her husband about the rape, he might or might not believe her; if she told the authorities about the rape, she would end up carrying the shame. And if she allowed herself to have intimate relations with her husband, she might possibly expose him to HIV, which she might have contracted during the rape. We opened the phone lines at various turning points of the story and allowed the listeners to enter into a role play situation, speaking on behalf of the woman, who we called Sarah in the show. Men, women, and young people called and said: "Hello, this is Sarah. I am afraid and I don't know where to turn. What will happen to my children, how can my husband suspect me of having an affair, etc.?"

This radio program allowed the listeners — men and women, teenagers and youth — to actually reflect on and discuss these issues. The discussions and reflections allowed each person to look into themselves and examine their own lives, their own responses, while empowering them to make informed and sovereign decisions about the adversities they faced in their own lives.

From an Integral perspective, what the radio show offered was an opportunity for each person to visit their own personal values and see how they were aligned or in dissonance with how they behaved externally, and vice versa. At the same time, it was about looking at what was dictated in our cultures, and how this culture was either represented or not by the systems we had put in place to support the society. In the example above, many listeners called in, wondering who they could go to, in order to report the rape without feeling ashamed. Where could they go to get treatment, therapy, and even justice, if possible? In fact, the audience was inherently asking about what systems were in place to help women who had been assaulted. What kind of support can a professional woman get for sexual harassment or abuse in the office? There were, of course, many other points being raised, and each issue raised pointed to a different aspect of society, of the systems in place, of our personal values, and the value systems of our culture. It is these comments and questions that allowed us to emerge a reflection in communities across the nation.

We witnessed many changes inspired by the programs we designed, and I would like to share a few of them in the following. The first is the story of a young woman who used to work in the red light district in the Kasanchis Area in Addis Ababa, where I made regular rounds in the night to talk to the women and the girls working as sex workers.

One night, at the end of my night round, I saw a girl on the ground being dragged and beaten by some police. We stopped the car and came closer to the scene and asked why they were beating the girl. I knew the girl very well and told the policemen that she was part of our program and that she was on her way to learning to live without working as a prostitute. They said to me that this girl was a hopeless case and that water would enter a stone faster than knowledge could enter the mind of this girl. At the same time, a man appeared and said that this girl was a thief and that after he spent so much money buying her dinner and drinks, she finally refused to do her part and provide him with sex.

At this moment, the girl interrupted the man – a disgruntled client – and spoke up from the ground where she had fallen. She said, "Don't believe anything this man says! He tried to get me drunk so that I would have sex with him without protection. I am the only child of my mother and I would rather die, being beaten by the police than die of the AIDS, which this man is trying to give me. You taught us the value of protection, you made us think about the future we can have, and I would rather die than give my life away to this man!"

This young woman had understood the choices she had, and instead of being bullied by her client, who had enough pull to engage the police to beat her up and tried to get her locked up, she chose to resist and stand her ground, even at the cost of a brutal beating. She could have just given in and agreed to go along with her client, but she did not, because she had been made aware of the choices she had.

I did not know how to get the girl out of her situation. I only knew that, if she got locked up, it could be a month before she got a trial and only God knew what she would face behind prison bars. So, I told the policeman with as much audacity as I could muster, that he should warn the man, because we had taped and recorded everything with the cameras we had with us in the car. In reality, I was only bluffing, but that was the only choice I had, because I knew that the life of the girl might be at stake. As I spoke to the policeman, the client interrupted me again and served me with a good number of insults. So, I turned and explained to him that, if he ever pressed charges against this girl and got her locked up, I would go to the press with our footage, and tomorrow, he would be welcome to watch it all on National TV, while having dinner with his wife. The man was fuming by now. He continued to insult me, so I turned to the policeman and said to him that he best warn this man seriously, because I had made a vow of honor not to strike anyone with anger when I graduated from my martial arts training – more bluffing, but at this point, I was desperate to save the girl. I told the policeman that, should this man push me to break my vows, I would take no responsibility for the physical harm that the man would incur. I had such a serious face that they were not sure whether to believe or not. In the end, they decided to leave the girl, and let my team and me walk away with a last offering of profanities.

This is a story of resilience. Even though this young woman was stuck in the world of prostitution, she was aware and conscious enough to stand up against the bully client who threatened her, jointly with the police. She was standing up for herself, regardless of the situation, and was ready to pay whatever price to avoid having sex with this client. Her strength came partly from her knowing that she had choices and also of being aware of the consequences of those choices. And this is exactly what our program ultimately aimed to provide – awareness of choice and of the ability to make an informed and conscious decision about these choices.

The second story of change is about the youth in the communities. Most of the youth we worked with were either just out of school or about to finish their school. Between 16 and 20 years of age, most were unemployed and did not have much motivation or aspirations about the future. Our aim was to instill in these teenagers the awareness that they still had choices, and that they could either choose to stay in the state in which they were, or decide to work with us. EveryONE made this offer under the condition that, if they were willing to help us raise the orphan children of the community, we in exchange would pay for their training in various subject matters and life skills. We wanted them to know that there were choices regardless of the bleakness of the circumstances they lived in.

Even though we offered no payment for their support in raising the orphans of the communities, and only gave them payment in kind (e.g., training courses), many of the youth joined everyONE's organization. Many of them took various vocational trainings we offered, such as becoming kindergarten teachers, car mechanics, or entrepreneurs in small businesses. A number of these youth were physically handicapped, and still they were inspired and motivated to beat the odds.

This happened not because we preached to them about safety and HIV-prevention, but because we spoke about overall survival, overall living, and about building a life that they would be happy and proud of, in a responsible way. In dealing with the economic and social challenges that the most destitute population was facing, we also indirectly addressed the issue of HIV in their lives. It was about giving hope, and through hope, giving life its due value.

Our message was clear and simple. We told the communities, adults and youths, that there was always a choice and that one could always either walk away or just say "no" to the act of engaging in life-threatening sexual behavior. That approach, which grew from an Integral analysis of the situation, seemed to create change where more traditional communication program messages had consistently been less effective.

INTEGRAL THEORY AS A TOOL FOR AFRICA

Many, if not most, Integral practitioners live in the United States, Europe, Australia, and other Western countries, and not enough of them in Africa. The work and discussion of these practitioners keeps pushing the boundaries of our understanding of the Integral approach across disciplines. There is immense knowledge that circulates within this community, and my attempt has been to find ways to bring the knowledge and insights from this community to Africa. It is in this effort that I was inspired to try and launch Integral Africa, discussed in detail in Chapter Six.

Many in the Integral Community have a deep understanding of the dynamics that govern human systems and our world. The question is how we can bring this knowledge to serve communities that might not always be accessible to the Integral Community or even the international community at large. I feel that these same individuals with such an understanding of dynamics of human systems are able to foresee the way forward toward change and transformation. Yet, they might not always be aware of the importance of the knowledge they hold, and hence they might not feel moved to put this knowledge to use in far-away communities, of which they might not even be aware.

I saw the value of the knowledge they hold, because I know the situation of the communities that I work in. I can appreciate the possibilities that might arise if we could find a way to implement the Integral approach in many of the development programs. In my country, we say that the one who knows the value of a remedy or medicine is the one who has suffered from the illness. In a very similar way, I have experienced development challenges in my own life and in my work in a very tangible way. So, for me, it is very obvious that part of the solution for development challenges lies in our capacity to bring the lessons learned from the application of Integral Theories and its approach.

For me, I found that Ken Wilber is certainly an incredible human being with a most brilliant, intelligent mind and a huge heart. I knew that understanding the Integral approach he offered would allow progress in my own work, and even more so, open potential new opportunities in economic and human development work. I will never forget the day I met Ken Wilber, the founder of the Integral Institute, for the first time in Boulder, Colorado. He is a wonderful man with a heart, he was attentive, and he listened to me as the Universe would have listened.

At the first Integral Transformative Practice (ITP) seminar at the Integral Institute in Boulder, Colorado, I told my friend Terry Patten that I would not leave without speaking with Ken Wilber. At that time, I had no idea that Wilber was such a superstar in the Integral and philosophical community, so I did not fully appreciate the effort it would take Terry to arrange a meeting with him. But finally, Terry managed to set up a time for me to see Wilber, and was kind enough to come with me to the meeting.

Upon arriving at the house (well on time), we saw that the entire front door of the building was taped off due to fresh paint), and we had no way to ring the bell. We also had no way of calling either, because the one we were suppose to call to announce our arrival had mistakenly switched off his phone. So, as Terry would say, we had to get creative. We went around the premises and eventually found an open window of one of the lower-level apartments. Well, in order not to be late for the meeting, we just had to take a deep breath and jump into this apartment, not knowing whether we would find someone, or maybe even worse, be received by a large dog. We were lucky that the apartment was empty and there was also no dog in it. We politely crossed the living room and came out through the door to find ourselves in the hallway of the first floor. When we arrived in Ken Wilber's loft, there was a meeting going on with the entire team of the Integral Institute. Nonetheless, they were all very kind to let us have some time to talk with Mr. Wilber. Given the situation we have in Africa, given how the Integral Approach is revolutionizing and innovating how things are done in all sectors, my main message or question to him was about how could we manage to bring the Integral Approach to the stakeholders, the leaders, and the policy makers on the continent.

What came out of me as I spoke to him sounded like more of a plea for him to get involved more actively in spreading the Integral approach worldwide, since I saw the need for such tools to move forward on many development related matters. In this case, my message was more directly linked to the alarming spread of HIV/AIDS in Africa and the effects it has in our societies and countries. So I asked Ken Wilber how we could change the focus from making predictions and statistics about how many more people would be infected, how many more children would be orphaned, and how many more would die, to predicting how many will be saved, how many will survive, and how many will overcome this catastrophic epidemic.

I remember that, as I spoke to him, a lot of the deep sadness I felt personally and carried with me came out, a lot of the questions I had about the predicament of African nations, and I wanted him to provide me with his views on this. I just remember that he listened to me with a level of deep empathy that I had never seen before, and that is when I realized that he is a man with a huge heart.

Ken Wilber is someone with a serious following. I thought that, if he could do something to bring positive attention to the various issues facing Africa, we might find a way to strengthen civil society in African nations. I asked him literally, "What could you personally contribute to the need for change in Africa? Could you do something and support us in exploring solutions using the Integral approach? Or is the Integral Institute, which you are heading, rather going to remain a mind workout/new age brain gym for those of us pretending to seek enlightenment?" He was very kind and promised to always be ready to help. At the end of the conversation, I did not feel like I had a precise question for him, so I left the meeting telling him that when I had a serious list of questions compiled, I would come back to him. A few years later, I made arrangements to meet Ken Wilber again, but as I flew in from Freetown-Sierra Leone to Denver, Colorado to see him, I learned at the airport upon arrival that he was quite ill and had just been admitted to the hospital. So, I did not get a chance to present to him my consolidated list of questions, or one might also say, my wish of how he, in person, or the Integral Institute in general, could be involved in bringing much needed change to Africa. Even though in my first reaction I was quite concerned about his health condition, and at the same time I was quite disappointed about not meeting him again, I hope to see and sit down with him after this book is published, and gather more ideas and energy for the work lying ahead of us.

I feel that the more Integral theory and its applications are mainstreamed, the more precise our conversations and dialogues could be, and with this precision we could actually face and address some of the challenges at hand. When I refer to the "we" here, I am referring to the "us" of people from all parts of the world, committed to create a reality of greater good in a wider sense and not limited only to Africa. And holistic thinking and Integral approaches will become even more important with the challenges of how to address climate change.

The Integral theories and other related applications and practices all deconstruct and reconstruct the systems in which we exist, unveiling the leverage points and the structures beneath. When I participated in the GTC program in Seattle, I did not gain new knowledge per se, but rather additional perspectives, which have emerged as being even more valuable than I could have ever imagined. What the training offered me was a platform and the time to reflect on what was already within my mind. The seminar further allowed me to make sense of and expand the recognition of my own reality. As a consequence, I was able to see how we each have a role to play in co-creating the reality in which we live.

From my own experience, I believe that Integral thinking offers us the language, instruments, and mind maps needed to actually deconstruct reality at the moment when we enter a field of energy that allows transformation. Since Integral lets us consider the reality of the situation through the four quadrants, through Spiral Dynamics stages, and through other levels of thinking and cognitive models, we have the chance of not only seeing the gross forms, but also to visualize and discern the texture of the reality. The results are similar to science fiction movies, where people look at their computer screen or laptops with 3D-glasses and each aspect of reality is shown in depth and in different dimensions.

For example, from a Spiral Dynamics perspective, when a person is at an altitude in the spiral that is rather ego-centric, the main discourse within that person's internal structures is also at that same ego-centric level. As a consequence, it is nearly impossible for a development program to engage that person, using the language and logic from another altitude, such as a humanist, community-oriented level. Rather, a translation must be offered into discourse that is congruent with the person's ego-centric perspective.

For example, a person who might be in the ego-centric level is preoccupied with power and asserting his/her power over others, regardless of whether that comes through arms, money, or other means. On the other hand, a person who might be in a stage of development which is more interested in humanistic issues and community welfare is most likely more concerned about the greater good for everyone and how each person can find their place in the community. Often such people promote participatory approaches — they want to discuss, they want to "hold hands", they want to make sure that there is consensus on the issues at hand. Most charity and volunteer organizations are associated with this type of value system of a humanistic/community-oriented level of development.

A good example to illustrate this dynamic is the story I told earlier about the girl who was being dragged and beaten by the police for refusing to have unprotected sex with an ill-intentioned client. Had I tried to talk it over with this client and tried to negotiate with him to let the girl go, he would have never listened to me or taken me seriously. Instead, the message that got through to him was one that portrayed me with a power that he felt challenged by: my willingness to go to the press with the hypothetical footage of the incident, and my hypothetical martial arts practice, both of which had potential consequences that he was worried about. As ego-centric as he was, this was the only way of communication that allowed me to get through to him. It was necessary for me to "show teeth" and to demarcate the power that I held, it was simply about the perception that the man/client had to realize when being confronted with me. And that was all that mattered. If this man thought that I should not be challenged, and if he could perceive the danger that I presented, then he would back off. But how could I know that he was ego-centric? The way he behaved was simply completely ego-centric: he was using his money, his connections, and his physical size to coerce the helpless girl into unprotected sex.

It is through Integral's holistic and comprehensive lens that we can see with our human eyes that which the divine heart creates — miracles for the taking. My experience with GTC has led me to think that, if more people in Africa had access to this type of program, they too would gain multiple lenses and further capacity to understand our paradigms. I strongly believe that this type of perspective would have the potential to initiate an organic harmonization of efforts among development practitioners in Africa. It is the emergence of such a group of individuals that would potentially create the critical mass of change agents needed to move African nations and their people forward.

OVERLAP WITH AFRICAN WISDOM

Interestingly, the four quadrant Integral map is not very different from how I have witnessed elders of African communities thinking. When our elders address a situation, they always consider the personal or individual aspects of the reality, and at the same time they also look at how the problem translates for the collective, just as Wilber suggests. Our elders look at the reality within, which is the subjective side of the world, while simultaneously considering the external and tangible aspects of reality. It is in using such a kaleidoscope that the elders were able to find resolutions to conflict, solutions to crisis and guidance for the future.

In 1993, my grandmother, Almazesha, was arrested in Ethiopia, along with over 2000 men and women, as they were all members of the All Amhara People Party (AAPP). My grandmother was the founder of this organization and had established the party in response to the ethnic- and religion-based attacks that had started taking place throughout the country, targeting Christians of Amhara ethnicity, during that time. Initially, Almazesha had wanted to call the party the "All Ethiopian People Party," but she was told that the party had to reflect an ethnic group in its name. So, against her will, and just for the sake of establishing the party, she complied with the rules and ended up calling the party AAPP, instead of allowing the name to encompass the nation. The party decided to appoint as their leader one of Ethiopia's most renowned surgeons, Professor Asrat. Eventually, Professor Asrat was arrested and detained. On the occasion of one of his court hearings, the party organized a peaceful protest (more of a gathering) outside the courtroom. At the end of the court hearing, soldiers informed my grandmother that there was unrest outside, and it was best to leave through the rear door of the courtroom, for her personal safety. She followed instructions, only to find herself facing a line of military trucks. I learned later from people who were present at that time, that the soldiers asked Almazesha to jump on the truck first. While doing so, they tried to rush her and they also pushed her around.

A man who was part of the police force at the time, and who later worked with me, and was present at the scene, told me what he saw. He said: "Our mother [Almazesha] just turned to the soldier and said to him—'My son, don't push me, after all, I could be your mother, if not your grandmother. Give me time to climb up.'" This policeman went on to explain that despite the fact that my grandmother was small in height and was not very healthy, she just jumped up on the truck in a way that would surprise anyone watching. She went in the truck peacefully without aggravating the soldiers and without any anger or resistance.

Following that, the soldiers just rushed more people into the truck, pushing and shoving them in. A man ended up being pushed onto my grandmother. Later on, she explained to me that the man was terribly stressed because he did not want to crush her. He suspended himself over Almazesha throughout the ride to their first detention place, apologizing endlessly as his sweat trickled onto her a drop at a time. She told him not to worry and tried to comfort him.

My grandmother remained detained for close to a month, and I went to see her soon after her release. She told me that soldiers are like remotely controlled machines, whose behavior is only a reflection of their superiors and the orders they have received. She told me that we therefore should not blame a soldier for doing his job, remembering that they are our sons as well and a part of our society. With this example, she taught me that we must understand that only by remaining calm and realizing the other's perspective, can we make sure that they have some clarity about our own situation. Guns are cursed, and if you aggravate someone with a gun, you don't really leave him room to think — he will just react with pulling the trigger.

Then she spoke of the process of climbing on the truck. She reminisced about her youth and smiled and said to me, "They don't know that I used to ride my horse bareback and that I am a sharp sniper myself." In fact, she was trained by her grandmother, around the time Ethiopia was at war with Italy. "They are trying to do the best they can, these soldiers. They are only carrying out their orders."

And then she smiled and spoke of the man who was pushed onto her. "The poor man was so distressed. He was so polite and gentle, at the same time that it was so difficult for him to be in that situation. I tried to help him and told him that I am a mother of many and that he too could be my son. He should not worry, I told him, but by the time we arrived at Sendafa[42] *his arms must have been in bad shape."*

In the situation above, my grandmother held no grudge or angst toward the soldiers. In fact, she understood that any resistance from her side or aggravation would lead the soldiers to lose their calm. Her ability to deeply understand what was happening on the surface and how that related to the deeper issues, such as the government's attitude toward independent parties, as well as the new political direction of dividing the country along ethnic lines, this perspective is what allowed her to remain calm. The same understanding also allowed her to bring out the compassion she had towards others, almost as in the Biblical sense, which teaches us to love our neighbors, no matter what. Later on, I heard from many who were at this scene, that, in fact, the soldiers ended up having a lot of respect and compassion towards Almazesha.

In that tense, dramatic and dangerous moment, Almazesha automatically held both the individual level (her assets, the soldiers as individual sons and fathers) and the collective level (the societal structures of governmental leadership, creating the police state) mentality. She considered both the internal (keeping her own calm) and the external (keeping the soldiers calm) dimensions of the situation she found herself in.

To me, the wonderful thing about the Integral approach is the fact that it allows us to deconstruct and dissect reality so that we are able to speak of the bottom line; something which our wise elders do inherently and almost naturally. Instead of speaking of that wisdom intuitively and without empirical foundation, the Integral thinking offers a kind of theoretical foundation for achieving a better understanding and for better analyzing a problem from various angles.

I am not saying that Integral theory and its application are the only

[42] Sendafa is a community outside Addis Ababa. It is also a place where they were detained in the Police Training College.

answer to the issue of development in Africa, but rather that as far as the work in Africa is concerned, the combination of traditional local African approaches with the Integral approach, can bring us a deeper understanding of complex realities, which in itself could open the way for innovative and sustainable development initiatives. I really believe that Integral approaches have the potential to generate initiatives that would reflect such recognition of knowledge in the tools and instruments developed to bring transformation in the human systems of developing countries.

Therefore this book is also speaking out to the Integral community, including the Integral Institute, to join hands and make the benefits of the Integral approach accessible to Africa. Through this book, I hope to ask this community: "What will it take to bring your attention to applying the genius of Integral to economic and human development in places where it is direly needed?" I would like to see the Integral conversation be more than a mind exercise for a modest number of intellectuals, out of reach of most communities in development countries. It would be such a missed opportunity to not find a practical way to share this approach with development practitioners across the African continent. Both the advances made in the applications of the theory and the developments in deepening the theory itself should find a way to be transferred from the "developed" parts of the world into developing countries.

If we explore the theory and discuss its applications from an African perspective in a systematic and persistent way, the true practical benefits of this theoretical construction could emerge. Through collaborative efforts and a cross-cultural exchange, we could adapt, contextualize, and implement well-designed programs that could potentially change the lives of thousands, if not millions of people. This may not be the only answer to the issues challenging African development, but the Integral approach, applied wisely and in combination with inherent African wisdom, could actually boost the efforts underway by the various development partners right now.

A great example of the application of the Integral approach to a development issue is the work done by UNDP in the context of HIV/AIDS. I was really fortunate to be working with UNDP at the time the programs were launched in Addis Ababa. The basis for the initiative was to make all constituencies and stakeholders understand the underlying dynamics and balances between the internal and external realities, as well as between the individual and the collective dimension. Understanding these dimensions allowed us to check whether the individual values and attitudes about HIV/AIDS were in line with the individual external behaviors, and whether this individual alignment was also coherent with the collective's culture and external structures, within the context of the societal systems. Applying the Integral approach for the first time in the African context was a great eye-opener for many of us. We realized that the different components of the HIV/AIDS pandemic were often not coherent, and in the discordance, we found the leverage points to establish programs that would yield change and transformation.

Even though people were concerned about contracting the HIV virus, it was apparent that many men engaged in sex with multiple partners, because the underlying culture celebrated the macho-type of man with many partners, as opposed to a man in a monogamous relationship. In the same vein, even though there were many campaigns for voluntary testing, the campaigns could not deliver results, because the testing centers were either not client-friendly or were not as confidential as the public and the Ethiopian society wanted them to be. Identifying such discrepancies and interrelationships is quite fast and straightforward using the Integral mapping approach, and, once the core issues and inter-linkages are identified, solutions can be implemented.

When we speak of Integral theory, it must be clear that we are only talking of a map, a tool, a complex instrument to work with human systems. But, it is the use of the Integral approach, in combination with African ways of thinking, that can actually bring about substantial and durable changes. Integral theory offers us such a map, through which we can navigate by using our own wisdom and knowledge of the world and circumstances we find ourselves working in. It is at the same time a lens that allows its user to look at the world from a distant and yet close perspective, and derive results from this unique viewpoint.

CHAPTER FIVE

Change Begins Within: The Integral Monster In Me

"African development calls for innovative, bold, and forceful solutions to address our development problems"

–K.Y. Amoako

The following is an excerpt from Dr. K.Y. Amoako's[43] address at the Africa Renaissance Institute in Pretoria, South Africa on October 11, 1999.

"...This renaissance is not a mirage. Indeed, the groundwork for change has been partly laid. There is a wide recognition of the problems we face, and a greater consensus within Africa on the overall direction for the future. As a result of the new thinking, recent years have seen tangible progress made by many countries in reforming their economies, and in putting in place the requisite enabling environment to bring about equitable growth and poverty reduction. This has resulted in very encouraging growth rates over the last five years — Africa's best economic performance since the late 1970s.

Yet these accomplishments cannot be assumed to mean that the aggregate African economy has crossed the critical threshold to self-sustaining poverty

[43] Kingsley Y. Amoako (b. 1944 Accra) is a Ghanian-born international civil servant who led the United Nations Economic Commission for Africa (UNECA) in 1995-2005 at the rank of UN Under-Secretary-General. He played a key role in the design of the New Partnership for Africa's Development (NEPAD) and created several new forums allowing African policy makers to engage in productive dialogue, including the African Development Forum, which has been a dynamic force for ICT in Africa, gender equality, and for regional integration. He led the ECA in developing indicators to track Africa's economic performance, promoted the need for donor policy coherence in providing concrete improvements in the delivery of aid, and backstopped and supported African negotiations in international trade. (http://en.wikipedia.org/wiki/K._Y._Amoako)

reduction. To make our vision a reality, we need to recognize that poverty is multidimensional, and that its reduction is a long-term effort requiring sustained capacities in the delivery of essential social services. Macroeconomic stability and structural reforms are also essential to move to a higher path of sustained growth. Broad-based participation of civil society and strengthened governance, including improved budgetary management and public accountability, are equally important to the implementation of an effective anti-poverty strategy.

Harnessing our storehouse of intellectual talent and expertise on the continent or in the Diaspora, is critical to meeting these challenges. President Mbeki put it eloquently when he said at Midrand in August 1998 that 'Africa's renewal demands that her intelligentsia must immerse itself in the titanic and all-round struggle to end poverty, disease, and backwardness.'

So what strategies should we employ to enhance the role of research in promoting African development? What if we were to create a network of networks, which links regional research institutions and universities as a means of strengthening quality, cost-effectiveness, and inter-disciplinary knowledge, through broad information sharing between knowledge-producing centers? What if we set out strategies to strengthen mechanisms through which analytical work from African research networks and universities impacts on public policy decisions and activities of civil society? And what if we could simultaneously identify strategic studies needed to address urgent development issues?[44]

For several years, this statement of needing "bold, innovative, and forceful economic solutions" was one of the cornerstones of my argument for a holistic approach to development. But, over time, I came to realize that the word "forceful" may not be appropriate. Integral theory and Integral approaches encourage us to focus also on the interior, individual aspects of problems at hand.

Creating change might not be about force, but rather about depth and authenticity in our interventions. It is not about force, but about turning to "within" to find the solutions instead of keeping our binoculars trained on far horizons. The solution is also inside, and it is those inner solutions that will allow us to devise durable and "organic" means to overcome our

[44] http://www.africaaction.org/docs99/eca9910.htm

multifold challenges.

In addition, from a Spiral Dynamics perspective, the dominant mode of discourse in today's world is one that may be at the ego-centric level. Those offering solutions come from a post-modern worldview, wanting to do good but held back by their inability to identify with their own shadows. In order for change to be successful, we must initiate a conversation between these two disparate groups. And the communication between these positions will rely on the ability of change agents to work through their own interiority, their own shadow sides, so that they are no longer held back from contributing to change. This chapter therefore focuses on the change within, as a means of facilitating change in the world.

COPING WITH COMPLEXITY, FRUSTRATION, AND PAIN

The first man I met living with full-blown AIDS in Ethiopia, was Hailu. He was about 45 or 50, and he looked physically terrible. His face was scarred, his body was frail, his skin was peeling, his eyes stared out of their sockets and he had a bad smell resulting from unattended sores and lack of regular facilities to wash himself or his clothes. In his eyes, one could see the pain he was going through, the tough life he faced, the experience he had with the illness, and the pain of rejection he was constantly confronted with. In his eyes one could also see his resilience and his surrender to what he was confronted with.

I learned that Hailu had been a driver for one of the international NGOs, and that upon becoming ill, he was given a financial settlement before getting fired. I heard he was from an area called Lasta (near Lalibella, in Northern Ethiopia). He had a wife and children, but decided not to go back to them to spare them the shame and the burden of caring for him. He preferred, rather, to carry the whole burden himself.

One day he came to talk to me in my office. I had put the word out that I wanted to get in touch with a person living with HIV to come teach, discuss, and share experiences about the virus on all levels with the women in our program — about personal protection, testing, caring and supporting for AIDS patients, and also about being aware of discrimination. Maybe Hailu came to my office following this call; maybe it was for another reason. I am not sure.

We had a long conversation where he explained to me that he had been thrown out of the house he had rented. He told me that for some time he had been sleeping on the street. In my head, I kept thinking of the spare room I had in my house. I kept vacillating between telling him to come with me and calling my husband first to involve him in the decision of whether to open our home to this total stranger. I was newly married and was very mindful of not just running my own show. So, I called Matthias quickly, and to my most pleasant surprise, he agreed with me and said I should take Hailu home with me. So, Hailu and I went home together.

The better part of the fiasco was still to come. Once I reached home and announced to my staff that Hailu would be living with us, and asked them to support him to the best of their capacity, my cook resigned and the caretaker/guard said that he would not stay unless "this man" goes.

Initially, I did not understand their harsh reaction. If you know that HIV is only transmissible through body fluids, how can you be afraid of a person living with HIV? I thought, what is the use of fasting on Wednesdays and Fridays and for weeks on end for various holidays, as practiced according to Ethiopian-Orthodox tradition, or of praying to God when we can't even go beyond our own egoist fear to care for another? I thought, what makes us Christians, and when does this Christianity translate into action for the needy? In a nutshell, I was sad, and at the same time furious. The cook left our house. The caretaker/guard stayed on. I suppose he stayed on from guilt, as he had been referred to me by my grandmother to take care of me and my home. I suspect he did not want to let her down.

So, Hailu stayed with us for about a month. We gave him one of the rooms in the service quarters with a proper toilet and shower. His room was comfortable with proper furniture and lots of light. Hailu was comfortable. Since the cook had left, I was getting food sent from either my parents' house (they lived across the street) or from Laïbet, my grandmother's place. At times we ate together and shared meals with Hailu, discussing and learning more about what he was going through. Things were ok. But eventually, he felt the pressure from the community around us and decided to leave to find a place to live on his own. I helped him rent a small place and arranged that some of the furniture I had was delivered to his new place

This time we spent with Hailu was my first experience in witnessing the power of discrimination and how, in the face of fear — often a result of lack of knowledge and compassion as well as ignorance — people change dramatically and unexpectedly.

This little episode was a snippet of what lay ahead in the coming years for entire nations and the African continent, which has been hardest hit by the HIV/AIDS pandemic. We speak of HIV and talk of prevention. We speak of the care for AIDS patients, and yet at the time, it seems that people would have been more comfortable if those with AIDS would just go away. In a sense, through those living with HIV or AIDS, it seems that we witness our own fears and shadows related to our impermanence in this world. It is as though when we see someone with HIV we are reminded of death, of our own inevitable death, which some of us might want to push away as far as possible. As it is, anyone who was told they had a terminal illness, that is, contracting HIV, at that time it meant the end of their life. Of course, things are different now and with the right lifestyle and medication, anyone with HIV can continue to have a healthy and productive life. Is the discrimination anchored in our own incapacity to accept our mortality? Or, rather, is it realizing the possibility that we could lose all we have by one sex act?

After one of the GTC seminars, the wonderful woman who sponsored my participation in GTC invited me to dinner. She invited me in order to have a chance to talk in person, to meet and discuss my plans with Integral Africa (see Chapter 6). We went to a fancy restaurant, and eventually the conversation focused on the issue of Integral Africa. As I described to her the hopes and aspirations I had, I was filled with tears — desert tears that never fall, but remain suspended on the doorstep of the soul. The woman looked at me with such compassion, gazed deeply into my eyes, and said to me: "You cry because you're pregnant with dreams and ideas. You are just full of hopes and you are waiting for ways to bring them to the world."

And indeed, I felt all these emotions, because I held hope for my people, for my country and for all other communities around the continent, and for Africa as a whole. I still do believe a prosperous and healthy Africa is yet to emerge. Inside of me lived the hope that tomorrow would be better than today, and I thought I had a hunch about how to help make all the necessary changes happen. The tears were an expression of both the genuineness of the vision, and of the truth of the frustration of holding such a vision and of knowing that as a finite human constrained in my flesh, it would take an army of willing men and women to bring such a vision to fruition.

Emotions fly high when we talk about things which we hold deeply in our hearts and which we hope to grow into a living being for all to see and experience. It is the ups and downs, following the initial conception of the vision, that leave wrinkles on the heart and that tire the soul. At the same time, it is also the same ups and downs of the path that builds endurance, while making us wiser, stronger, and kinder. Those of us who want to bring change must learn to cope with the complexity, frustration, and pain, which are inevitable parts of such an endeavor.

SWALLOWING THE RED PILL AND RELEASING THE SHADOW SIDE

In the movie, *Matrix*, Neo had a choice between the blue pill of blissful ignorance and the red pill of painful truth. With the blue pill, it would all end there; with the red pill, Neo would gain a way to actually do something about the situation. As spirit incarnates in flesh, we have the option to choose whether we take the blue or red pill; then we pray for serenity, courage, and wisdom to bear and be part of the subsequent unfolding of the choices we make.

What is there to know and learn to be best prepared for understanding the complexities at hand? There is everything to learn and everything to question and touch — touching the good and the scary, experiencing love and knowing betrayal. You must experience the pain of crying in order to fully appreciate the blessings of laughter. And you must have loved and hated, to understand the dynamics of relationship, the texture of love and the texture of rejection or loss. In essence, it is the extremes, or the challenges of life one has to personally experience, in order to appreciate the blessings of life. Wealth and poverty, health and illness—it is all one and the same, just different axes of that which we call life. In essence, life is all there is and it is eternal. When we forget that life is eternal we are subjected to our egos. We are reduced to the flesh.

I have always chosen the red pill. In fact, my earliest memory of choosing this path of learning and knowledge goes back to my first day in preschool.

Until that day, I had spent my days mainly in the compound of my grandparents' house. Until that day, as the first grandchild and the only baby around, I can say that I had more attention than I could handle. I just remember playing and playing and playing with everyone. Then, I was told I would go to school and I was prepared for it. My uncles and aunts taught me how to write my name and taught me the alphabet. I was very proud to know all this and to be able to count.

On the first day of school, I must have been escorted by no less than eight uncles, aunts, cousins, etc. They took me to my classroom and left me there. I was very enthusiastic to see all the other children. During break time, I rushed out to play with the children. But, sadly, each little group that I went to play with told me, in one way or another, that they did not want to play with me and I should go away. One group of little girls told me that I could not play with them because I did not have pigtails (hair parted in two and tied with a ribbon). Well, I did not have pigtails because I did not have much hair—I had proper nappy hair with a hairline that was far, far, very far back.

I remember clearly a moment of choice: I knew I could either spend the rest of my days running after the other children to get them to play with me, or I could have my own way and play on own. I chose the latter. Soon, I had a flock of invisible friends with whom I played. I think the conviction with which I played struck the others. Eventually, a few days later, they came asking if they could play with "us" (me and my invisible friends). I told them they could, and that was the end of the story.

Looking back now, I know that what happened, in fact, was that I was able, only God knows why and how given my age at the time, to set my own boundaries—to take the rejection and make it into my starting line. And if there were no real human friends to play with, I had no problem inventing some.

This attitude of going full force into life, taking and facing whatever challenge came my way very consciously and turning that into a new start, never changed in me. As I did in preschool, I still do today. As the years passed, I have always been willing to learn whatever was needed for me to understand my world, which centered around Africa. I have been always willing to come full on and learn, in order to further develop my capacity to live fully and bring deeper consciousness for the blessings of life. I have always been open to experience new challenges, and consequently, I was and I am still willing to swallow the red pill of life, in order to make me prepared also for the shadow sides of life. Choosing this path has been like looking into the reflections of my features on a little pond, and being yanked into the water by an unexpected force—a loving and a challenging one. But a force nonetheless that has dragged me through the caves, the depths of oceans, and the heights of skies. A few years down the road on this intense journey, I believe I see some light. My life, as for everybody, has been a very peculiar journey, one that undoubtedly will still hold plenty of surprises and challenges, for which I have to be prepared, in order to take this challenge.

What I have learned is that for any dream to take root in the manifest world, the dreamer and carrier of these dreams must come free of baggage, free of our own self-ness, free of our egos, and free of toxicity. It is almost like flying with a big balloon, which only takes off and rises into the skies once you drop the ballast down to the earth. It is when we travel without baggage that we reach our destination faster. It is when we travel with lightheartedness about our being that we benefit from a flexible heart and mind, and it is when we travel without toxicity that we can benefit from empowering energy to fuel us more smoothly throughout the journey of life.

Sometimes it takes our sharing the not-so-pretty personal experiences, the not-so-successful aspects of our work and of ourselves, in order to delve to a deeper space of existence. From this deeper space we can speak from authenticity, standing at the source and looking out to the lost horizons, which we hope to recreate.

So, this book tells in a way my story and presents my dreams. Dreams that I entertain but that are also not different than dreams many Africans have for this continent. It is a process of self-reflection in order to better understand my personal self in its internal and external dimensions, from an individual and a collective perspective, and be better prepared for the coming decades of my life.

We as individuals and we as Africans must face our shadows to move forward. Part of what gives way to our vulnerability might be our incompetence, this incompetence or unwillingness to raise our sleeves and get the work done. Instead, many of us Africans rather talk and talk and talk about potentials, while failing to invest ourselves in making our visions become reality. So, we need to face our shadows and bring them to the light in order to make the necessary next steps towards progress and development. It is our ability to face, accept, and integrate our shadows to our being that allows us to emerge in our fullness and allows us to move away from the perpetual stagnation we are trapped in.

Part of this incompetence is a result of the existing systems. For example, in gender-related work or in epidemics such as HIV, professional preparedness and capacity are not necessarily required. It is enough to be a woman to work on gender, as much as it seems to be enough to be sexually active to work on HIV. Public awareness and involvement has been limited by the messages presented in the news, which is mostly the news that is "convenient," but might not always give us the inconvenient truth, since many TV channels are still fully state controlled.

For example, during the time I worked with MSF on the project for the women of the red light district, there was a lot of judgment passed on the women. Sometimes, when I held gatherings or meetings with our women participants, I could hear comments such as: "She's brought her whores again," or "I can't believe there is a project for such women," or "Don't bring such women here!" — the list is long. What I did not understand then, and what I found so hurtful at the time, was how others perceived these women. Others, meaning some colleagues and some of the people in our office, the various authorities we had to deal with, and even the people that we rented the meeting rooms from. They saw these women merely as money-oriented and vicious prostitutes, and, at times, even as whores with no rights. They saw them as undeserving and also as women who brought shame to our society.

The problem was that the people, who made such harsh comments, were not even willing to recognize the prostitute that existed within them. Many of us tend to hide in our righteousness, our perceived uprightness, our denial that we, too, could be in a situation of prostitution. Prostitution is in fact not only the sale of sex, but also the trading, bending, and violating of our own principles in order to gain something. So, when we engage in false friendships or false associations in order to gain something out of that association or friendship, this is equally some form of prostitution in some way. When we turn our eyes away from injustices or discrimination, or remain silent when we see unfair treatment around us, this is also prostitution to a certain extent, because we are turning a blind eye and silencing our principles so that we can remain in our status quo. So, prostitution cannot be just reduced and simplified to the trade of sex. If we were willing to realize this, and could also conceive that in extreme situations, such as war, hunger, and so on, we too might engage in selling our bodies, maybe then it would be possible to relate to the women of the red light district without being burdened by biases, prejudices, and judgment.

When we reflect on our shadows and welcome them into the light, we will be able to be counted and be present in all of our greatness, and also be able to make room for our weaknesses. In such a situation, we are empowered to develop, to create in place a positive and fertile ground for change and growth.

Vulnerability arises when someone touches a blind spot; it is scary when light comes to the shadow, and sometimes the pain is too much. For example, we condemn, rightfully, the 1994 genocide in Rwanda, the on-going tragic and bloody conflict in Darfur, and such brutal wars. However, we fail to realize that given the circumstances, many so called normal people can be drawn or led into participating in such atrocities. Anytime there is strain, pain, and unease within a human being or a community, it is easy for situations to escalate. Anytime we cannot forgive ourselves we are not able to forgive others. We may not find in ourselves a big enough heart to understand the pain that perpetrators often carry deep inside themselves. Our inability to move beyond what is apparent at the surface and reach a level of understanding how *"other-ing"* another human being or another community can lead to the greatest atrocities.

In 2003 in Addis Ababa, I met a woman from Rwanda, Berthilde Gahongayire, who had come to participate in an HIV/AIDS Regional Conference I had organized as part of my assignment with the UNDP-SURF. It was Sunday when we met. She had just arrived and we had lunch together. After a while, I told her that I would not be able to stay and that I would be leaving, because every Sunday all my family meets at my grandmother's house to just be together. She seemed to go off in her thoughts for a while, and then she said to me: "I also used to do that with my family before the genocide, but now I have lost eight brothers and sisters. Such family gatherings are now only alive in my memory." I was stunned and did not know what to think or even how to process this information.

Then she said to me, "But we have to re-build our lives, we have to forgive and continue our lives", which made me even more stunned. I just could not even imagine forgiving, let alone rebuilding together.

It is difficult for most people to forgive and rebuild a community after such traumatic and tragic events, because we are unable to see the perpetrators as part of us. But how many times have we been in a space where we turn other individuals into objects of hatred, into "others," into something that is not part of the "us?" And, how far would we go (subject to the context of course) to get rid of these human beings that we label as "others?" Whether it is making a distinction of "us" against "them" based on skin color, ethnicity, religious backgrounds, or even sexual inclinations, as is often seen between hetero and homosexual people — it is all about this "other-ing" that is a dangerous path for humanity.

Today, Rwanda is a new country. With the leadership of President Kagame, the country is going through a re-branding exercise, whereby it seems to emerge as one unified country with one people, whereby communities are empowered to move on and to build their country, and not dwell on or be stopped by what took place in the past.

"We will not forget the genocide," President Kagame responded to questions about 1994 and Rwanda's image, "but we will not be defined by it."[45]

[45] http://www.africanloft.com/re-branding-nigeria-lessions-from-rwanda/

So, the question becomes: what else are we beyond the image and perceptions that we hold of ourselves or that others hold for us? Are we able to embrace both our strengths and weaknesses and see the opportunity that an integrated view of the situation and reality offers us?

Accepting our weakness and embracing the weakness we have is a fertile ground to transform the situation. For example, in Sierra Leone one of the key issues for people living here is access to the airport; we have to travel across a huge River Estuary of more than 20 kilometers in order to reach the airport. The option to drive by car instead can take up to five hours. Other alternatives include the utilization of a helicopter service, taking the ferry, or using a speedboat to reach the airport on the other side of the river mouth. None of the alternatives are perfect, and many travelers experience serious frustration about these circumstances, when traveling to Sierra Leone.

During a discussion with a government official, I asked him if it would be possible to bank on this need to cross the river and create an entertainment cruise catering solely to passengers as well as to members of the community who want to have a short break on a short cruise. Would it be conceivable and realistic to use the weakness of the current limited access to the airport, to bring in a product that could support the branding of the country as a viable tourist destination?

In a comparable way, when we speak of the red light districts, many of us shrivel up when we come in contact with a woman selling her body. Prostitution is not acceptable in the Ethiopian society, because selling sex is often seen as a taboo. Yet we fail to realize that a lot of these young girls sell their bodies for pure survival reasons. As such, the sex they have with their clients feeds their families. In contrast to this, men are willing buyers of this product or service, because we want to get something which we do not get otherwise in our lives. Our judgmental view of African sex workers slightly changes when we think of the time we bypassed our principles in order to get something we desired. So are we in fact prostituting ourselves? As a consequence, should prostitution remain limited to the exchange of sex for money, or shall we rather be honest with ourselves and accept that humans tend to exchange or bend our principles to attain something that is otherwise unattainable? If a woman sleeps with a man to get a job, that might be considered close to prostitution, but if she makes a dinner and wines and dines a man so that her husband gets the job or the promotion, then it is called lobbying and public relations.

Again, it is what remains hidden in our shadows and tucked away in the dark that comes to sabotage our own world. When such shadow attributes are brought forth to the light our ego could flare up and act like a puff-adder disturbed in its sleep – defensive and aggressive. Learning to use the shadow and the light is one of the necessary paths to move towards forgiveness, towards healing, and eventually towards transformation and change.

As a spoiled and pampered child tends to cry about not getting its way, most Africans also tend to shout, fuss, and whine about every economic, political, or social challenge we face, and of course, we perpetually continue to blame the "white man" for all our problems. But does this "white man" really still exists? Or are we in a state where we only project the "white man," which is already within all of us? It is true the "white man" exploited our resources for centuries, but we are not willing to realize that today, our own people, the elite of Africa, have become collaborators in this game and often engage in comparable exploitation of the natural resources, participating in illegal land selling and land grabbing as well as allowing conspicuous business to take place at the detriment of local communities and the environment.

At the TED[46] *conference in Arusha, Tanzania, the Irish campaigner and musician, Bono, made a presentation about his work in Africa. He spoke of the value of aid and compared Africa with where Ireland used to be in the past, while making the point that it is only through aid that Ireland got on its feet. In the same way, Bono was suggesting that Africa, too, can benefit from aid. One man from the audience stood up to make a comment and blasted Bono saying that Africa needs no aid and that the only way forward was trade. The man in the audience was not willing to discuss the issue, however,*

[46] www.ted.com – TED Conferences are annual conferences that bring together people from all parts of the world and from all kinds of professions to discuss ideas and concepts for humanity. In 2007, the TED Arusha conference was the first TED Conference in Africa.

and this exasperated Bono who eventually said that part of the problem is that "Africans can get touchy."

And Bono was right, Africans do get easily touchy, and we are touchy. We are touchy because most of us continue to live in a paradigm of scarcity instead of living in a paradigm of abundance. We remain in a space of denial about what is so in the reality. So, there is never enough, it's always someone else's fault, and we are never responsible. In meditation and contemplative practices, there comes a time when one realizes that such touchy-ness comes from ego. The ego acts up when it feels threatened.[47] We only get touchy and flare up when our wounds are exposed, but we continue to nurse our wounds and deny the healing process, because it is easier to continue nursing the wounds than to take steps to actually heal them. We Africans have been wounded through history – no one can contest that. The resources of our countries and communities were exploited like no other part of the world; our brothers and sisters, forefathers and ancestors were sold into slavery, and millions perished in the most inhumane ways. All that is true, and it is time to take steps to remain cognizant of history and the scars it has left on our faces, while, at the same time, we must start living in the present moment in order to have a chance to create a different future, something other than a reenactment of the past.

Despite all the trauma that the people of the African continent have been subjected to from all the various historical incidents and events, what is it that prevents us from overcoming these traumas and building our countries and communities as people on other continents did? For example, what are we willing to do about children orphaned by AIDS? We may express our frustrations about the issue, but how many of us have taken the initiative to care for even one child orphaned by AIDS? Instead of thinking of what we can personally do on our own scale, we rather wait for someone else or an organization to take the lead. There are enough well-to-do Africans who could financially afford to provide care for one child, but how many really do this? Our own lack of self-initiative is part of the shadow that we must recognize, accept, and deal with. The same goes for many other is-

[47] Eckhart Tolle, *New Earth* (Penguin Group, 2005).

sues, whether it is the issue of health care, education, environment, or infrastructure, just to name a few. How many of us are willing to do something about it, and how many just wait for the government or some aid agency to take on the work? It is time to face our shadows so we can be empowered through that understanding, and to move forward in creating change.

HARNESSING THE PAIN BODY: EMBRACING PAIN AND BLISS

As African elders believe, words have their own energies; in a word of contradiction, only contradiction can emerge in action. For positive action to come out of a word of contradiction at all, it requires great pain and labor. I know this, as I look into myself and try to understand why I wanted to work in an "NGO" in the first place. What was it in my being that felt attracted to that idea? Was my desire purely to help, or were there some hidden motives that related to shadows of the Savior Syndrome? Did I need to save myself from my own life and my own agony? Did I even know there was agony?

It took some time for me to realize that there was in fact pain and agony in my own being, the same as the agony we carry by being human and living in this world. I was angry with society, angry that we could not do better, angry that we did not want to treat these destitute people as we would want our own loved ones to be treated. I could feel my throat coiling up in knots. I could not stop my usual tears from flowing. I could not stop wanting to quit and leave for good for a place where the air is fresher.

Eckhart Tolle speaks of the Pain Body, the body that has inherited all of the suffering of humanity in time across the past and the future. He speaks of an inter-relationship between the ego self and the pain body, and how together they work in collaboration to make us believe that they hold the meaning of life. Yet, when led by the ego and when unable to see the pain body in action, we remain prisoners of our minds, and live, trapped in our bodies, without ever tapping into our divine being, which is Spirit.[48]

Some pain is full of texture, other pain comes with grooves. It comes from somewhere so deep that we might not even know where to look for;

[48] Eckhart Tolle, *New Earth* (Penguin Group, 2005).

it is like trying to find the source of the Nile. Where does this great river find its source? Where does our great flow of life find its source and where does it acquire all its alluvials? My grandmother tells me that someone who has not experienced pain cannot feel for others. She tells me that someone who has not known, who has not been oiled and anointed by life, who has not been tested and challenged might remain unripe, unless of course the gift of understanding is graced by living experience. I was not sure where to look to make sense of the pain and frustration I sometimes face. I did not find a direction to aim for, as I threw my line in the water, hoping to fish out a sense of relief and some knowing that an answer was on its way. I wanted to talk to God in person, maybe just for a moment, to hear from the source what all this was about, and most pressingly: why? Why all this?

In Caroline Myss' work about our sacred contracts, she argues that we all have agreed to come into this world with a specific contract, and that we come with helpers to allow us to fulfill these contracts. As our spirit descends to this world, it must compress itself to fit into this world, and in that process, it fragments itself like crystals shattering into small pieces. Where the pieces land, we do not know at first, but as we go through life, we start collecting the pieces here and there through experiences we gain, through encounters we make, through people we meet, and through the journey of life in general. And with each piece, we find the many parts of ourselves that must be reintegrated to our being in order to reach wholeness, in order to reach a state of completeness and peace.[49]

My work with the women in the red light districts of Addis Ababa was a way to relate to that part of me that is so destitute, so broken, and so ostracized by society. It was also a way of acknowledging the existence of choice and the fact that, whatever circumstance we are in, we always have a choice to turn the wheels. I say this now, but it took me close to a decade to come to this realization, and to stop making excuses and also learn to categorically refuse to accept any further justifications and reasons for myself to fall short of all that I am. And, given the state of reality in many African countries, I wish that many others, especially young people with a great future and po-

[49] Caroline Myss, *Sacred Contracts: Awakening your Divine Potential* (Sounds True, 2001).

tential, will do the same. Yes indeed, average African nations are poor from a Western point of view, but it is up to us, each man and woman that cares to be counted, to change this pattern for tomorrow's generations.

One of the major personal challenges for each one of us is to see the opportunities for change and to find the inner peace and balance to realize the potential that lies in this very unique continent. We must face the ephemeral obstacles between us and reach a common ground to translate these potential into real and sustainable development. It is absolutely necessary to find this peace and confidence in the feeling that our hands are tied in moving forward with African development, a feeling that has come over me countless times in my life.

One day, I had to catch a flight to Istanbul and my connection was through Casablanca and Royal Air Maroc. When I arrived at the Lungi International Airport of Freetown at about 3:00AM to take the flight due to depart at around 5:00AM, the lights at the airport were still off and the staff was either not there or sleeping on the floor. The Royal Air Maroc plane we were supposed to take was due to arrive in less than an hour, and the airport was literally total blackout. I looked at the manager of Royal Air Maroc, and we both just shook our heads. This was a moment beyond stress, a moment where greater letting go has to take over in order not to burst some cells in our brains. How could the airport not be ready when an international flight was due to arrive within an hour?

One of the main challenges for me was to be able to harness the revolt I felt inside, in a way that would be constructive, as opposed to just turning me into an "unpredictable loose cannon," as many might have labeled me during that time. But anger alone is not productive in creating change, unless we use the energy and turn it around to bring a positive impact and a different result. Yet such a maneuver is not always easy. It takes reflection. It takes patience and it also takes compassion. It takes resources and also a firm stand to say "no" to what is about to unfold, and a commitment to steer the situation to another more positive and humane direction.

Sadness and happiness are interwoven; unless we cry, we cannot possibly laugh. Marianne Williamson[50] says that unless we can understand and witness crucifixion, we cannot understand resurrection. Without the shadow, the words "we have overcome" would be meaningless to us, and we would remain condemned to the limitation of our boundaries, subjected to merely the gravity, which keeps us on the ground. True tears flow from the sources of truth, a truth that is universal and timeless. If you notice, the times that we truly cry, when our souls are touched and our entire being is noticing tragedy, these are moments when tears truly come from within. Then the tears emerge out of the depth of the universe. In the same way, the times when we really laugh, the kind of laughter that is so genuine that we find our bodies contorting in so many directions, the kind of laughter when tears flow out and when we even might not be able to breathe, that, too, comes from the very depth of the universe. Both tears and laughter come from the same place of authenticity — the authenticity that is within all of us. However, this authenticity, despite its existence in all of us, requires consciousness, awareness, and mindfulness in order to emerge and be unveiled.

One night in February 2004, I had a long discussion with Terry Patten, who through the years became a dear friend of mine. On that particular evening, we were having our closing dinner for the GTC seminar, and this conversation was the first opportunity I had had to actually sit and talk with Terry. Throughout the seminar, I realized that he could understand a lot of what I shared in the group, even though he had never visited Africa. Sarah Keenan joined our conversation; she looked like a modern day fairy with long, red, bouncy hair and the kind of smile that is only in fairy tales or James Bond films, the kind of smile that oozes mischief and comes from a heart that flows with compassionate love. I have learned so much from Sarah and I count her as one of my dearest friends.

The three of us spoke deeply and intensively about topics that would be considered impossible for three people sitting around for the first time. There was truth in our eyes; there was a space of sacred opening to communicate at all levels. There was an active listening and an allowing for the words to land as they were spoken out or heard.

---

[50] Marianne Williamson, *A Return to Love: Reflections on the Principles of "A Course in Miracles"* (Harper, 1996).

We spoke of the great paradox of existence. We spoke of being able to see pain on one hand and also being able to witness and experience joy on the other hand. This was a completely new concept for me. I had never known how to process my experiences and express the scenes I had witnessed myself. The stories and experiences with the girls who ended up in the red light district, selling sex for about 0.10 USD; the Ethiopian-Eritrean border conflicts, where thousands of young men found death in the trenches of a World War I type of massacre. The stories of so many of my friends from Rwanda who lost so many friends and so many family members in the genocide and were also unable to retrieve the bodies of their loved ones. And let us not forget talking about the hunger and famine in the Ogaden region; the suffering of Hailu as he sat with his sores; and the suffering of many more AIDS patients. There is so much more. There are so many more stories that were too long to list. It is a collective tragedy of unimaginable scale.

Terry said that the Goddess can cry and weep on one hand, and know bliss and peace on the other. What is happening with our collective aura, and how much more will it take for us to awaken to what is so in order to revert towards balancing our world and existence?

I was stunned to think of what knowing and accepting this paradox would mean in terms of how I would define my reality and my life. Did Terry mean that in witnessing the most atrocious and saddest events of the world, I could also, on the other hand, accept and allow myself to witness the miracles? He literally said: "The Goddess weeps and laughs, she remains in the equanimity of the center and source of life. She is this and that at the same time." I asked him which Goddess and which world he was talking about. He answered that it is the Divine in all of us, the Goddess and the God that lives within us. In accessing this very being, we are able to stretch ourselves to fully witness both the joy and the suffering, to experience the beautiful and the ugly, and to immerse ourselves in the tension of being.

ASSESSING WHO WE ARE & KNOWING WHERE WE CAN GO TOGETHER: ESTABLISHING FLEXIBLE PERSPECTIVES

As the multiple facets of a diamond and the light reflections they generate define the diamond's value, so it is for us to recognize all of our facets that we may reflect the light in all its brightness. We are all multidimensional beings. We may not always be aware of all of our facets and how each facet affects the other, but it is in discovering all of these facets that we can enter the fullness of our being.

One night, in Belle-Ile, France, I had a very long conversation with an old girlfriend of mine named Claire-Noelle Jamoulle. We talked about life, about our children, and about so many other things. Claire-Noelle told me that I change all the time, and that she didn't know which one of me was truly me. I explained to her that I am all of what she has experienced and even a hundred other ways more. She felt that I should be just one way and that is the "true self," and she explained to me that if I change all the time, then I might want to consider therapy. Somehow, I did not manage to explain to her that we are all faceted, and the fact that the light reflects more on one facet than the others in a certain circumstance does not in any way mean that the other sides of me or the wholeness of me would be diminished; it might only be under-reflected at this point in time.

This conversation reflects the fact that we may indeed not always be aware that we are whole and are also fragments of the whole. From the perspective of Holons, Claire-Noelle could only relate to the parts of me that she knew. She only knew "the me" in the way that I appeared in the environment and system we had shared together a couple of years ago. But there was no way she would be able to recognize the other parts of my being that come out in other systems, be it in my family systems or in the system of my work environment. I shared with her a "whole" that was defined by the social circles we shared and the way that we all behaved within those circles, but that whole was also just a part of who I am. If I am reflected in a large mirror, and the mirror should shatter on the floor, the pieces are still my full reflection. It is this reflection of our inner self that might free us from the hold of the role society has assigned us to play.

I mention this, because unless we raise our awareness to our wholeness and become parts within that wholeness, we might not be able to have the flexibility required to flow through the myriad of circumstances that will arise on our path. The question is: what side, part, aspect, or facet of "me" needs to arise to best address a situation.

Yene Heran Kidist Assegid is the name I have been identified with, a name that has its own operating system, by which I must abide in order not to disturb the status quo of the world I live in. However, I am a lot more than just this name. Through the various names and affiliations I have, different roles have been assigned to my person. Ababi, my grandfather, called me "Mamishet," a nickname derived from Mame, which is often given to the firstborn child. However, my grandfather only used this name for me and my Aunt Elene. In his world and our world with him, our system recognizes this name as equated with some "title" or rank in the hierarchy of closeness. The name represented our complicity and the texture of our relationship with him. On the other hand, Almazesha calls me "Mimiye," which is a term of endearment from Mame, similar to adding the "ito/ita" in Spanish. She has a way of saying it that highlights my relationship with her and the role that we play for each other, a role that is completely different from the relationship established with Ababi. My father calls me "Mim," and it reflects my relationship with him, a very casual, humorous, and friendly one. My mother calls me "Mimi," which is the name unchanged and again reflects the relationship we have, a rather serious and orderly one. My friends call me Yene, Heran, or Mimi, and the names they use reflect the phases of my life when I met each of these friends.

And I am all of these names and all of these roles, separately as well collectively. I am — I am that and I am more, and I am also none of it. So, my names or my nicknames illuminate the type of relationship with a certain person; to them and to me, that name refers to my being in the context of that word that refers to me.

I am more than the word, more than that name and that context. I talk about this, because our actions in this world might be limited or framed by how we identify ourselves with our names and how we perceive our roles in the context of the name(s) we answer to. Rigidity in how we identify ourselves, and hence in our worldview, takes away from our ability to truly respond to a situation from a deep source and may leave us stuck on the surface or shallow levels.

In the same way, it is essential for us to have flexibility in the origin identities that we are led to adopt. In Addis Ababa, I am "Ye Shola Lej," a term that refers to the neighborhood I am from. In Ethiopia, I am an Amhara with Harari and Tigray ascendants. In Africa, I am an Ethiopian. In Europe and the rest of the world, I am an African. Among my friends I am a girl, and among my sisters I am the oldest. To my daughters, I am their mother, and to my employees, their boss. I am all that and I am also more than that. To an alien from another planet, I might be an Earthian.

If we do not have attachment to the circles that we belong to, then we can have the freedom to operate from a place of truth. So, in a nutshell, it is all about perspectives. Which perspective are you anchoring yourself on, as you look out into the reality? Can we change perspectives at will and assess reality in a myriad of ways?

When Claire-Noelle told me that I continuously change, she said that when she sees me with my parents, she sees a child; when she sees me in the office, she sees a workaholic; when she sees me at parties, she sees this unbelievably extroverted person; when she sees me with my sisters, she sees a moderate person; and with her, I am all that and more. Indeed, I am all of that and more, and none of it really, because that which I am is intangible and must manifest in fragmented little ways in order to exist in our paradigm. It goes back to Integral's four-quadrant perspective — horizontally and vertically as well as in depth, outer and inner. How far this understanding of self and other all goes, depends on the consciousness from which we stand to look out of, or into, reality.

FOLLOWING THE INNER VOICE: NOT-KNOWING AS AN ALLY

After I received my master's degree in 1988, my parents did their best to set up meetings with potential employers, and I too did my best to send as many applications as possible. None of it really amounted to anything.

One day, I went to a senior official of WFP *in Addis Ababa, hoping to apply for an internship. I wore the one suit I had bought for interviews. I looked odd in it. I don't like suits and I don't think they like me either — somehow it always looks like they are hanging on me as opposed to my wearing them. The man received me in his office, sitting behind his pile of papers and buzzing office machines, phones, faxes, and telexes, and engaged the conversation. I sat up straight and hoped with all my heart that this one interview would work. He asked, "What would you like to do?" I answered, "I would like to contribute to the development of Africa." He stared at me, and his body language reflected how cliché my answer was to him. Days later, I learned that this attempt, too, was yet a flop.*

I wondered what it was that was preventing me from working. I had graduated with excellent grades in my Master's and offered an array of capacities of language, interpersonal skills, and commitment. So, the level of disappointment I felt was immense. At this time, most of my college friends were still in school and not very concerned about work. But, here I was, out of school, not yet employed and having to busy my days with filling out applications. At one point, I just abandoned my job search, and thought I would just set up my own work.

My parents, family, and friends worried about me. They thought of me as someone reckless and irresponsible, and who might possibly embarrass them at interviews. After several other interviews, they stopped offering their help and I stopped asking for it. As a consequence, I became withdrawn in my own world, a bit rebellious and very distant to everyone. I challenged everything, and sometimes acted carelessly, maybe subconsciously inviting trouble.

Looking back in retrospect, I find that these years were very important in teaching me resilience and persistence. The struggle gave me a chance to experience the deep sadness resulting from not being able to express my work and my vision. It gives one a load of humility and deference to the Universe. It forced me to surrender and allow myself to flow with what came as opposed to trying to paddle against the river of life.

Flexibility in identity and perspective goes hand in hand with viewing not-knowing as an ally. When I think of the situation in Africa, and I am sitting alone, I often wonder about what it will take to change things on the continent. I wonder whether my caring is a case of the martyr–savior in me trying to emerge, or whether there is truth in what I say and envision. There are so many other qualified and brilliant Africans. So at times, I also wonder whether it really matters what I say. Well, it may not matter on a large scale, and that is okay. But it matters in my own world and planet, because I cannot watch the situation and do nothing, even though I am conscious about the fact that my personal universe will eventually die and cease to exist, once I pass away. I believe that part of the crux is that too many Africans, particularly those living in the Diaspora, have already lost their hope and confidence that the situation in Africa will ever change to the better, and instead build their new lives abroad. There are just too many Africans that don't care anymore, or can't care, about the future of their place of origin. And at times, I believe that some of the expatriates might be even more concerned about the future of Africa than Africans. As much as there might be expatriates that are not being helpful at all, there are also many who come to Africa to work very hard and work in areas and under circumstances that few Africans would be willing to do.

When something inside nags us daily, or when there is discomfort in just sitting, we can either find distractions to stop hearing the impulses within, or we can respond to them. Responding to these impulses, for me, is partly insane, partly scary, and partly foolish, or all of the above. In the Bible, in Exodus, God speaks to Moses and tells him to speak to the Pharaoh to let his people go. Moses initially resists and, in fact, he tells God that he is not ready to speak to the Pharaoh, and in fact he tells God that he doesn't feel he would know how to address Pharaoh and might not know what to say, almost like wondering why God couldn't pick someone else. And God tells Moses that he should just have faith and that once in front of the Pharaoh, God will be there to speak through him. There is a Moses in all of us, there is a cause that we all want to stand up for and go tell the Pharaoh. At the same time, God may have not spoken so clearly to many people since the time of Moses, and instead his communication has come as whispers in our hearts. Many of us have heard these whispers, but how many of us actually listen to the whispers and garner the faith to enact them? I am sure a lot more people have heard the whisper than those willing to admit it. Sometimes the whispers can be a call to do something as simple as calling someone to check on them. Sometimes it's about giving support to a person, or it can even be something on a much larger scale, such as engaging in one cause or another. Whatever the whispers may be, it is our unconscious speaking; it is the God within us speaking to our hearts.

Many of us hear these inner promptings subconsciously. The difference is in how we may have reacted to the whispers. Do we find distractions to drown the whispers, or do we ask for quiet to listen better, to press our ear to the wall to better decipher the message? My sister once asked how we would know that we actually heard the voice of God, the voice of the Divine and higher being, as opposed to hearing the voice of our own ego. Well, in my experience, the difference is very subtle and it takes being still and quiet to know the difference. I know for sure that when we follow the whispers we hear from the God that is within all of us, then it seems as though the universe opens to us because the universe is kind and intelligent, and wants us to operate from truth. The universe is within us and the ego tries to ignore that; it must ignore it in order to sustain the importance it claims. In the surrender, when the ego comes to alliance or when it is dead, then the universe can emerge into our deepest being, into our unconscious, transcending and including the flesh into spirit.

My sister, Fofi, tells me that it is ok to have no answers, because answers come and go, based on our mental configuration, and there is no right and wrong. All is one in the universe. The lack of clarity due to being in a space without answers should not be a source of frustration, but rather a space of knowing that what we need to know and find, will emerge in due time. It is necessary to pose questions for which there are no definite answers. It is finding comfort within the discomfort of this reality that will allow us to sit with the inquiry until the wisdom emerges from the well of Time.

THE INTEGRAL MONSTER IN ME

Saniel Bonder[51] speaks of the Second Birth: the birth that happens as we, our current self, dissolves and dies, rots and decomposes. The reason for this is so that from this death a new birth can arise of a self that is aware of ego, conscious of the divine, and able to work with the divine, all-capable spirit within the confines of a human body. Viewed from an Integral perspective, this concept illustrates our development and our evolution through the different stages of our personal growth. As we go through our own fragmentation and then re-emerge from that shadow space with a

[51] Saniel Bonder, *The Second Birth* (Trafford Publishing, 2005).

renewed self, all the experiences, knowledge, and images, associated with the stage we are transcending, get defragmented when we die. Then, as we re-emerge, these experiences, knowledge, and images get integrated in our fabric at our deepest cellular level. The result is that, as we re-emerge, we re-emerge being what we know, instead of having a separation between our being and our knowledge. To me, this process is how we evolve through the spiral of the development of our consciousness.

I mentioned earlier that in April 2008 we had a wonderful gathering of Integral practitioners in Istanbul. In this gathering, we all came to discuss how our work was going and present some of our successes and challenges. I had always been very eager to learn. I had been eager to know more, to understand more — it was always more, more, more. But during this gathering, things changed. I did not care so much about learning new things and I was not there to present any of my findings. I was not there to get acknowledged or encouraged. I was not there to learn more. There was something else I did not expect. Initially, I felt that I was just there, but that my presence did not really matter. And that is when the magic happened. I realized that I had just come home, full circle to where I started. I was at emptiness. I did not care. I did not want. I did not ask, but mainly, I did not want. This freed space in my being to actually allow more understanding, not from the brain, but from within, from somewhere much deeper inside.

I had not prepared a PowerPoint presentation ahead of time. Instead, I made it while I was waiting for my turn. The interesting thing for me was that this was the first PowerPoint I made without trying to give the audience a special message. But instead, I just remained with the truth that I felt applied to my life at that moment in time. At the end, it was the easiest presentation I ever made and I had fun. I actually even felt relieved and supported by the others. When giving this presentation, I felt ready to engage in the next phase of my life. All the tears that I may have shed, all the frustration that I may have felt, and all the toxicity that I may have accumulated from wanting and from grasping too much, suddenly it was all released.

Since I was not "trying" to do anything in particular, and was rather in a mood of surrender, and since I was not there to convince anyone of my visions, I felt free to tell "my" own truth. Suddenly I was able to speak freely about the challenges of setting up my Integral Africa program. I was able to talk about all of those issues that mostly do not find room in our usual presentations, such as speaking about personal struggles, about the questions that haunted me, about the disillusionment I often experienced. The entire experience of this gathering, including the presentation I made, was the first time I was able to bring my full being among my colleagues and friends. And I believe this was the case because I did not necessarily attempt to speak using the Integral jargon, but was ready to speak about my progress in my own words. While doing so, the Integral thinking that underscored my work, came through more clearly than it ever had before. It all made sense and it gave me a sense of relief: the relief from striving for success, from the fear of failure, and even from the fear of success.

In that moment, creating the PowerPoint from my heart's truth, I found a friend or a part of myself that I called Integral Monster in Me (iME). The image I used to represent iME in my PowerPoint was that of an alien looking like a small, scruffy, and scared animal in the last stages of severe stress. The animal's hair had fallen out, it was emaciated and clearly unhealthy in every way. This image was a representation of what often happens, certainly to me, but also to many of my peer development practitioners, as we follow the usual path of pushing for change and transformation. There is a difference when we push for something or flow with it in conscious surrender. Pushing or forcing for change is a sure ticket to find the iME in all of us; it is unhealthy and ineffective. The trouble is that rarely can we realize that we are pushing or forcing. Often we mistake that for being persistent or determined. The difference between pushing/forcing and being persistent/determined is very subtle and the only way we know which is which – is when we listen to the rhythm of our hearts and pay attention to the color of the aura that we reflect. Flowing with a path, no matter how challenging or how hard, offers an inner, unshakable peace within and endows us with the strengths and courage we need to move forward. On the other hand, pushing too hard or trying to force things is strenuous on the soul. It brings stress. It reduces us to a constrained being and robs us of our capacity to fly with our ideas.

It is often common to find that when we first hear about a new theory or even a new way of doing things, for that matter, many of us can become overly enthusiastic and become evangelists about that new theory or new way of doing things. We may not always be always conscious of the initial honeymoon phase and are unaware of the high waves that will come crushing in as we get deeper into the new approaches or theories. Learning new ways can remain in the mind or transcend to being a part of us. It is the process of making the learning a part of us that demands "us" to change first, and then we can continue to offer that learning to others in our community and the world.

The challenge of internalizing learning is really once we engage on the path and truly enact what we preach, and the change starts taking place. Then we are talking of a whole new ball game—it becomes a different story. We often neglect to factor in the discomfort of change and the growing pains of a new way. We often forget that knowing is one thing, but that doing is another, and being that which we preach is yet another level of existence. Difficulties arise that can lead us to extreme states of exhaustion and frustration.

As I tried to work with the Integral Theory, I sensed that I went through all the stages of being skeptical at first, to then being enthusiastic, and eventually to experiencing severe frustrations as I tried to bring what I knew and learned from the Integral Theory to the scale that I wished to see it applied. In the midst of the frustration, I literally burned out. I completely exhausted my energy and found myself literally on the ground.

Saniel Bonders speaks about the Second Birth; until the time I spoke in Istanbul, I was only in the space of fragmentation, fully immersed in the pain of not having overcome the challenges I faced in launching Integral Africa (see Chapter Six). It is in Istanbul that my Second Birth, per se, took place. In intuitively wanting to remain in my truth during my presentation and not force myself to talk about progress, I allowed this truth that I felt to emerge. This allowed me to speak about my own personal journey and present to my colleagues the state I felt myself in at that moment.

When iME came up on the screen in Istanbul, I used a lot of humor and we laughed senselessly. We laughed because iME is not only mine but exists in all of us. As to allow you to better understand the frustrations I went through, the next chapter describes my personal struggle to initiate and implement a leadership transformation program based on my vision of change for our continent. It speaks of my struggle in creating a form of a program for leadership development, called Integral Africa. While trying to set up Integral Africa, I came up against some of my own internal, shadow-side obstacles. In the following discussion, the insights I gained from that experience are applied to the task of moving forward in creating change and transformation for Africa.

It is important for us to reflect on our respective "Integral monster within" because it is through that part of ourselves that we can further explore more ways of learning, expanding, and growing. For me, I know that through the process of reflecting on the process of Integral Africa through the writing of this book, I have reached a point where I take responsibility for the successes and the failures of the first incarnation of Integral Africa. As Terry Patten puts it, it's about moving from the "drama triangle" of victim psychology to "the empowerment dynamic" of choosing to see ourselves as the creators of *everything* in our life. David Emerald presents this concept of "drama triangle" versus the "empowerment dynamic" in his book *The Power of TED.*[52] It is our ability to see that we are the authors of our stories and the creators of our lives which allows us to find and leverage the power that is within us.

In an email exchange about this book and about Integral Africa, Terry Patten said something that I found very touching and very inspiring for continuing my journey. This same message might also inspire you in your journey. Here is what he said:

> "When your way of seeing the first cycle of Integral Africa is to see its (temporary) failure as *something you alone created,* when you see yourself with the same unblinking clarity with which you see others, *then you* will really be ready to manifest it, *then* you will be in the process of midwifing it into being, then your dreaming will awaken into the world of form. So I invite your curiosity to turn upon the deeper reaches of the shadow "what you can't see that you can't see" because

[52] The Power of TED. 2nd Edition. Bainbridge Island, WA: Polaris Publishing, 2009.

that's where important new power can be found; I'm sure of it."

What Terry says is not only true for me or Integral Africa. I think it holds true for many of us, maybe even all of us. It is really our ability to truthfully reflect on our doings and beings; to genuinely see ourselves, both in terms of the light and the shadow aspects of our being, that will allow us to be fully empowered to create, to innovate in ways that best serves those we choose to serve.

CHAPTER SIX

A Vision of Change for African Leadership: Integral Africa

It is one thing to talk about Integral theory or approaches and reach levels of theoretical complexities, but how do we intend to take it further and actually apply Integral to the issues of poverty, of epidemics, of conflict, and of economic development and prosperity in an African context? Is there at all an opportunity to bring the approach to Africa? Can it be heard, can it be understood, and can its value be appreciated by those who might be able to benefit most from it? I believe that we can create the opportunities, so that this approach can be scaled up in areas where it might make a difference in the lives of millions of people living under challenging conditions.

Something has to be done to open the gates of knowledge and create a platform where learning can take place, at least for those who want to learn and further develop themselves. When such a sharing of knowledge and learning is made available, it can create a fluency in our ability to use the tools, the approaches, and the applications. This in turn might open the path to further innovations and creative applications for the Integral approach today to support development in Africa. Since 2004, I have been pursing such a platform through a program I call Integral Africa. It has been quite a difficult journey to bring Integral Africa to fruition, and this chapter tells the story of that journey and the wisdom I have gained from it on my way.

THE BEGINNINGS OF INTEGRAL AFRICA: FOCUSING ON LEADERSHIP DEVELOPMENT

As outlined earlier, after years of work in the field of HIV/AIDS prevention, current HIV and AIDS prevalence rates indicate that many efforts might not sustain their results. During the time I had been working in this field, I experienced total disappointment concerning the lack of peer support and regional exchange of lessons learned and best practices applied in the field. Of course, there were a number of online networks, but this was just not enough. For my work, it would have been helpful to actually see and meet peers from various corners of Africa and to be able to learn from each other, to exchange experiences, and to just be there for supporting one another. There was no way to travel easily from one African country to another as the costs were too high. There were also few opportunities to connect in person, apart from the rare occasions when attending a regional meeting or a conference. So there was very little chance to know one another and to learn from each other, respectively to not repeat the mistakes others made earlier. Of course, as I mentioned, there were conferences and a number of electronic web-based forums, but none of them provided the genuine exchange I believe was needed. The Internet was not yet as mainstreamed in the nineties as it is today, and my annual visits to MSF headquarters in Brussels brought me little relief.

Throughout those years, it became apparent that there would be a need for a means, which would allow people to connect to each other and network at a deeper level. And even though the Internet is now in place, I strongly believe that a kind of exchange platform is needed, where one can call for peer support. This support might then materialize in a kind of brainstorming platform, which allows each to be heard and to hear each other, a platform to be able to stand for one another and to exchange best practices as well as to share good and bad lessons learned, in order to synergize in a way that would benefit Africa and consequently other countries as well.

In reading Wilber's and other Integral theories and approaches, while spending time reflecting on what we had done so far, I reached a point where I knew there had to be something else, other than what we had been focusing on so far. I believed that there was something holding us back from finding lasting solutions for our problems. Even though I did not know what exactly was needed, I was convinced; I just knew that HIV/AIDS could not be existing in a vacuum, and that a more systemic approach to understanding our reality was needed, so as to find a durable solution for addressing the challenge of HIV/AIDS in Africa and the world.

It was partly a time of giving up and a time during which I was trapped in disillusions. Although I went to conferences, nice talks and conversations here and there were often the only thing that resulted out of these events. Eventually, I started thinking that HIV/AIDS might certainly be linked to our current collective mindset and how we do things as a collective. It is our laws, our structures, our cultures, and our traditions that might be influencing, in one way or another, the reality which provides a good seedbed for the virus to spread. And as long as the collective level of consciousness remains as it has developed over the years, we are unlikely to find solutions for the problem. The core issue is really in finding the root cause of HIV/AIDS, which is surely in one way or other, linked to conflicts, poverty, and malnutrition. It all reverts to leadership and to how our leaders chose to structure our systems and how they chose to address the problems. It therefore is the systems that have to be reconfigured in order to allow a new order to emerge, where a new consciousness about this disease can emerge.

Leadership is one of the key capacities to be developed, since it is a catalyst for change and transformation in economic and human development. Without effective, strong, positive leadership at the community, national and regional levels, the future of Africa will be the same as in the past. It is, in fact, through leadership that change can be channeled. Leadership is needed to guide our capacity to clearly see the current reality and adopt lenses that will allow us to identify leverage points, to see the challenges, to make distinctions between adaptive and technical challenges, and also to have the wisdom to select and prioritize the problems to tackle. We have to delve to the root causes of our problems, and this, in turn, will give us the basis to find long lasting and sustainable solutions to the challenges we face.

I am suggesting that most of the problems and challenges we face on the African continent should be addressed by tackling the issue of leadership first. Because it is about peace, about opportunities, and about change, I believe that leadership is the cornerstone that needs to be laid in order to move forward in our development. Our understanding of leadership must be as subtle as understanding the existence of various realities. And one thing is certain—leaders must not be scarce, it will take plenty of leaders, a critical mass of leaders to change things on the continent. It is absolutely essential to have a critical mass of leaders at all levels, in order to change the balance and to influence the reality toward a new consciousness or evolution of our societies and mindsets.

During the early phases of my endeavor, I remained with the open question on how best to engage this kind of consciousness and how to mobilize and build such a critical mass of leaders. An Ethiopian saying says that *"Soldiers who have shared trenches are brothers for life,"* and that *"Those who grew up together are also brothers for life."* In order to have a tight pool of change agents, to start building up this critical mass, it is essential to create mechanisms for bringing such people together. This could be kick started by short seminars and workshops on Integral theory and practices in the context of African development, leadership, and governance. Taking the African context in consideration, I am advocating for something that is attainable through a network of individuals, something that does not require massive financial resources and governmental cooperation.

Africa is a continent of paradoxes. The pictures range from the largest deserts to the longest river, from extreme beauty to extreme poverty. And its people, as well as the current and potential leaders, fall into a paradox as well.

It is often said that African leadership is poor and corrupt, but this is an inconvenient truth, showing up frequently in this world. However, it is also true that Africa has brilliant, capable, and intelligent people who are willing to serve and to provide the chance for improvements in the lives of their people and for the betterment of the continent. Many people with this untapped potential, however, either give up, burn out, or, even worse, are "eliminated" from the arena.

Men like Sankara[53] and Lumumba[54] had the passion, courage, intelligence, and drive to bring change to their nations. The aspiration of Integral Africa is to find and bring together the African men and women with comparable leadership competences to the Sankaras, the Nyereres, the Mandelas, and Lumumbas of Africa. It aims to bring together men and women who have the comparable courage, integrity, and conviction such as the Fikes and the Meazas and the Elsas. Such men and women are all over the continent; they work relentlessly in the various ministries, in the private sector companies, and in the civil society and NGOs. Integral Africa can offer them the tools, frameworks, and methodologies to sharpen their decision-making skills and finesse their ability to strategize.

Integral Africa is also about men and women who are open to relate to one another to jointly develop common visions and connect with each other to make a positive difference. It is about men and women relating to one another coming from the same basic knowledge and understanding, and having the same ultimate goals. It is not only about high-level leaders, but also about the grass roots leaders such as Fike, Elsa, and Meaza. It is about finding the right people who can make a difference, every day, and who can draw together the practice and the lessons of leadership from different sources of wisdom.

Integral Africa is my personal vision of evoking a much needed platform to allow dynamic African leaders to collaborate in solving their challenges by combining historical, cultural, and modern resources, as to encourage and coach one another. There is indeed so much to learn from our

[53] Sankara Thomas Isidore Noël Sankara (December 21, 1949–October 15, 1987) was the leader of Burkina Faso (formerly known as Upper Volta) from 1983 to 1987. With a potent combination of personal charisma and a social organization with some participatory democracy, his government undertook major initiatives to fight corruption and improve education, agriculture, and the status of women. His revolutionary program provoked strong opposition from traditional leaders and the country's numerically small but powerful middle class. Added to friction between radical and more conservative members of the ruling junta, these factors led to his downfall and assassination in a bloody coup d'état on October 15, 1987. (http://en.wikipedia.org/wiki/Thomas_Sankara)

[54] Lumumba Patrice Émery Lumumba (2 July 1925–17 January 1961) was an African anti-colonial leader and the first legally elected Prime Minister of the Democratic Republic of the Congo after he helped to win its independence from Belgium in June 1960. Only ten weeks later, Lumumba's government was deposed in a US CIA-sponsored coup during the Congo Crisis. He was subsequently imprisoned and assassinated under controversial circumstances. (http://en.wikipedia.org/wiki/Patrice_Lumumba)

past to create a better future.

Both Thomas Sankara and Patrice Lumumba were eliminated at a very young age and before they had a chance to implement their vision and dreams. I believe that their fate would have been different, if they had had a circle of peers, friends, and a good number of trustworthy colleagues to be around them, particularly in the not so good times. These extraordinary Africans were led by their vision and by their strong belief in the future of their countries.

How many visionary and committed leaders, be it in the public, private sectors, or in civil society, do we have in Africa today, who are sincerely ready and able to serve their respective nations, our communities, and our continent? And what would it take us to spare the time and effort needed, to support such type of leaders in implementing their dreams, in manifesting their inspiration and in executing their plans? Can we afford to wait until the right time and the right leaders come or shouldn't we rather think of changing the way we look at our reality and find the leaders, the change agents, already on the ground, working quietly? Are we ready to bring such change agents on board established political systems, into our organizations and our companies? Are we ready to bring these change agents who are, in a way, comparable to the imaginal cells of the caterpillar, together? Such change agents, or the human version of the imaginal cells, hold the capacity to transform our living conditions, our economies, and our reality, from one that is comparable to a caterpillar dragging on the ground into one that is comparable to a butterfly. It is the coming together of such leaders, such change agents, and, in a way, the connecting of the human version of the imaginal cells that would allow us to see the butterflies fly over Africa. It is the connection among the change agents that will allow us to create a transformed and changed reality in favor of economic and human development.

I strongly feel that it is important, and even key, to emerge a new kind of leadership for the continent, a leadership style anchored within a philosophy coherent with the overall culture of African communities. Although it is true that there is no such thing as "Africa" per se, and that it is more "les Afriques," as it is said in French, there is nonetheless a common ground featuring the main characteristics of the people of this continent. I believe that courage, resilience, wisdom, respect for elders, resourcefulness, kindness, and compassion, just to mention some major ones, are all traits reflected in African communities all over the continent.

The Integral Africa framework is meant to identify and develop a new kind of leadership culture and style in Africa. The approach would be meant to enable decision-makers to invoke the possibility of a transformed and strong environment, through a philosophy that recognizes the value of continuous leadership capacity development and a compassionate approach to development work. It is imperative to revive ways and find traditional passes that are based on indigenous African culture and traditions, and to infuse that wisdom with modern beliefs and technology.

It is time to create an organic network of professionals who have their feet on the ground, their minds in the sky, and their hearts firmly planted in the dream of a remarkable transformation for all of Africa and its people. In a nutshell, we need a critical mass of leaders who have the commitment, willingness, and ability to imagine the unimaginable for Africa. We need a critical mass of people, who have the courage to be bold and innovative in their ideas. We need dedicated men and women, who have the inner strength and courage to follow through, no matter the obstacles that are bound to confront them on their way. In fact, it is the current obstacles and problems that will be our opportunity to grow our capacities in dealing with the complexities that we face now, and to also prepare for those challenges we will still be facing throughout time.

Integral Africa is about finding and developing such leaders. It is about awakening our imaginal cells, to connect and change into the butterflies. The former Under-Secretary-General of the United Nations, Mr. K.Y. Amoako, once said that what Africa needs is bold and innovative leadership. Integral Africa is about finding such caliber of leaders that are bold, strong, passionate, and creative.

The key to an effective solution to Africa's main developmental challenges is by creating a platform and by developing an enabling environment from which African leaders can operate. This should be an environment that will permit them to showcase their best and dare to go beyond. Such leaders would have to be committed to facing the complexity of the matter at hand. It will take courage, tenacity, and vision. If, as ordinary citizens, we manage to create such a platform, and if we manage to change our current environment to one that is enabling, then I believe we will be halfway there. The rest will only be a question of time, logistics, and pure sweat equity.

STRUCTURE OF INTEGRAL AFRICA

Integral Africa is supposed to be a formalization of previously random networks of like-minded individuals who share Integral thinking and have holistic visions for sustainable development in Africa. It is very common to see many conferences and initiatives for donor harmonization, for aid effectiveness, for regional integration, for creating grounds for collaboration, etc.. Thousands of people flock to these meetings and conferences, only to revert back to their work and offices with a stack of business cards and new contacts. It is rather the exception that people follow up on the connection made at a conference, at least, it seems not to happen organically. In a different sense, it is also common to meet with individuals with whom we resonate, and in this case, follow-up conversation happens automatically, no matter how many months or years go by. Once we connect with another person with whom we truly resonate, or once we physically see the person behind the e-mail, the connection can be maintained without much effort. And it is exactly this type of connection that allows organic collaboration and natural harmonization of efforts to happen.

Imagine if we could look into the future and identify the people in leadership positions, and then backtrack to the present, to see these same people in the early years of their careers. We could find character traits and behaviors that might lead us to prospect on their life direction. What Integral Africa tries to do is basically just this: identify today the leaders of tomorrow and offer them a platform to form relationships, to form grounds on which they can build on each other's support. This platform would be coupled with both education facilities in terms of technical knowledge and use of decision-making tools, and also with adequate resources to allow each member of the network to excel in their pursuit of their visions and dreams.

As such, Integral Africa comes as a strategic initiative to galvanize organic means for change and transformation, through influencing and affecting actively the systems in which we each operate as individuals. Integral Africa is a way to formalize the natural networks that already exist. It is not necessarily about networking as in the traditional style, but rather about networking in terms of building relationships. Based on this, the objective is to build a web of connected transformation nodes, working toward a common development goal.

The intention of the network is also to allow each of its members to guard himself or herself from frustration and anger related to how things are today. The intention is further to find a place to re-source our energies so that we are controlled in mind, led by heart, and act through intelligent means with a shared vision of how Africa can best emerge.

For the sake of efficiency, the network of change agents is to be built in a way that favors partnership with all stakeholders working on development. The change agents might belong to African institutions, public bodies, civil society, private sector, but they can also be individuals. The focus of the network is to create the ground for opportunities for transformative leadership development, collaborative regional networking, and personal and professional growth.

The centerpiece of the network revolves around leadership and leadership capacity development, while at the same time finding anchors in key development issues. As the world changes, as technology evolves, and as globalization changes our planet to the size of a village, the African leaders of the future are also individuals affected, empowered, and changed by the global movement. Tomorrow's leaders might have similarities with our former leaders, but in addition, these men and women are world citizens in a global village. They are souls who want more for Africa and at the same time, also, for the entire world. These men and women can envisage how the world can also benefit from a healthier and stronger Africa, which plays a responsible role after having evolved from post-colonial times and from an era where African leaders saw the continent as a victim of world politics. Nevertheless, while we establish this communication platform, we also have to find ways to emerge out of poverty, conflicts, and disease; instead we have to highlight our commercial and cultural capacities. The essence of Integral Africa and the network described here is to facilitate the emergence of the next generation of leaders who will take Africa into a place of prosperity, where the quality of everyones' life is raised.

DIFFICULTY MOVING FORWARD

I faced significant challenges in trying to make my vision of the Integral Africa program move forward. It did not make sense to me to try and get African participants to the United States, as the financial and travel logistics would not be reasonable. So, I instead suggested making Integral Africa an online program, supported by face-to-face seminars, over the lifetime of the course. The resulting pool of participants would be the inception of the critical mass of change agents, and it would be through them that the Integral thinking and approaches would spread over the entire continent. This was, and still is, the core of my vision to contribute to planting the seeds that will induce the necessary changes in Africa.

Once I had drafted the outline of the idea, a lot of effort went into forming the organization and formulating the program. Between 2004 and 2007, I was actively working on setting up Integral Africa, working with colleagues from Pacific Integral in Seattle, who had designed the GTC program. Even though the idea of trying to create some system to allow the emergence of an African Leadership network had been in my heart and mind for many years, it was indeed my personal experience with the GTC program that gave me the critical spark to work on Integral Africa. When I began initiating and designing this program, it was this same circle of friends from GTC and the greater Seattle area that came forth in the early days.

As a learning program of two years, Integral Africa was designed to bring together Africans committed to change and development, and offer them the latest leading-edge tools to support them in defining their strategies, as well as improving their decision-making and personal development skills. At the onset, the program was based on the structure of the GTC program, and Integral Transformative Practice (ITP, as discussed above) was also an important part of the curriculum at that time. Integral Africa aimed to bring together and form a network of imaginal cells throughout Africa. These imaginal cells, or change agents, were supposed to be brought together two or three times a year for face-to-face seminars, while, during the rest of the year, online seminars and courses for practicing the acquired skills and exchanging experiences, would characterize the program.

As mentioned earlier, the GTC program combined with my experience working at the grassroots and in the communities inspired me in conceptualizing the Integral Africa program. Based on my long-term practical working experience for African development, the GTC approach seemed to me the best available curriculum for teaching innovative skills to planners, decision-makers, and leaders, so as to bring change in Africa. As much as I learned from the Integral programs I attended for myself, I also brought my own wealth of experience with me into the world of Integral, and tried to use Integral in a way that would allow synergies with the work I had already done. The cumulative experiences I have discussed above led me to parenting Integral Africa and creating a movement with a code of ethics among members of this platform. We also took a stand to be accountable for our time and resources spent. As much as we are a sum of all the learning experiences we have experienced and gone though in our lives, in the same way, Integral Africa is a result of my own experiences and learning opportunities, combined with the experiences from GTC and other learning sessions in the Integral world.

In the years following its inception, I spent a lot of time and energy pitching the program to senior African Leaders within multilateral organizations as well as in the private sector. However, for some reason things were not moving forward; Integral Africa did not materialize as planned or as it had been designed. It is hard enough to conceive something alone, so imagine how difficult it would be to try to conceive something collectively as a group. Part of the challenge was that the process felt like conceiving something that we *felt* was needed, that I thought I *knew* was needed, and which was also completely new and never put together before. The whole concept was very unconventional and that was, in hindsight, part of the challenge.

It was indeed a great program concept, and for a while many senior personalities in Africa gave their endorsement. Many participants also signed up, but gaining funding for the program seemed close to impossible. The problem was that the change the program promised would only be visible within ten or so years, and investors/donors usually want to see changes and progress within a shorter time frame. In addition to that, I believe that the vision that we held and reflected through the program required us, the people on the ground and the team working together, to live up to it—which was not always easy.

Since funding was not readily available not much could be done. The team of volunteers dissipated little by little until more or less I was left alone with the concept and idea of Integral Africa. The choice I faced was to chuck the program and forget about it, or continue to see what else could be done to manifest the vision of the program. Even though it did not work quite well in the first instances, I must say that I will be forever indebted to my friends and colleagues who supported me while working to set up Integral Africa, and who have continued to support me. In a sense, this book is one of the steps I am taking to express the frustrations of the journey, the dreams that kept me going, and also to manifest the vision of Integral Africa and keep it alive. Maybe it will come in some different shape, sometime in the future. The fact is, there is a need for a platform to connect us and whether it is through Integral Africa or another such initiative, the aim is to connect, to network, and to start working together.

As we all know from our own experiences, the time is not always right for new and innovative initiatives. And I also now realize that organic growth needs its own time and must come from inside. Likewise, an initiative like Integral Africa, which is meant to connect men and women throughout Africa, must come from inside, from within the continent and its people. Whether it is a kind of naïve youthful eagerness to get started or simple impatience, I was just in such a rush to start, that I myself was not willing to slow down and take the time needed to put all the details in place. I liked the people I worked with, I did not want to loose momentum and their commitment, and consequently, I did not want to look beyond. I must admit, that at times, I felt that it would have been better to initiate Integral Africa with a different and more diversified group of people, but I was hesitant in doing so. Maybe the hesitation came from not wanting to tamper with the status quo. Maybe it came from thinking that things would work out themselves. Maybe I was afraid to lose the support of the group that had formed around Integral Africa, and maybe I wanted it to work too much to make the impossible possible against the many odds we were facing during that time? I realize now that I was in fact not detached enough and that my commitment became too rigid, and not inclusive enough of opinions, thoughts, or alternatives.

My inability to explain how I perceived the current challenges in Africa, combined with the limited knowledge that our team had about Africa, became an inevitable source of an increasing blind spot and growing frustration for all of us. On one hand, I was pressing to get things started as soon as possible, and on the other hand, our team was working to ensure that we created something as Integral as possible, without sufficient exposure to the African realities on the ground. And in addition to all of this, we used completely different ways of communication.

What was missing in the entire process of designing and formulating the programs of Integral Africa, was our ability, as a team, to work from within the fullness of our beings. We may not have been owning the light and shadows of our own individual selves, nor that of the group. We may also not have been willing to question and inquire about our blind spots, and we certainly may have missed fully honoring the vision of the Integral Africa program. These lessons inspired me to think about the need to examine the shadow within, in order to create change without, as discussed in detail in Chapter Five. For the reasons listed above here and due to some more aspects to be discussed below, the program did actually not yet start.

Suzanne Cook-Grueter,[55] who is a wonderful teacher, told me during one of her seminars that unless I was willing to own my vision and stand up to it, despite all the shadows, all the questions, and all the potential insecurities in launching something of this scale, I would lose the chance of a lifetime to be a channel for change and transformation. She was right,

[55] Suzanne Cook-Greuter developed the SCTi-MAP that builds on the work of Jane Loevinger. The method she uses assesses a person's level of development through the analysis of the complexity of language the person uses; http://www.cook-greuter.com.

because I realize I have lost time in not having the courage to be fully who I am. I might have been caught up with how I was raised to behave: nice and courteous, gracious and kind. In fact, at times, there are moments that called for being straightforward, short, and explicit. But I could not manage to act that way in those years with Integral Africa, as I was just too cautious and concerned about how the other person might feel. But at the same time, these past five years have allowed me to go deeper into myself, to understand more, to learn more, and to emerge as a stronger, calmer, kinder, more compassionate person. So, although Suzanne was right about losing an opportunity to make change, I can say that through the writing of this book, I hope to step into my full being and inspire many others to step into their greatness to collectively bring the change and transformation we need in Africa and probably some other parts of the world.

Maybe it was not yet time for Integral Africa, and maybe there were still other lessons to be learned before it could manifest. In either case, I decided to write about the stories, the reasons, and the inspirations that led me to conceive of Integral Africa in the first place. I am hoping that through this book and its stories, I can inspire you to get involved, to speak up and act up in ways that can build communities, create healthy environments, and allow our system to evolve.

"No problem can be solved from the same level of consciousness that created it," stated Albert Einstein.[56] This also means that the issues in Africa cannot be resolved with the same level of consciousness that created them. We need to address these matters from a different paradigm, with different and higher levels of consciousness. The aim of the Integral Africa program is, and will remain, to actually gather change agents in Africa and offer them not only a platform to interact, collaborate, and think together, but also do give them access to the latest models and theories that offer systemic ways of thinking. More systemic approaches will help us be more effective in supporting change. We would then have the option to apply our combined knowledge and co-create, addressing the challenges faced by the countries of sub-Saharan Africa.

---

[56] http://www.einsteinalive.com/quotes/einstein-creativity.htm

When I talk of Integral Africa, I talk about a philosophy but also of a methodology and strategy to unchain the realm of possibilities, and to transform the current operating system, which led once proud African nations to the bottom of Human Development Index. I do not propose a radical change or to adopt another way of working and thinking. However, the best and most economic way forward is rather to evolve what already works into something that would work even better. A healthy community of development practitioners can actually be the channels through which we can facilitate the emergence of healthy nations and regions—such leaders are already in place, working independently all over Africa. They are young, emerging, talented individuals who are the human "imaginal cells," and it is the vision of Integral Africa to be the network that connects and actively supports them in their aspirations.

LESSONS LEARNED: EVOLVING INTEGRAL AFRICA

Although Integral Africa is the name of a specific program that I have designed and conceptualized, from here on I use the name in relation to thoughts of strategically supporting development efforts on the African continent. Integral Africa is thus a way to engage a conversation about the emergence of a new consciousness and the kind of leadership that might emerge with it in the coming years.

In a way, Integral Africa was originally designed like a classical orchestra, where the conductor or composer decided which instruments and which musicians would be included. It becomes clear that this is a kind of constraining approach. Today, I realize that the intentions of Integral Africa are still as valid as ever; however, the angle through which we put forth the program has to be slightly different. We basically have to change the format. Previously, Integral Africa was designed in a very structured way with online learning and regular face-to-face meetings. Now, I believe we must restructure the concept to be more fluid and organic; something like an improvised Jazz concert where the goal is to make music and the path is to follow one another in a harmonious collaboration, something that is more of an exchange or a conversation using musical instruments. This would be an organic process that might be unpredictable yet alive, similar to Jazz where musicians follow the sounds and express emotions in an intricate dance weaving in and out their collective expressions. It is very different from a process that might try to make the musicians and the instruments fit into a mold or be restricted exclusively to a possible preconceived idea of how one thinks the music should sound. This reflects a certain letting go of trying to orchestrate things. It reflects my realization that sometimes it is in letting go that we allow innovation to emerge; it is in letting loose that we make space for others (as well as ourselves) to take ownership, contribute and collaborate. This change reflects the core of African music, which is very participatory and democratic to a certain extent, as it brings everyone in to the melody and is accessible by all.[57] Such programs of leadership development as Integral Africa or others will succeed better following an African model: accessible, participatory, fluid, and flexible, without being constrained by rigid structures of learning.

Integral Africa has to be open. It has to be flexible and allowed a life of its own, so that it can draw the musicians—change agents—to play tunes that will transform reality in the various contexts on the African continent. When the musicians from Africa play in concert with each other and also invite other musicians from beyond the continent to contribute to the music, then we will have found the way to write the tunes of transformation; a transformation sourced from the depth of each player's greatness and gift. To me, this is the kind of transformation that will not only sustain itself through the years, but also happen painlessly and naturally, and include all who want to be part of it.

It *is* possible to see such change in our lifetime and I believe that we are already on the right path. We each hold part of the solution, part of the pigments needed to retouch the picture of the current reality. It will take letting go of our own egos, letting go of our own personal agendas, and allowing ourselves to focus on the greater vision, the common good that can be achieved through our collective efforts. It will also take tolerance and understanding of ourselves and those around us.

---

[57] Mutombo M'Panya, *Mirrors of Distortion: Western Delusions, African Reality* (unpublished manuscript).

The vision of Integral Africa, or any such initiative, is perfectly feasible; however, before such a program can truly unfold, we must first look in the mirror and assess whether we truly care and truly want this change, since the work must be done from conviction and not because it is yet another nice program to have. We must get involved because it matters to us, and regardless of the question of whether we will still be around when the results emerge—we, as Africans, must want to be part of such a program.

I have found that part of the reason why I did not manage to launch Integral Africa as I had hoped, in spite of all the effort and support it received, is because I, personally, may not have been ready for the changes myself. There was a lot more I had to learn and experience in order to truly serve such a vision. Our team may not have truly understood how vital such a program would be once launched. In addition, because our team did not experience the challenges and difficulties that exist on the ground in most African countries and communities – they could not really genuinely understand the situation, merely because they had not lived through these challenges. Hence, their support may have certainly been full of compassion and empathy, but I am not sure whether they could truly appreciate the urgent need to get started. At the same time, I was so focused on getting started, that I lacked the patience it would take to put such a program together. Lastly, a good number of the African colleagues and peers I was trying to enroll in the program may not have truly believed that change was possible. This might be due to the fact that the strategy for change I was suggesting might have looked unrealistic and possibly too far out of the box.

It is always so disappointing not to see the expected results after putting so much effort into an endeavor, let alone taking the lack of results as failure. And I am no exception to the rule and must admit that it took me some time to realize what I had actually gained from the exercise of putting Integral Africa together. The first lesson is that nothing worthwhile can be put together overnight. It takes Time to prepare; it takes Time to adjust, study, and revise; it takes Time to plant the seeds, and Time to allow the seeds to take root. The issue of development in Africa is an issue that hundreds of organizations have spent billions of dollars on, and where thousands of men and women have put in countless effort and sweat equity—a complex matter, it needs an approach that can correspond to the complexity at hand.

Second, before we talk of tools and methods, an understanding of the complexity must be reflected in our own individual being. How much do we really understand what is at hand? How much are we really willing to stand for the vision? How much are we willing to surpass our own personal limitations to reach stages of consciousness that will allow us to create programs to support the change agents we target?

This initial effort, despite the fact that it lasted almost four years, may have been just the first try; there is still time for a second, better-informed try. And when the time comes for the second try to enact a program like Integral Africa, we will be able to leverage the lessons learned from our past setbacks; we will be able to leverage our experiences in order to make the second try a success. On my side, I know that I will be able to work from a state of abundance and flow, as opposed to working from a state of scarcity and need. I can see how I will be able to change the urgency I felt for the program, so that instead of it being limiting, it will be more of a springboard and an enabling factor.

Third, instead of looking for resources and funds from outside Africa, I think we have found the way to get the resources from within the continent. We will be able to be committed, yet not attached, and it is this non-attachment that will allow more creativity, more innovation, and more boldness in our work. What I have learned now is that the intentions of Integral Africa and its vision are still alive more than ever. What has changed is the way that the program might start. Instead of beginning with seminars and activities, which would demand funding, the program will now start with this book, which is partly an effort to allow Integral Africa to emerge in the form most true to the needs on the continent and most helpful to bring the necessary mindset changes.

Lastly, and in some ways most significantly, Integral Africa's theoretical foundation was mostly the Integral approach. Now I realize that one has to also contextualize the program, as to honor everything that is already in place on the African continent and to support things that are already waiting to emerge. Before the program is put on the ground, I believe a conversation also needs to start about the changes that African men and women from across the continent wish to see and are willing to commit to. There are hundreds, if not thousands of African change agents all around the world, who could bring an organic sort of transformation; but yet, they might not be fully aware of their potential roles and responsibilities. So, this book is just one of the many catalysts that may spark the coming together of such change agents.

During one of the discussions about Integral Africa, my friend Sally, who had been listening to our heated discussion about the way forward with the program, once asked me whether I was planning to include existing African traditions and wisdom into Integral Africa. At that time, I was so taken by the Integral theories and practices that I must have been kind of blinded by them. So, my response to her was that what we need in Africa is a systematic way of making decisions, of looking at reality, of understanding our environments, so that we can devise better and greater programs, policies, and means of governing ourselves. What I missed was realizing that Africa has its own systems, and it is within and together with these systems and traditions that we have to design various means to bring transformation where it is needed.

I was not wrong in my answer to Sally, but I missed seeing that there may already be ways and means within African traditions to actually make these sound decisions and have a comprehensive understanding of the situation at hand. The answer we seek is usually within. But I had apparently been so discouraged by the years I worked at the grassroots level – mainly with MSF – that I wanted something new. I wanted something fresh, and the Integral theories and practices looked very attractive to me. I thought that we would find all the solutions we would need only by understanding the theory and by successively applying the practice. What I know now as I write these words, is that it is not about a particular tool or method; it is not about this theory or that one, but rather about a mindset and a commitment to a journey for transformation. Once the journey is started, the tools, methods, and theories can be used to address and benefit progress along the way. But the main issue remains the mindset, the commitment, and the spirit for change, and the conviction that it is reachable and achievable given the right mix of individuals and hard work.

Today, about five years down the line, I understand Sally's question and I fully admit that I failed to see the insights in her comment. As much as I wanted Integral Africa to manifest, I had not been proportionally eager to integrate within the program of Integral Africa the wisdom and traditions of African ways of leading, managing, creating, and negotiating. Now I understand that, yes, Integral theory and practice hold a lot of potential for African development, but it is only the combination of Integral with the existing knowledge/wisdom of African communities that will herald the path of advancement in the fields of economic and human development. It is therefore also very much about integrating and combining African traditional wisdom, culture, and knowledge with what modern programs such as Integral Africa might offer.

The process of writing this reflection has allowed me to come full circle and to reach a point of understanding of "why it didn't work," and why Integral Africa did not come to fruition the first time. I am excited to apply what I have learned to take Integral Africa forward and answer the question, "When will it happen?" and how shall it be designed this time in order to best serve the needs of our communities and our nations?

AFRICAN WISDOM: A TWO-FOLD PLAN FOR TRANSFORMATION

Tremendous amounts of resources are spent for development programs—resources of funds, of sweat equity, of hope, and of continued effort. Integral Africa and the concepts it holds aim to add to this effort a new way of thinking, a holistic approach of looking at development, change, and transformation. This more holistic view looks to African traditions for guidance, for inspiration, and for wisdom to move forward.

My sister, Fofi, says that we are accountable to not only ourselves, our peers, and our family, we are also equally accountable to the thread of our ancestors. Thousands of years ago, people in greater Africa had societies structured to provide rules of law — indigenous democracies where men and women lived in security with their basic needs addressed.

My ancestors, as those of many Ethiopians, were often involved in battles that were fought to acquire and gain new territories or to protect the nation from enemies, both African rivals and European invaders. During the times when European invaders had to be fought as well as the smaller provincial African rivals, the time for conflict was based on many factors, including the time of year, seasonal needs being met, and religious days. In consideration of these circumstances, the battles were planned respectfully for both enemy and foe alike. This respect often was exhibited in the course of the battle, as well as its outcome. Long before the Geneva Convention was formulated, the African warriors had an understanding of how to behave at war. Most battles were like a crusade.[58] Our battles were fought for a cause, and only after first attempting to resolve the differences through negotiations. Only when words and council failed did the communities revert to battle to bring matters to term and completion.

Growing up, when I stayed with Grandmother Almazesha over the weekend she used to sometimes tell me the stories of these ancestors of ours who were a part of such battles. The stories remain with me to this day. What I remember the most is that there was the Copper Pots. These Copper Pots exemplified the humanity of the warriors of Ethiopia, which I learned about from Almazesha's stories. I first saw one of the Copper Pots that had belonged to her grandfather and was used when he went into battle. Copper pots were essential parts of the battle equipment, as necessary as any weapon. Their purpose was to feed all members of the caravan going into battle. In Ethiopian tradition, as it may be in most African cultures, one cannot possibly fight with those with whom one has shared a meal or gone to battle with; so mealtime in battle and in peacetime was a way to bond. During the preparation of the meal, everyone had a different responsibility for the copper pot: some for stirring, others to provide ingredients, others still for preparing the meat or vegetables to go in, some others to keep the fire going, and still others to eventually serve the meal.

[58] I am not denying the bloodshed of it all, especially for children; I am merely noting the relationship of a cause. It is also true that rival tribes would fight or raid each other, especially during the slave trade era in order to take prisoners to sell to slave traders. But overall, the battles were truly like a crusade, fought for a cause and only fought when negotiations failed.

The Copper Pot is thus for me the symbol of what we are trying to accomplish now in Africa, a symbol to reflect our crusade against poverty, deficits in development, epidemics, illness, and conflict. The Copper Pot is also a reflection of the importance that each one of us must take responsibility to create the new Africa. We cannot go into battle without this provision and commitment from a critical mass of men and women who represent the continent. It will take all of us, Africans from throughout the continent as well as our global allies and peoples from around the world, to create and serve our vision so that it appropriately satiates the hunger for development that has been so endemic to Africa.

In African traditions, problems, challenges, and enigmas experienced and unsolved are brought to elders; it is the circle of elders that direct, guide, and show the path to possible solutions. In the same way, I feel that this problem of leadership and the related development challenge must be brought to our senior leaders, our senior local community leaders and spiritual leaders. Their wisdom, their experiences, and their stories, will give us insights and clarity, and open the way to an adapted, more suitable approach to leadership development in Africa. I trust that our well respected elders will share with us a genuinely African strategy and action plan to mesh together the principles of African leadership with other leadership principles to best address our needs.

Stories house wisdom, they offer gems of knowledge, and they hold precious gifts of insights. Stories commonly find their way from one generation to the next through our oral tradition of storytelling. It is to this tradition of storytelling that I want to revert, to arrange all the findings in a sacred mosaic, a starting ground for reflection and action geared to advance African leadership capacities for nation building that can eventually emerge to larger dimensions. The best way I see to begin this sacred mosaic is to lay a foundation, a background setting that represents and opens the path for the integration of the wisdom, experience, and insight our elders offer to the next generation of African leaders.

Others will join me in further developing this mosaic — its colors, patterns, and texture — to gain clarity, direction, and guidance for the way forward. I also hope that others follow and continue to add their stories to the mosaic of life in Africa. There is hope and a clear path, and together the mosaic will remain long after we are gone and be available for many more years and many more generations as a sacred space for Africa, for the world, and for humanity to the wisdom within.

The journey of living Integral from Africa, with dreams for this continent that may sometimes seem unreasonable, is a journey that has affected me personally. It has been a process of being, disintegrating, and re-emerging again, and returning back again as a new self. It has been a story that is renewed and anointed with the beauty, the wounds, the misery and the wealth, the humor and the tragedy, the violence and the love, the compassion and the selfishness, the envy and lust, the jealousy, anger, and generosity of being human.

I am still committed to bringing the concept of Integral Africa alive in order to create a platform of conscious and intelligent, compassionate, and resourceful change agents, once the time is right. But this time, I hope to do it from a space and heart of abundance, a field of love, energy, and miracles as opposed to a space of scarcity, anger, and subjugation. It is the attainment of detached commitment that is allowing me to write these lines and to peacefully exist in both my limited humanness and in my unlimited divinity. I cry as much as I laugh, I dream as much as I breathe, and each time I dare to follow the whisper of my heart and take each step forward with one hundred percent conviction, commitment, and persistence.

NEXT STEPS

The idea of creating an online, or other, platform of change agents through a program like Integral Africa is important in order to support men and women working to move the development agenda forward in Africa. It might not be easy, but there is a call for something to be done, something to be started, created, and birthed in order to allow conversations on the necessary change and transformation to take place. .

By the time you read these words, a website will be available as an initial platform for discussion under *www.butterfliesoverafrica.com.* Please join the discussion and bring your experiences, your dreams, and your challenges to this forum. Join us also to support and coach one another on the forum.

It is my hope that within two to three years of the publishing of this book, we will have our first gathering. During this gathering, it would be wonderful to create a mechanism of working together and supporting each other in our respective endeavors and challenges. What happens next is up to each individual as a part of the collective community of African citizens, each of us as individuals and as a part of the network of imaginal cells for Africa.

Acknowledgments

A moment of appreciation, a time for acknowledgements

In Africa, when a child is born, that child is the child of the community. Sisters, brothers, grandparents, relatives, neighbors, aunties, uncles, and friends feel equally entitled to the child as much as the biological parents do; because of this, I am blessed knowing that I have been raised by such a community, as it was done for centuries and is still done in most parts of the continent. This upbringing, this introduction to life and the world, adds to the collection of treasures in my life coming from not only my parents alone but also from a greater circle of friends, family, colleagues, mentors, teachers, guides, role models—light and shadows that sparkle on the mosaic of my "being" like stars in the far sky. Every day I am thankful for all these wonderful souls that have shaped and molded me into the person that I am today.

Recognizing that we are all that we are and all that we do is a result of the people who have been part of our lives, part of the contexts and environments we have lived and worked in; I am very conscious that I am the result of the collective and the space in which I have existed, and so it is to this collective that I want to present my appreciations and acknowledgements. It is this collective as a whole that I must thank for the inspiration, the wisdom, and the insights it gifted me with as well as for the permission it granted me to make mistakes, as we often all do, and draw precious lessons from the experience. To me, this collective is like a village without boundaries that stretches across our planet, a village that goes from Africa, through Europe, to Asia, through the US, across Australia, through Latin America and back again to Africa. My village extends to the World, with different neighborhoods where learning took place, still takes place today, and will always take place with friends and family, peers and mentors within the community of development practitioners, as well as with the Integral Community and many non-stated Integral souls who have been applying the essence of Integral living.

In writing this acknowledgement section, I think of all the individuals I want to thank and realize the amazing number of individuals I have been blessed with. This book is really a reflection of my life and the lessons I have learned for the past forty years or so. The process has been comparable to looking back and reviewing the assortment of influences that have touched me, and also attempting to look ahead and trying to envision the path ahead.

Hence, I bring you to this space of reflection and invite you to share with me this moment of appreciation. The following quote best describes what I am trying to say about the importance of the collective dimension and how this collective has so enriched me as an individual. While this perspective can be found in many cultures, it is deeply rooted in an African worldview that asserts:

> *I am because we are; and because we are, therefore, I am. "I" is the individual and the infinite whole. We "is" the individual and collective manifestation of all that is. Self includes all ancestors, the yet unborn, the entire community, and all of nature. In my being is my worth, because I am not a separate, finite, limited being, but an extension of—and one with—all that is.* (Myers, 1993, p. 20)[59]

My perspectives and understanding of my world might appear very biased towards Africa, I must confess. No matter where I am in the world, my outlook seems to be anchored in an African perspective. At the same time, I genuinely appreciate and realize how other societies, communities

[59] Myers, L. (1993). Understanding an Afrocentric world view: Introduction to an optimal psychology. Dubuque, IA: Kendall/Hunt.

and peoples, anchored in different worldviews, might perceive the reality on this continent of ours. I have lived and worked in so many parts of the world and have been interacting with such a broad range of individuals coming from all over the world, that I can't help but see the multitudes of vantage points, perspectives, and ways of being that can exist in relation to the same moment or situation.

As human beings, we understand things, see things, and do things in a way that is totally subject to who we are and what we know, to our cultural and traditional background, and to our level of consciousness and mindset. In the past, having these multiple perspectives had been sometimes challenging to me. It was hard to make decisions, because in my heart I could feel why each different side had a point. In time and with enough moments of paddling through rough rivers of frustrations and disappointments trying to make sense of my world, I have learned to befriend the perspectives that swirl in my life as a revolving door that disgorges a different person each time it turns. These perspectives help to deepen my understanding and to draw meaning and uncover insights about life, about work, about development—about everything that matters in my own little existence. It is these perspectives that have unveiled to me the importance of linking cultures, the importance of advocating more understanding of the "other", the importance of knowing that although some of us might be led to be in a paradigm of "us against them" – solutions will only be found when we learn to see that there is no "us against them" and that we are part of one consciousness, one world, one holistic system where our mindsets, our values, our behavior, and our actions are bound to affect us all.

Once we understand that there is no separation, it is possible to delve into spaces that allow us to work more effectively and in a more sustainable way. This is true for everything, and it is even truer for the work that we do in the context of economic and human development in developing countries around the world. Personally, my work has focused on Africa. And as I look back at all the experiences and lessons learned, several points emerge as key, starting from the importance of looking within for answers, the importance of creating understanding, of nurturing compassion, humility, resilience, appreciation of one another, as well as the importance of having the courage to stand up to injustices, corruptions, exploitation, and ill-doings. We can't possibly expect to do good work that serves our communities and peoples if we don't come with our hearts first. It is our hearts that will open the doors, that will monitor and evaluate the human value added that we bring and establish, and ensure excellence in the results we deliver.

My deepest gratitude goes to God; not only for this book but for everything in my life. I thank God, I thank the inner Spirit that has guided, encouraged, and inspired me throughout my life, throughout all the ups and downs, throughout all the projects I undertook, throughout all the accomplishments, but even more so throughout the countless mistakes or failures I have gone through. To me, God has been like an inner compass, a subtle energy which dwells within all of us; that is always there to point us the way. My relationship with God has certainly been a rocky one. It has been one that keeps maturing and evolving through lived experiences, through the errors I make and challenges I encounter. This relationship has been a source of humility, insights, kindness, hope, and audacity. I thank the Divine, Spirit, God – however we choose to refer to this Loving Being - for allowing me to complete this project of *Butterflies over Africa*. It is this God, this Divine Being that allows me to remain hopeful about the future and keeps me going each day with faith for a better tomorrow.

My sincere appreciations go to my husband, Matthias Reusing, and my daughters, Rosi and Leoni. "Rosi, Leoni, Matthias, I don't have words to thank you enough. You have been there for me throughout the years with patience, compassion and understanding. What can I say other than I love you so very much and that you mean the world to me...." Matthias, thank you so much for going through all the drafts of this manuscript and giving me meticulous feedback and comments. Your help has been priceless to me. I thank greater family, my sisters, my aunts and uncles, my cousins and especially my parents, Sally Makonnen and Assegid Tessema, for their continuous support, encouragement, and love. My grandmother, Almaz Haile-Mariam, who has been for so many of us a guiding light and a beacon of hope, will remain forever the source of my inspiration.

Anna Fitzpatrick, my editor has been just a precious person to know and work with throughout the writing of the manuscript. Anna, thank you so much for bearing with me through so many revisions and edits with patience, kindness and gentleness. Deborah Rose and Cynthia McAfee, thank you both so much for your support in doing the last edits before printing.

I have been blessed to know and work with Dr. Russ Volkmann, my publisher, who has been so encouraging throughout the process of shaping the stories and writings into a manuscript. Russ, I count myself as fortunate to know you and be working with you because you are such a source of knowledge, a soul with a generous and loving heart, and a wonderful mentor. Thank you, Russ, for your great gift in leading and coaching anyone working with you to deliver writing that comes from the depth of our being and not merely from the surface of the intellect.

I extend my thanks to the Pacific Integral team. All the principals of Pacific Integral (at the time I joined the program), Dr. Terri O'Fallon, Dana Carman, Geoff Fitch, and Joseph Friedman, have been great teachers and will always remain as such in my spirit and heart. All the members of the first GTC group have been such supporters of the work that I have been trying to do in the context of the children's charity organization, *everyONE,* I established in Ethiopia as well as the program of Integral Africa.

In the work of Integral Africa, I thank all the members of the GTC programs who supported the initiative. My deepest thanks to all the GTC peers who hosted me, helped me run fundraising campaigns, and stood by the vision of the organization. Thank you all so much and know that even if it may not be called Integral Africa, I trust that we will one day soon have the network of change agents that we have been working to create. A special thanks to Laura Johnson, Jesse McKay, Shawn O'Fallon, Gail Hochachka, Susan Canon, Adam Jones and Heather Johnson, for working with me with such commitment to the vision and goals of Integral Africa. I want to thank Rama Rothe and her family, Donna Zahara and her family, Dana Carman, Sarah Keenan, Deborah Boyar and Terry Patten, Elisabeth Ferguson, Saniel and Linda Bonders, Suzanne Anderson, Raj Shaw and Kim Adams for their immense support, encouragement and continued faith in my work. Special thanks to Dr. Marilyn Hamilton.

In terms of the support of Integral Africa from the African side, I had the chance to present and discuss the concept with Africa's senior leaders such as the team of the then Executive Secretary of the United Nations Economic Commission for Africa, (UNECA) and a number of former African Heads of States. During the work on Integral Africa, Mr. K.Y. Amoako, who was then the Executive Secretary of the UNECA and Under Secretary-General of the United Nations, along with his team, Mme Josephine Ouedraogo, Deputy Executive Secretary, and Elene Makonnen, Principal Advisor to the Executive Secretary offered me priceless insights into how to institutionalize and sustainably establish a program such as Integral Africa. Thank you for your time, consideration, and willingness to listen to the ideas and thoughts. In the same breath, I also want to thank Bob Berg for his continued support and guidance throughout the years.

I am indebted to Dr. Ibrahim Mayaki, CEO, Nepad, and Former Prime Minister of Niger. I met Dr. Mayaki through my research for my doctoral dissertation on the issue of leadership in Africa. He was not only gracious and generous enough to allow me time for an interview but also agreed to read this manuscript and send me his thoughts and comments. I am truly humbled and honored. Dr. Mayaki, thank you so much for all your encouragements and support. I can't thank you enough for all the inspiration. I feel much honored to have your words as the forward of this book.

I present my genuine gratefulness to the following family members, friends, peers, colleagues, and mentors who have been so kind in reading the manuscript and offering me feedback, comments, and suggestions: Joan Baxter, Jessica Horn, Ina Ismael, Rita Mazzocchi, Fouad Ismael, Matthias Reusing, Dana Carman, Assegid Tessema, Terry Patten, Deborah Boyar, Josephine Ouedraogo, Laurent Labourmene, Kelo Kubu, Thati Mokgoro, Judy Lendzian, Lusanda Ganda, Justice Yvonne Mokgoro, Dr. Joanne Gozawa, Kim Slater, Fabian Assegid, Noel Assegid, Lily Assegid, Quentin Moore, Consolata Bakareke and Abdul Rahman Turay, Dr Chikwe Ihekweazu, Nick Streets, Benedicte Ausset and John Drummond, Kim Slater, Rahel Samara, Etiye Yeshiye Samara, Chloe Rumak, Kim Thue, Jordanos Zerom, Hortense Niamke, Rahel Terefe – Thank you all so much for your support, encouragement, and feedback. I send my thanks and appreciation to Terry Ann Hayes for working with me across the oceans in designing the wonderful layout, cover, and graphics work.

It's our ability to rely on our support group that allows each one of us to make modest steps outside of our comfort zone. And it is in this space outside the comfort zone that we often can have access to breakthroughs, insights, and opportunities to shift paradigms. For me, it was my collective network of friends, family, and colleagues that gave me the encouragement to come forward in expressing my thoughts and engaging in writing this reflection. I hope that we each manifest our support networks, and through these networks, engage on the path of changing our behaviors, mindsets, and ways of being, in the present time, so that we can create the future we want to see emerge; so that we can create the future we hope to bring about for our children and their children, and the future that holds the economic and human development conditions and realities that we know our communities deserve and are capable of generating. It all happens when we choose to connect. It all happens when we dare to be counted and when we commit to remaining in our truth, in our essence, and in our deepest self as we take on our daily work.

About the Author

Born in Ethiopia, Yene was raised in Europe. She completed her university education in the United States. While her educational background is Finance and Investment Analysis, her professional work focused on civil society programs and international agencies' initiatives/projects aiming for social change issues for disadvantaged and destitute members of society. Presently, Yene spends most of her time consulting, coaching and conducting research on means to leverage leadership capacities in favor of transformation and change in the context of economic and human development.

She is the founder of *everyONE* (*www.everyonesworld.org*), a humanitarian organization based in Ethiopia; currently supporting the livelihoods of over 10,000 boys and girls affected by AIDS or orphaned by AIDS; as well as several disadvantaged communities affected by poverty, physical disability, leprosy and HIV/AIDS. Part of the proceeds from this book is committed to starting an Endowment Fund to support Children's livelihood programs both within *everyONE* and other such organizations worldwide.

Yene lives in Freetown, Sierra Leone with her husband Matthias Reusing and their two daughters Rosi-Selam and Leoni-Almaz. To contact or more information please go to: *www.butterfliesoverafrica.com*.

www.ingramcontent.com/pod-product-compliance
Ingram Content Group UK Ltd.
Pitfield, Milton Keynes, MK11 3LW, UK
UKHW020144250726
13967UKWH00002B/855

9 780578 039930